LABOR AND INDUSTRIAL RELATIONS JOURNALS AND SERIALS

An Analytical Guide

Compiled by

Michael C. Vocino, Jr.

and

Lucille W. Cameron

Annotated Bibliographies of Serials: A Subject Approach, Number 14
Norman Frankel, Series Editor

G
P

Greenwood Press
New York • Westport, Connecticut • London

D0002871

19920035

Library of Congress Cataloging-in-Publication Data

Vocino, Michael C.
    Labor and industrial relations journals and serials.

    (Annotated bibliographies of serials, ISSN 0748–5190 ; no. 14)
    Bibliography: p.
    Includes indexes.
    1. Industrial relations—Periodicals—Bibliography.
I. Cameron, Lucille W. II. Title. III. Series.
Z7164.L1V6   1989   016.331'05   89-11887
ISBN 0–313–25986–0 (lib. bdg. : alk. paper)

British Library Cataloguing in Publication Data is available.

Library of Congress Catalog Card Number: 89–11887
ISBN: 0–313–25986–0
ISSN: 0748–5190

First published in 1989

Greenwood Press, Inc.
88 Post Road West, Westport, Connecticut 06881

Printed in the United States of America

The paper used in this book complies with the
Permanent Paper Standard issued by the National
Information Standards Organization (Z39.48-1984).

10 9 8 7 6 5 4 3 2 1

To my parents
Michael Vocino and Dorothy Connaughton Vocino
who are counted among my best friends
and
JRP, still the focus of the quixotic dream

MV

I dedicate this book to my parents
Louise Baldwin Cameron
and the late Hugh Alexander Cameron
who sacrificed so much for me
and to my husband, James Robert Doris
who is always a strong and loving support

LWC

C

CONTENTS

SERIES FOREWORD

The effects of the "information explosion" have been pronounced in the area of serial publishing. Encouraged by the availability of word-processing and computer printing, masses of material have been flowing from the presses. Many of the new journals and serials have proved to be ephemeral, ceasing publication as a result of financial difficulties, mergers, or loss of interest by the editorial staff. However, a large number of useful new publications remain, augmenting older titles, which have undergone important editorial changes. On-line bibliographic databases and electronic publishing have also affected the direction of serials publishing. Despite modern technology, as the amount and type of material in most disciplines have proliferated, subscription prices for serials have been maintaining a steady upward trend while library budgets generally have been declining.

The intent of the ANNOTATED BIBLIOGRAPHIES OF SERIALS: A SUBJECT APPROACH series is to make the task of serial selection and use more systematic through identifying, collecting, annotating, and indexing currently published English-language serials in the major fields of knowledge: social, natural, and applied sciences; humanities; medicine; and business. The scope of the series is worldwide. Serials cited are from the many countries where English is a primary or important language, notably the United States, Canada, the United Kingdom, Ireland, Australia, New Zealand, South Africa, Nigeria, India, Pakistan, and Israel. It is worth noting that journals of international importance from areas of the world where the national language is not widely understood outside the country are often published wholly or in part in English.

Each series volume provides comprehensive coverage of the English-language serials in one subject area with extensively annotated entries for each serial. Titles are included if their primary focus is on the discipline of the particular volume. Many fields overlap, and it is sometimes difficult to decide where the dividing line should be. Occasionally, the same serials will appear in more than one volume, with the annotation pointing to its applicability to the subject area in question. The comprehensiveness of coverage and informative annotations, both exceeding that of other guides to serial literature, will aid librarians in deciding whether a particular title is appropriate for their collections and aid scholars in determining whether the title will be useful for their research.

For the purposes of this series, "serial" is applied to periodicals having a frequency of issue of at least one per year. This includes journals, publication of professional associations, magazines, selected newsletters, almanacs, and conference proceedings. Newsletters are included only if they publish significant articles or have unique features. The newsletter literature is voluminous, and in many disciplines would provide enough material for a separate volume. The same can be said for government documents. Only the most important government publications are included in these series volumes.

The serial entries are culled from extensive searches of manual and computerized information sources. Basic indexing and abstracting services, thorough searches of the most important resource collections, contacts with library associations and other professional associations in the pertinent disciplines, all have been utilized by the volume authors. Wherever possible, volume authors have personally examined representative issues of each serial and have acquired information directly from publishers.

Frontmatter contains introductory material including a "How to Use This Book" section, a table of abbreviations, and directories of microform and reprint companies and/or databases as appropriate. Abbreviations or acronyms for indexes, abstracts, and databases may be included in the table of abbreviations or, if an extensive list, may be given in one or more separate tables. Depending on the subject matter, some volumes are divided into chapters according to classified sub-disciplines while others are arranged in one unclassified sequence. Entries are alphabetical by title. Most volumes will include a geographical index, an index of publishers and a subject index or classified title index. Depending on the organization of the volume, an alphabetical title index may be added.

It is hoped that the information provided by ANNOTATED BIBLIOGRA-
PHIES OF SERIALS will facilitate access to and help strengthen bibliographic control of the rapidly growing body of serial titles.

Norman Frankel
Series Editor

PREFACE

Eminent British social scientist, Richard K. Brown, identifies labor relations and industrial relations as the terms most often used to describe the economic interaction or "social relations between employers and employees, management and workers, or their representatives." He further asserts that "...the study of labor relations has always been multidisciplinary."* Since labor relations has yet to establish itself as a distinct and separate discipline and must depend heavily on other fields, the labor and industrial relations serial literature is mainly drawn from other disciplines. It is this multidisciplinary nature of the labor and industrial relations literature that requires the examination of serials from such fields as economics, history, law, political science, psychology, and sociology to fully comprehend, analyze or interpret the field.

Preparation of this bibliography began with the identification of institutions that conduct serious research in the area of labor relations. If those institutions had libraries and if those libraries had lists of their serial holdings, the compilations were consulted. Among the institutions which are noted for quality programs are the New York State School of Industrial and Labor Relations at Cornell University; the Institute of Industrial Relations at the University of California, Berkeley; and the Labor Relations and Research Center at the University of Massachusetts, Amherst. The thirty-six page list, *Current Periodical Titles Displayed in the Silent Reading Room, August 1988*, published by the Martin P. Catherwood Library of the New York State School of Industrial and Labor Relations at Cornell University, was chosen as our major control group of titles to include in this bibliography. As an added check, we consulted *Ulrich's International Periodical Directory, 1987-88*, the *Social Sciences Citation Index*, and the *Social Sciences Index*.

---

* *The Social Science Encyclopedia* (London: Routledge, 1985):437.

This bibliography is selective and defined by the following criteria: Requests for sample copies along with questionnaires were mailed to the publishers of hundreds of serials identified from the aforementioned sources. Only those titles that could be personally examined were included. Where publishers did not respond with sample copies, an attempt was made to locate titles in area libraries. If not located, such titles were added to a list at the end of this bibliography. Only serials published primarily in English were considered, including those in English from non-English speaking nations.

In addition to the traditional academic journals, this bibliography also encompasses newsletters, some newspapers and several bulletins. There are some publications from local and state governments, almost always statistical in nature. These publications are not necessarily listed because of outstanding quality but rather as an example of the kinds of literature available in labor and industrial relations at the state and local level. Nearly all states and most major cities publish such information. What is true of state and local publications in this area is also true of labor unions. Virtually all labor unions publish at least a newsletter. Others such as the United Mine Workers publish substantial journals, and these union publications are incorporated when warranted.

The United States government is the most prolific publisher of labor related information, especially statistics. The publications of the Bureau of Labor Statistics are voluminous. Only major U.S. government publications such as the *Monthly Labor Review* are included in this bibliography. Those interested in labor statistics generated by the U.S. government should consult the *American Statistics Index* published by CIS (formerly the Congressional Information Service, Inc.).

Annotations are designed to appraise the publication in such a way that the reader can easily determine the audience for which it is written. Each annotation conveys a general sense of what kinds of articles each serial publishes. To help the reader ascertain flavor and scope, the actual titles of some articles and delineated topics are furnished whenever possible.

The bibliography is arranged in a numbered, alphabetical sequence. The title entry for each serial usually conforms to AACR II (*Anglo-American Cataloging Rules, 2d Edition Revised*). There is a full subject index, a publisher's index and a geographic index. The title index includes current titles and previous entries for title changes or mergers.

With the publication of *Labor and Industrial Relations Journals and Serials: An Analytical Guide*, a heretofore existing gap in the bibliographic literature has been filled. This resource should be useful to academics, specialists, students and librarians interested in the serial literature of labor and industrial relations.

Michael Vocino
Lucille Cameron
Kingston, Rhode Island
March 1989

ACKNOWLEDGMENTS

We have had the support of a number of people without whom this book would not exist. The series editor, Norman Frankel, has been most cooperative in responding to our inquiries and in offering us the wisdom of his experience. The University of Rhode Island has been most accommodating in supporting this project. Dr. Arthur P. Young, Dean, University Libraries, has offered us not only moral support but also some very practical advice and suggestions. The physical production of the manuscript is the work of a very talented group headed by Barbara George and assisted by Sheila Felice and Joan Fink. We are deeply indebted to them for their attention to detail and for the long hours of service spent at the computer while maintaining normal job responsibilities.

It is a pleasure to acknowledge the enormous efforts of Dr. Robert M. Gutchen toward the completion of this bibliography. His mastery of typography and style has made this production much better than it otherwise might have been.

We owe a debt of gratitude to several faculty members at the University of Rhode Island who have been very generous in offering suggestions that were incorporated in this bibliography: Dr. Alfred Killilea, Dr. Carl Gersuny, and Professor John B. Etchingham, Jr. Without the computer expertise of Professor Miu Lan Millie Kwan, this bibliography would not have been possible. We would also like to take this opportunity to extend our thanks to the faculty and staff of the University of Rhode Island Libraries for their support and encouragement during this endeavor. A very special and heartfelt thanks is due to our families and close friends for just being there and enduring.

HOW TO USE THIS BOOK

Industrial and labor relations serials are interdisciplinary. Because of this interdisciplinary nature, the titles in this volume are arranged alphabetically for easier access. There is a broad representation from the disciplines of sociology, psychology, political science, economics, and history. All of the journals are published in English. Selective publications from federal, state and local governments have been included.

All entries are arranged in accordance with the standard format used by each volume in this series. The format is divided into two parts. The first part contains the bibliographic information; the second part is an annotated description including the scope and purpose of the publication, the authority of the contributors, the editorial policy as well as its organization and special features.

The Title Index is arranged alphabetically and includes the current title and all previous titles. In the Geographic Index journals are arranged according to their place of publication and to the geographic area of focus. There is also a Publishers Index. All of these indexes also have entry numbers which refer to the entry numbers in the main text.

The format for the bibliographic data is listed below. It should be noted that if a journal does not contain one of the elements, that element is omitted from the entry.

1. ENTRY NUMBER: Utilized in the indexes.

2. TITLE: As provided by the publisher, or as listed in national bibliographic utilities, standard reference works, or on the title page.

3. DATE FOUNDED: As provided by the publisher, and verified by national bibliographic utilities or standard reference works.

4. TITLE CHANGES: Former titles and dates of publication.

5. MERGER: Names and dates of publication of prior titles which merged into present title.

6. FREQUENCY: Regularity of publication.*

7. PRICE: Subscription prices to institutions, individuals (personal), and members listed in U.S. currency whenever possible.

8. PUBLISHER: Name and address as provided or found in standard reference works.

9. EDITOR: Individual listed in this capacity.

10. ILLUSTRATIONS: Used if there are pictures, graphs, tables, figures, etc.

11. INDEX: Used if indexed in each issue or cumulatively.

12. ADVERTISEMENTS: Used only if paid or exchange advertisements are included.

13. CIRCULATION: Regular circulation as provided by publisher or found in standard reference work.

14. MANUSCRIPT SELECTION: Who decides what articles are published?

15. MICROFORMS: Are back issues available on microform? If so, from what source?**

16. REPRINTS: Are reprints available? If so, from what source?**

17. BOOK REVIEWS: Is there a book review section?

18. SPECIAL ISSUES: Does the serial publish special issues or supplements? How frequently?

19. INDEXED/ABSTRACTED: Where is the serial indexed or abstracted?***

20. TARGET AUDIENCE: Who is the intended readership?*

21. SAMPLE COPIES: Used only if sample copies are available free to libraries or individuals.

---

*   See Table of Abbreviations
**   See Directory of Microform and Reprint Publishers
***   See Table of Abstracts and Indexes

ABBREVIATIONS

Frequency of Publication

a	annual
bw	biweekly (every two weeks)
d	daily
m	monthly
q	quarterly
sm	semimonthly (twice per month)
w	weekly
2/yr.	two issues per year
3/yr.	three issues per year
5/yr.	five issues per year
6/yr.	six issues per year
8/yr.	eight issues per year
9/yr.	nine issues per year
10/yr.	ten issues per year
11/yr.	eleven issues per year
15/yr.	fifteen issues per year

Target Audience

AC	academic
GP	general public
HS	high school
SP	specialist

Currency

Can. $	Canadian dollar
Dfl.	Dutch florin
DM	Deutsch mark
£	English pound
NZ $	New Zealand dollar
R	Rand
SwF.	Swiss franc

INDEXES AND ABSTRACTS

AAR	Accounting Articles
AbAnthro	Abstracts in Anthropology
ABCPolSci	ABC Pol Sci. Advance Bibliography of Contents Political Science and Government
AbCrimPen	Abstracts on Criminology and Penology (Now: Criminology and Penology Abstracts)
AbHlthMgtS	Abstracts of Health Care Management Studies
AbHyg	Abstracts on Hygiene and Communicable Diseases
ABIn	ABI Inform
AbPopCult	Abstracts of Popular Culture
AbsBoRvCurrLegPer	Abstracts of Book Reviews in Current Legal Periodicals
ABSCAN	ABSCAN
AbSocWor	Abstracts for Social Workers
AccDataProAb	Accounting and Data Processing Abstracts
Access	Access: the Supplementary Index to Periodicals
AccI	Accountant's Index
AdolMentHlthAb	Adolescent Mental Health Abstracts
AdvManR	Advanced Management Report
AHCI	Arts and Humanities Citation Index
AmBibSlav	American Bibliography of Slavic and East European Studies
AmerH	America: History and Life
AnnBibEngLang	Annual Bibliography of English Language and Literature
AnthroI	Anthropological Index to Current Periodicals in the Library of the Museum of Mankind
APAIS	Australian Public Affairs Information Service (Now APAIS: Australian Public Affairs Information Service)
API	Alternative Press Index
AppMechRev	Applied Mechanics Review

ArtArchTechAb	Art and Archaeology Technical Abstracts
ASEANMgtAb	ASEAN Management Abstracts
ASI	American Statistics Index
ASSIA	Applied Social Sciences Index and Abstracts
AustNatBib	Australian National Bibliography
BankLitI	Banking Literature Index
BI	Business Index
BibAg	Bibliography of Agriculture
BibDevMedChildNeur	Bibliography of Developmental Medicine and Child Neurology. Books and Articles Received
BioAb	Biological Abstracts
BioAg	Biological and Agricultural Index
BMTA	British Maritime Technology Abstracts
BoRvD	Book Review Digest
BoRvI	Book Review Index
BrAbMedSc	British Abstracts of Medical Sciences
BrArchAb	British Archaeological Abstracts
BrCerA	British Ceramic Abstracts
BrEdI	British Education Index
BrHumI	British Humanities Index
BusI	Business Periodicals Index
BusIndust	Business, Industry, Technology Service
CADCAMA	CAD CAM Abstracts
CanBusI	Canadian Business Index
CanPerI	Canadian Periodical Index
CathPerLitI	Catholic Periodical and Literature Index
CCLP	Contents of Current Legal Periodicals
ChemAb	Chemical Abstracts
ChemIndN	Chemical Industry Notes
ChildDevAb	Child Development Abstracts and Bibliography
CIJE	Current Index to Journals in Education
CINAHL	Cumulative Index to Nursing and Allied Health Literature
CISAb	CIS Abstracts (Now: Safety and Health at Work)
CLI	Current Law Index
CLOA	Current Literature on Aging
CMI	Canadian Magazine Index

CoalA	Coal Abstracts
CommAb	Communication Abstracts
CompBus	Computer Business
CompConAb	Computer and Control Abstracts
CompIndUp	Computer Industry Update
CompLitI	Computer Literature Index
CompRev	Computing Reviews
Compumath	Compumath Citation Index
ContPgEd	Contents Pages in Education
ContPgMgt	Contents Pages in Management
CREJ	Contents of Recent Economic Journals
CrimJusAb	Criminal Justice Abstracts
CurrCont	Current Contents
CurrIStat	Current Index to Statistics
CurrLitFamPlan	Current Literature in Family Planning
CurrPackAb	Current Packaging Abstracts
DataProD	Data Processing Digest
ECER	Exceptional Child Education Resources
EdAdAb	Educational Administration Abstracts
EducI	Education Index
ElecComA	Electronics and Communications Abstracts Journal
ElecElecAb	Electrical and Electronics Abstracts
EmpRelAb	Employment Relations Abstracts (Now: Work Related Abstracts)
EnerI	Energy Index
EnerInfoAb	Energy Information Abstracts
EngI	Engineering Index Monthly
EngIBioengAb	Engineering Index Bioengineering Abstracts
EngIEnerAb	Engineering Index Energy Abstracts
EnvAb	Environment Abstracts
ErgAb	Ergonomics Abstracts
ERIC	Educational Resources Information Center
ExMed	Excerpta Medica
FLI	Film Literature Index
FoodSciTechAb	Food Science and Technology Abstracts
ForLangI	Foreign Language Index (Now: PAIS Foreign Language Index)

FuelEnerAb	Fuel and Energy Abstracts
FutAb	Future - Abstracts
FutSurv	Future Survey
GeoAb	Geographical Abstracts
HiEdAb	Higher Education Abstracts
HiEdCurrAwareBull	Higher Education Current Awareness Bulletin
HistAb	Historical Abstracts
HospLitI	Hospital Literature Index
HRA	Human Resources Abstracts
HRIS	Highway Research Information Service Abstracts
HRRep	Human Rights Internet Reporter
HumI	Humanities Index
ICanLegPerLit	Index to Canadian Legal Periodical Literature
ICommLegPer	Index to Commonwealth Legal Periodicals
IDentLit	Index to Dental Literature
IEconArt	Index of Economic Articles in Journals and Collective Volumes
ILegPer	Index to Legal Periodicals
IMed	Index Medicus
IndPsyAb	Indian Psychological Abstracts
IndSAPer	Index to South African Periodicals
IndUSGovPer	Index to U.S. Government Periodicals
INI	International Nursing Index
InsurPerI	Insurance Periodicals Index
IntAbOpRes	International Abstracts in Operations Research
IntAeroAb	International Aerospace Abstracts
IntBibE	International Bibliography of the Social Sciences: Economics
IntBibPolSc	International Bibliography of the Social Sciences: Political Sciences
IntBibSoc	International Bibliography of the Social Sciences: Sociology
IntLabDoc	International Labour Documentation
IntPkgA	International Packaging Abstracts
IntPolSc	International Political Science Abstracts
INZPer	Index to New Zealand Periodicals

NursAb	Nursing Abstracts
OceanAb	Oceanic Abstracts
OperRes	Operations Research/Management Science
PAIS	Public Affairs Information Service Bulletin
PCR2	Personal Computer Review - Squared
PeaceResAb	Peace Research Abstracts Journal
PerManAb	Personnel Management Abstracts
PersLit	Personnel Literature
PhilI	Philosopher's Index
PhysAb	Physics Abstracts
PollAb	Pollution Abstracts
PolScAb	Political Science Abstracts
PopInd	Population Index
PovHumResAb	Poverty and Human Resources Abstracts (Now: Human Resources Abstracts)
Pred	Predicasts
PROMT	Predicasts Overview of Markets and Technologies
PsyAb	Psychological Abstracts
Psycscan	Psycscan: Applied Psychology
PubAdAb	Public Administration Abstracts and Index of Articles (Now: Documentation in Public Administration)
RecPubArt	Recently Published Articles
RefSo	Reference Sources
RehabLit	Rehabilitation Literature
ResHiEdAb	Research into Higher Education Abstracts
ResourceCenI	Resource Center Index
RevRelRes	Review of Religious Research
RG	Readers' Guide to Periodical Literature
RIAD	RIA Digest
RILA	International Repertory of the Literature of Art
RIO	Religion Index One. Periodicals
RiskAb	Risk Abstracts
RuralDevAb	Rural Development Abstracts
RuralExtEdTrAb	Rural Extension, Education and Training Abstracts

RuralRecrTourAb	Rural Recreation and Tourism Abstracts (Now: Leisure, Recreation and Tourism Abstracts)
SafSciA	Safety Science Abstracts Journal
SageFamStudAb	Sage Family Studies Abstracts
SagePAA	Sage Public Administration Abstracts
SageUrbStudAb	Sage Urban Studies Abstracts
SchPsyDig	School Psychology Digest (Now: School Psychology Review)
SCI	Science Citation Index
SciAb	Science Abstracts
SelWaterResAb	Selected Water Research Abstracts (Now: Hydro-Abstracts)
ShipA	Ship Abstracts
SocAb	Sociological Abstracts
SocEdAb	Sociology of Education Abstracts
SOCI	Social Sciences Citation Index
SocSc	Social Sciences Index
SocWAb	Social Work Research and Abstracts
SPDA	Social Planning, Policy and Development Abstracts
SRI	Statistical Reference Index
StatThMethAb	Statistical Theory and Methods Abstracts
StudWomAb	Studies on Women Abstracts
TexTechD	Textile Technology Digest
TraIndI	Trade and Industry Index
TropDisBull	Tropical Diseases Bulletin
UrbAffAb	Urban Affairs Abstracts
USPSD	United States Political Science Documents
WomAb	Women's Studies Abstracts
WorAb	Work Related Abstracts
WorBankAb	World Banking Abstracts
WorldAgEconRuralSocAb	World Agricultural Economics and Rural Sociology Abstracts
WorTexA	World Textile Abstracts
WritAmHis	Writings on American History

DIRECTORY OF MICROFORM
AND REPRINT PUBLISHERS

AMS   AMS Press, Inc.
56 E. 13th Street
New York, NY 10003

BLH   Bell and Howell
Old Mansfield Road
Wooster, OH 44691

California State Library
Library & Courts Building
Box 2037
Sacramento, CA 95809

CIS   Congressional Information Service, Inc.
4520 East-West Highway
Bethesda, MD 20814

Custom Microfilm Systems
3221 Kansas Avenue
Riverside, CA 92507

Elsevier Sequoia S. A.
P.O. Box 851
CH-1001 Lausanne 1, Switzerland

ERIC   Eric Document Reproduction Service
3900 Wheeler Avenue
Arlington, VA 22304

Founders Memorial Library
Northern Illinois University
DeKalb, IL 60115

ISI   Institute for Scientific Information
3501 Market Street
Philadelphia, PA 19104

JAI   JAI Press Inc.
         55 Old Post Road, No. 2
         P.O. Box 1678
         Greenwich, CT 06836

         Johnson Reprint Co.
         111 Fifth Avenue
         New York, NY 10003

KTO   Kraus Reprint Co.
         Route 100
         Millwood, NY 10546

LC   The Library of Congress
         Photoduplication Service
         20 First Street, S.E.
         Washington, DC 20540

MCA   Microfilming Corporation of America
         200 Park Avenue
         6th Fl., E. Wing
         New York, NY 10166-0015

MIM   Microforms International Marketing Co.
         Maxwell House
         Fairview Park
         Elmsford, NY 10523

         Micromedia Limited
         158 Pearl Street
         Toronto, Ontario M5H 1L3

OECD   Organisation for Economic Co-Operation and Development
         2, rue Andre-Pascal
         75775 Paris Cedex 16, France

         Paul Hall Library
         Seafarer's Harry Lundberg School of Seamanship
         Piney Point, MD 20764

PMI   PMI
         P.O. Box 43
         Drexel Hills, PA 19026

Princeton Microfilm Corp.
P.O. Box 2073
Princeton, NJ 08543

3-R   Record, Retention & Retrieval Corp.
           110 Melrich Road
           Cranbury, NJ 08512

           Reprint Services
           Personnel Administrator
           P.O. Box 1183
           Minneapolis, MN 55458

RPI   Research Publications, Inc.
           12 Lunar Drive
           Drawer AB
           Woodbridge, CT 06525

RRI   Fred B. Rothman & Co.
           10368 W. Centennial Road
           Littleton, CO 80127

           Routledge
           11 New Fetter Lane
           London EC4P 4EE, England

           Sheridan Press, Inc.
           145 Palisade Street
           Dobbs Ferry, NY 10522

           State Historical Society of Wisconsin
           816 State Street
           Madison, WI 53706

           Swets & Zeitlinger
           Heerweg, 347 B
           Lisse, The Netherlands

           Temple University Microfilm Series
           Samuel Paley Library
           Temple University
           Berks & 13th Streets
           Philadelphia, PA 19122

GPO   United States Government Printing Office
           Superintendent of Microforms
           Washington, DC 20402

UMI   University Microfilms International
           300 N. Zeeb Road
           Ann Arbor, MI 48106

           University of Wisconsin
           Memorial Library
           728 State Street
           Madison, WI 53706

           World Microfilm Publications Ltd.
           62 Queen's Grove
           London NW8 6ER, England

WSH   William S. Hein & Co., Inc.
           1285 Main Street
           Buffalo, NY 14209

YALE   Yale University Library
           Publications Office
           Box 1603 A, Yale Station
           New Haven, CT 06520

Labor and Industrial Relations
Journals and Serials

BIBLIOGRAPHY

1   *AALC Reporter.* DATE FOUNDED: 1965. FREQUENCY: 6/yr.
PRICE: Free. PUBLISHER: African-American Labor Center, 1400 K
St., N.W., Suite 700, Washington, D.C. 20005. EDITOR: John T.
Sarr. INDEX. CIRCULATION: 1,000. TARGET AUDIENCE. SP.
SAMPLE COPIES: Libraries, individuals.

This concise, pro-labor newsletter reports on the activities and policies
of the labor situation in Africa. It is composed by its in-house staff and
would be of value to those seeking concise, current information. It is simultaneously published in English, French, and Arabic.

A recent issue contains information on South Africans studying organizing techniques in the U.S., reports on trade unions in various African
countries, a list of visitors to the African-American Labor Center, staff
changes, and union training programs in Africa.

2   *AAOHN Journal: Official Journal of the American Association of Oc-
cupational Health Nurses.* DATE FOUNDED: 1953. TITLE
CHANGES: *American Association of Industrial Nurses Journal* (1953-
1968); *Occupational Health Nursing* (1969-1985). FREQUENCY: m.
PRICE: $45/yr. institutions, $32/yr. personal. PUBLISHER: Slack In-
corporated, 6900 Grove Road, Thorofare, NJ 08086-9447. EDITOR:
Geraldine C. Williamson. ILLUSTRATIONS. INDEX. ADVER-
TISEMENTS. CIRCULATION: 12,300. MANUSCRIPT SELEC-
TION: Editor, Editorial Review Panel. MICROFORMS: UMI.
BOOK REVIEWS. INDEXED/ABSTRACTED: CINAHL, CISAb,
CurrCont, ExMed, INI, NoiPolPubA, NursAb. TARGET AUDI-
ENCE: AC, SP.

AAOHN is written for specialists. It is directed at the continuing
education and issues of importance to occupational health nurses. It is
published under the sponsorship of the American Association of Occupational Health Nurses. It is a companion to the *Journal of Occupational
Medicine* for occupational health and safety literature with a clinical
perspective. Titles of interest recently published include: "Maternity
and Parental Leave Policy," and "Employee Health Practices: Relationship Between Attitudes, Perceptions and Behaviors."

Each issue publishes eight to ten articles of varying length, usually under ten pages. News items for association members are a regular feature as are product news and a calendar of events. There are two to three book reviews. They are signed and of one-half page in length.

3   *Academe*. DATE FOUNDED: 1915. MERGER: *AAUP Bulletin* (1915-1978). FREQUENCY: 6/yr. PRICE: $38/yr., $10/yr. American Association of University Professors members. PUBLISHER: American Association of University Professors, Suite 500, 1012 14th Street, N.W., Washington, D.C. 20005. EDITOR: Paul Strohm. ILLUS-TRATIONS. INDEX. ADVERTISEMENTS. CIRCULATION: 55,000. MANUSCRIPT SELECTION: Editor, Advisory Board. MICROFORMS: UMI. BOOK REVIEWS. SPECIAL ISSUES. INDEXED/ABSTRACTED: AmerH, CIJE, ContPgEduc, CurrCont, EdAdAb, EducI, HistAb, PAIS, ResHiEdAb, SRI, WomAb. TARGET AUDIENCE: AC, SP.

Academe is the bulletin of the American Association of University Professors. Its articles are written by American academics for American academics. Typical articles include: "Higher Education and the Public Interest," "Student Assistance in Uncertain Times," and "Merit Pay: Reaganomics for the Faculty?" This is a union publication for its membership.

Each issue publishes an average of five conceptual and empirically based research articles. They are usually under ten pages in length. Each issue publishes a section for reports from the union's divisions. It also publishes on a regular basis university administrations censured for union violations, a news update, and a listing of academic vacancies. There are several signed book reviews, two to three pages in length in each issue.

4   *Academy of Management Executive*. DATE FOUNDED: 1987. FREQUENCY: q. PRICE: $38/yr. PUBLISHER: Academy of Management, McCool Hall, Mississippi State University, P.O. Drawer KZ, Mississippi State, MS 39762-5865. EDITOR: W. Warner Burke. ILLUSTRATIONS. INDEX. ADVERTISEMENTS. CIRCULA-TION: 8,650. MANUSCRIPT SELECTION: Editor, Editorial Review Board, Refereed. BOOK REVIEWS. TARGET AUDI-ENCE: AC, SP.

The *Academy of Management Executive* serves as a link between the academic community and the executive. It publishes articles on theory, research, and practice. The articles reflect the broad spectrum of interest of its readership covering topics on union-management relations, organizational effectiveness and efficiency, and consequences of societal changes on executives. Its perspective is that of management as is apparent from the title and publisher.

Each issue contains five to seven articles averaging ten pages in length, as well as two or three shorter articles. Some issues devote themselves to an in-depth look at one issue, a lengthy review article, or an extensive case-study. There are an average of six books reviewed per issue. These critical, signed reviews are more than one page in length.

5   *Academy of Management Journal.* DATE FOUNDED: 1957. TITLE CHANGES: *Journal of the Academy of Management* (1957-1962). FREQUENCY: q. PRICE: $38/yr. PUBLISHER: Academy of Management Journal, P.O. Drawer KZ, Mississippi State University, Mississippi State, MS 39762. EDITOR: Richard T. Nowday. ILLUS-TRATIONS. INDEX. ADVERTISEMENTS. CIRCULATION: 6,500. MANUSCRIPT SELECTION: Editor, Editorial Board, Refereed. MICROFORMS: UMI. REPRINTS: UMI. INDEXED/AB-STRACTED: AbHlthCareMgtS, ABIn, BI, BusI, CINAHL, CommAb, HiEdCurrAwareBull, HospLitI, MgtC, MgtMarA, OperRes, PAIS, PersLit, PsyAb, Psycscan, SOCI, WorAb.

This journal publishes articles in fields of interest to members of the Academy: business policy, entrepreneurship, health care administration, international management, management education, management history, managerial consultation, organization and management theory, organizational behavior, organizational communication, organizational development, personnel and human resources, production/operations management, women in management, social issues and technology in management. Power negotiation and conflict management as well as research methods are covered by AMJ.

Each issue contains an average of ten articles of twenty to forty pages in length. "Research Notes" and indexes are included in each volume.

6   *Academy of Management Review.* DATE FOUNDED: 1957. TITLE CHANGES: *Journal of the Academy of Management* (1957-1962); *Academy of Management Journal* (1963-1975). FREQUENCY: q. PRICE: $38/yr. PUBLISHER: Academy of Management, P.O. Drawer KZ, Mississippi State University, Mississippi State, MS 39762-5865. EDITOR: David A. Whetten. ILLUSTRATIONS. INDEX. ADVERTISEMENTS. MANUSCRIPT SELECTION: Editor, Editorial Review Board, Refereed. MICROFORMS: UMI. RE-PRINTS: UMI. BOOK REVIEWS. INDEXED/ABSTRACTED: AbHlthCareMgtS, ABIn, AccDataProAb, ASEANMgtAb, BusI,

HospLitI, MgtC, PersLit, PsyAb, Psycscan, RefSo. TARGET AUDI-
ENCE: AC, SP.

The *Academy of Management Review* is a management and organizational
theory journal published by The Academy of Management. *AMR* does
not publish reports of empirical investigations or articles written primarily for practicing managers. These are published in the *Academy of
Management Journal* and the *Academy of Management Executive*, respec-
tively. Topics covered include: business policy and planning, organization and management theory, production/operations management,
conflict management and among others, women in management.

Each issue has an average of eleven articles, usually under fifteen pages
in length. There is also a list of "Publications Received" and usually five
or so signed book reviews per issue.

7   *Administrative Sciences Quarterly*. DATE FOUNDED: 1956. FRE-
QUENCY: q. PRICE: $62/yr. institutions, $35/yr. personal. PUB-
LISHER: Samuel Curtis Johnson Graduate School of Management,
Malott Hall, Cornell University, Ithaca, NY 14853. EDITOR: John H.
Freeman. ILLUSTRATIONS. INDEX. ADVERTISEMENTS.
CIRCULATION: 5,300. MANUSCRIPT SELECTION: Editor,
Editorial Board. MICROFORMS: UMI. BOOK REVIEWS. IN-
DEXED/ABSTRACTED: ABCPolSci, ABIn, AccI, AmerH, ASSIA,
BI, BusI, CIJE, CINAHL, CommAb, CurrCont, EdAdAb, HistAb,
HospLitI, IntAeroAb, IntPolSc, KeyEconSci, MedCareRev, MgtC,
MgtMarA, PAIS, PerManAb, PersLit, PsyAb, Psycscan, ResHiEdAb,
SagePAA, SocAb, SOCI, SocSc, SocWAb, SPDA, WorAb, Writ-
AmHis. TARGET AUDIENCE: AC, SP.

Published by the Johnson Graduate School of Management at Cornell
University, *ASQ* is "dedicated to advancing the understanding of
administration through empirical investigation and theoretical analysis." Recent articles have included: "The Role of Value Congruity on
Intra-organizational Power," "The Changing of the Guard: Turnover
and Structural Change in the Top-Management Positions," "Predic-
tors of Job Satisfaction and Organizational Commitment in Human
Services Organizations" and "The Organizational Bases of Ethical
Work Climates."

Each issue contains six to seven articles of thirty pages or less. A fourth
of each issue is devoted to several signed book reviews. Another feature
included is "News and Notes."

8   *Advanced Management Journal.* DATE FOUNDED: 1936. TITLE
        CHANGES: *Society for the Advancement of Management. Journal* (1936-
        1939); *Advanced Management* (1939-1961); *Advanced Management-Of-
        fice Executive* (1962-1963). MERGER: *Modern Management* (1945-
        1949). FREQUENCY: q. PRICE: $29/yr. PUBLISHER: Society for
        the Advancement of Management, 2331 Victory Parkway, Cincinnati,
        OH 45206. EDITOR: Moustafa Abdelsamad. ILLUSTRATIONS.
        ADVERTISEMENTS. CIRCULATION: 11,000. MANUSCRIPT
        SELECTION: Editorial Review Board, Refereed. MICROFORMS:
        UMI. REPRINTS: Publisher. BOOK REVIEWS. INDEXED/AB-
        STRACTED: ABIn, AccDataProAb, AccI, BI, BusI, CompLitI, Dat-
        aProcD, MgtC, MgtMarA, PerManAb, Pred, PROMT. TARGET
        AUDIENCE: AC, SP. SAMPLE COPIES: Libraries, individuals.

        This scholarly journal publishes articles dealing with theoretical and
        pragmatic issues. Materials are written equally by U.S. business man-
        agers and academics. The major focus of the publication is to enhance
        the professional development of managers through the exchange of in-
        formation.

        A typical issue contains an average of eight articles. There are generally
        two signed book reviews, each consisting of one to two pages.

9   *Advances in Industrial and Labor Relations.* DATE FOUNDED:
        1983. FREQUENCY: a. PRICE: $56.50/yr. institutions, $28.25/yr.
        personal. PUBLISHER: JAI Press, Inc., 55 Old Post Road, No. 2, Box
        1678, Greenwich, CT 06836-1678. EDITOR: David B. Lipsky. IL-
        LUSTRATIONS. INDEX. MANUSCRIPT SELECTION: Editor.
        TARGET AUDIENCE: AC, SP.

        Advances in Industrial and Labor Relations is an annual volume in the same
        format as other *Advances in...* published by this press. The title indicates
        its subject focus. The majority of writers are from the academic
        community. There are a wide variety of topics covered, each of which
        surveys the existing literature. An important aspect of each lengthy
        paper is an exhaustive listing of references.

        A recent annual covered the areas of American collective bargaining,
        unionism and teacher compensation, and a general theory of industrial
        relations. Each paper is twenty-five to fifty pages in length.

10   *Affirmative Action Register.* DATE FOUNDED: 1973. FRE-
        QUENCY: m. PRICE: $15/yr. PUBLISHER: AAR: Affirmative Ac-
        tion Register, 8356 Olive Boulevard, St. Louis, MO 63132. EDITOR:
        Warren H. Green. ADVERTISEMENTS. CIRCULATION:

50,000. INDEXED/ABSTRACTED: RehabLit. TARGET AUDI-
ENCE: AC, SP.

This title is published as a recruitment tool for administrative, managerial and professional positions and directed to females, minorities,
veterans and the handicapped. Job advertisements are mainly from
American universities, colleges and research centers. It claims an
"audited readership of over 3.5 million."

11   ***AFL-CIO News.*** DATE FOUNDED: 1894. TITLE CHANGES:
American Federationist (1894-1976). MERGER: *CIO News* (1937-
1955); *League Reporter* (1949-1951); *AFL-CIO Weekly News Service*
(1951-1951); *ARL News-Reporter* (1951-1955); *AFL-CIO American Fed-
erationist* (1976-1982). PRICE: $10/yr. PUBLISHER: AFL-CIO
Headquarters, 815 16th Street, N.W., Washington, D.C. 20006.
EDITOR: John R. Oravec. ILLUSTRATIONS. ADVERTISE-
MENTS. CIRCULATION: 75,000. MANUSCRIPT SELEC-
TION: Editor. MICROFORMS: UMI. INDEXED/AB-
STRACTED: MagInd, MedCareRev, PersLit, WorAb. TARGET
AUDIENCE: AC, SP.

AFL-CIO News is the official weekly newspaper of the American
Federation of Labor and Congress of Industrial Organizations. It is the
vehicle through which the central AFL-CIO gets news and information
to members in a variety of affiliated locals. It is tabloid in format with
articles such as "Advisory Panel Says 'Yes' to Vital Role of Unions" and
"Import Surge Fuels Deficit."

Each issue runs eight pages in length. An article with broad appeal is the
recently published, statistically impressive "How Union Members
Voted." Good, broad union perspective is found in this publication.

12   ***Akron Business and Economic Review.*** DATE FOUNDED: 1970.
FREQUENCY: q. PRICE: $6/yr. PUBLISHER: College of Business
Administration, The University of Akron, Akron, OH 44325. EDI-
TOR: J. Daniel Williams. ILLUSTRATIONS. INDEX. CIRCULA-
TION: 2,500. MANUSCRIPT SELECTION: Editorial Review
Board, Refereed. MICROFORMS: UMI. REPRINTS: UMI. IN-
DEXED/ABSTRACTED: AAR, BI, CurrCont, PAIS, RiskAb, SciAb,
SOCI, WorAb. TARGET AUDIENCE: AC, SP.

The *Review* is dedicated to the promotion of the interchange of ideas
between businessmen and academicians. Its objective is to publish
commentary on contemporary problems, applied research and the
results of research in all areas of business and economics including labor

relations. Recent articles have included: "Combining Human Credit Analysis and Numerical Credit Scoring for Business Failure Prediction" and "The Impact of Past Performance on Expectations of Future Success: An Investigation of Australian Managers."

There are nine articles per issue of ten to twenty pages in length. Contributors are specialists and academics.

13   *Allied Industrial Worker.* DATE FOUNDED: 1958. FREQUENCY: m. PRICE: Free/institutions, $6/yr. personal. PUBLISHER: International Union, Industrial Workers (AFL-CIO), 3520 West Oklahoma Ave., Milwaukee, WI 53215. EDITOR: Anne Bingham. ILLUSTRATIONS. CIRCULATION: 80,000. MANUSCRIPT SELECTION: Editor. MICROFORMS: Publisher. REPRINTS: Publisher. BOOK REVIEWS. INDEXED/ABSTRACTED: WorAb. TARGET AUDIENCE: SP. SAMPLE COPIES: Libraries, individuals.

This tabloid newspaper aims to inform its union members and their families on many issues which affect them as workers, consumers and citizens. The majority of articles are relatively short and support the position of organized labor, specifically AFL-CIO. The articles are authored by U.S. labor union professionals.

Like most newspapers, there are about sixty to eighty items in each issue. Recent issues cover union strikes, profiles of members prominent in the labor movement and congressional debate on trade and minimum wages. Articles also provide information on international consumer issues such as health plans, a union credit card, and the purchasing of life insurance. There are regular features including stewards/officers notes, health and safety column, and labor union information. The highlights of the issue are translated into Spanish.

14   *American Business Law Journal.* DATE FOUNDED: 1956. TITLE CHANGES: *Bulletin-American Business Law Association* (1956-1962). FREQUENCY: q. PRICE: $20/yr. PUBLISHER: American Business Law Association, Inc., c/o Jan Henkel, Department of Insurance, Legal Studies and Real Estate, University of Georgia, Athens, GA 30602. ILLUSTRATIONS. INDEX. ADVERTISEMENTS. CIRCULATION: 1,600. MANUSCRIPT SELECTION: Editor, Staff, Refereed. MICROFORMS: UMI. BOOK REVIEWS. INDEXED/ABSTRACTED: ABIn, AbsBoRvCurrLegPer, AccI, BI, BusI, CLI, CurrCont, ICommLegPer, ILegPer, LegCont, LRI, MgtC, SOCI, TraIndI. TARGET AUDIENCE: AC, SP.

American Business Law Journal is the official publication of the American Business Law Association. It is written by and for mainly academics teaching business law outside of law schools. Academics from other disciplines do contribute and those interested in labor law would find this journal worthwhile. Recent articles include "Employee Urine Testing and the Federal Appeals Court," "AIDS in the Workplace, Legal Limitations on Employer Actions" and "Facilitating the Flow of Truthful Personnel Information."

There are four to eight articles per issue of twenty to thirty pages in length. Two or three signed book reviews of substantial length are included in each issue.

15   ***American Economic Review.*** DATE FOUNDED: 1908. MERGER: *Economic Bulletin* (1908-1910); *American Economic Association Quarterly* (1908-1910). FREQUENCY: 5/yr. PRICE: $125/yr. institutions, $75/yr. personal, varying rate for American Economic Association members. PUBLISHER: American Economic Association, 1313 21st Avenue, Suite 809, Nashville, TN 37212-2786. EDITOR: Orley C. Ashenfelter. ILLUSTRATIONS. INDEX. ADVERTISEMENTS. CIRCULATION: 26,000. MANUSCRIPT SELECTION: Editor, Board of Editors. MICROFORMS: UMI, Johnson Associates, MIM. REPRINTS: UMI. INDEXED/ABSTRACTED: ABIn, AmBibSlav, AmerH, BankLitI, BI, BoRvD, BusI, CREJ, CurrCont, EnerResAb, ExMed, GeoAb, HistAb, IEconArt, IntLabDoc, KeyEconSci, MagInd, MgtMarA, OperRes, PAIS, RecPubArt, RiskAb, RuralRecrTourAb, SelWaterResAb, SOCI, SocSc, TraIndI, WomAb, WorAb, WorBankAb, WorldAgEconRuralSocAb, WritAmHis. TARGET AUDIENCE: AC, SP.

This is the premier publication of the American Economic Association. Its other publications are the *Journal of Economic Literature* and the *Journal of Economic Perspectives*. This journal publishes on the full spectrum of economics from the micro to macro perspectives. Empirically based articles are usually written by American and occasionally international university faculty. Examples of recent article titles are: "Unemployment in the Soviet Union: Evidence from the Soviet Interview Project," "Innovation in Large and Small Firms: An Empirical Analysis," and "Family Economics and Macro Behavior."

Each issue has usually fifteen articles of varying length with most under twenty-five pages. In December, titles of economic dissertations written by recent graduates are included. There are usually ten to twelve shorter papers of less than ten pages.

16   *American Historical Review.* DATE FOUNDED: 1895. FRE-
QUENCY: 5/yr. PRICE: $43/yr. institutions, $17/yr. American His-
torical Association members. PUBLISHER: American Historical As-
sociation, 400 A Street, S.E., Washington, D.C. 20003. EDITOR:
David L. Ransel. ILLUSTRATIONS. INDEX. ADVERTISE-
MENTS. CIRCULATION: 16,000. MANUSCRIPT SELECTION:
Editor, Board of Editors. MICROFORMS: UMI, MIM. REPRINTS:
UMI. BOOK REVIEWS. INDEXED/ABSTRACTED: AHCI,
AmBibSlav, AmerH, AnnBibEngLang, BoRvD, BoRvI, CurrCont,
HistAb, IEconArt, MagInd, PeaceResAb, RecPubArt, RefSo, RG,
RILA, RIO, SageUrbStudAb, SOCI, WomAb, WritAmHis. TAR-
GET AUDIENCE: AC, GP, SP.

Published since 1895, the *American Historical Review* is not only the
official journal of the American Historical Association, it is one of the
world's premier journals devoted to the study of history. Its authors are
a virtual who's who of American academe. It is important for labor
history. Recent titles have included: "Long-Term Silver Mining
Trends in Spanish America: A Comparative Analysis," and "Feudalism,
Capitalism, and the World System."

Each issue has an "AHR Forum" devoted to a special topic and usually
three articles of thirty to fifty pages. The "Articles" section is also
usually three of the same length. Book reviews are numerous, signed
and substantial. They make up nearly half the publication.

17   *American Journal of Sociology.* DATE FOUNDED: 1895. FRE-
QUENCY: 6/yr. PRICE: $64/yr. institutions, $32/yr. personal. PUB-
LISHER: University of Chicago Press, Journals Division, P.O. Box
37005, Chicago, IL 60637. EDITOR: William L. Parish. ILLUSTRA-
TIONS. INDEX. ADVERTISEMENTS. CIRCULATION: 7,300.
MANUSCRIPT SELECTION: Editors, Refereed. MICROFORMS:
JAI, MIM, UMI. REPRINTS: ISI, Kraus, UMI. BOOK REVIEWS.
INDEXED/ABSTRACTED: AbAnthro, ABCPolSci, AbCrimPen,
AmBibSlav, AmerH, ASSIA, BoRvI, CIJE, CLOA, CrimJusAb,
CurrCont, EdAdAb, GeoAb, HistAb, IntLabDoc, LLBA, PAIS, Pop-
Ind, PsyAb, ResHiEdAb, RuralRecrTourAb, SageFamStudAb,
SageUrbStudAb, SocAb, SocEdAb, SOCI, SocSc, TropDisBull,
WomAb, WorAb, WorldAgEconRuralSocAb. TARGET AUDI-
ENCE: AC, SP.

This is one of the flagship serial publications of American sociology. It
is the oldest sociology journal in the world. Interdisciplinary in scope,
it focuses on analysis, research, theory and history. Empirically based
research articles are both quantitative and qualitative. Recent articles

have included "The Psychological Effects of Traditional and Economically Peripheral Job Settings in Japan," "The Ecology of Organizational Mortality: American Labor Unions, 1836-1985," and "The Stability of American Markets."

There are usually six substantive articles per issue of varying lengths. It also includes one or two "Review Essays" per issue. The twenty-five to thirty signed book reviews per issue usually run one and one-half to two pages in length.

18   *American Labor.* DATE FOUNDED: 1976. FREQUENCY: 6/yr. PRICE: $9.95/yr. PUBLISHER: American Labor Education Center, 1835 Kilbourne Place, N.W., Washington, D.C. 20010. EDITORS: Matt Witt and Debi Duke. ILLUSTRATIONS. ADVERTISEMENTS. CIRCULATION: 5,000. MANUSCRIPT SELECTION: In-house. REPRINTS: Publisher. BOOK REVIEWS. SPECIAL ISSUES: Occasional. TARGET AUDIENCE: AC, GP, HS, SP. SAMPLE COPIES: Libraries, individuals.

This newsletter focuses on labor issues from a progressive, activist point of view. It includes practical information and strategies which have been used by union members. The short timely articles are written in-house by labor educators. A limited number of articles deal with labor unions in Europe, South Africa, and Central America.

Recent past issues cover such topics as teachers' unions in schools, unions in the public and private sector, labor in Nicaragua, and organizing the unemployed. Most issues include a limited number of annotated reviews of books and pamphlets, audio visual materials, periodicals, and labor reports.

19   *American Political Science Review.* DATE FOUNDED: 1906. FREQUENCY: q. PRICE: $80/yr. institutions, $10/yr. American Political Science Association members. PUBLISHER: American Political Science Association, 1527 New Hampshire Avenue, N.W., Washington, D.C. 20036. EDITOR: Samuel C. Patterson. ILLUSTRATIONS. INDEX. ADVERTISEMENTS. CIRCULATION: 20,000. MANUSCRIPT SELECTION: Editor, Editorial Board, Refereed. MICROFORMS: UMI, MIM. REPRINTS: Publisher. BOOK REVIEWS. SPECIAL ISSUES. INDEXED/ABSTRACTED: ABCPolSci, AbsBoRvCurrLegPer, AmerH, BoRvD, BoRvI, CommAb, CurrCont, EnerInfoAb, EnvAb, FutSurv, HistAb, IEconArt, IntPolSc, PAIS, PersLit, RecPubArt, RefSo, RG, SciAb, SocSc, SocWAb, USPSD, WritAmHis. TARGET AUDIENCE: AC, SP.

The *American Political Science Review* is the flagship publication of the American Political Science Association. It publishes scholarly research and writing of "exceptional merit" in a broad range of subjects of interest to political scientists. Recent titles published which might be of interest to those studying labor/industrial relations would include: "Class Compromises in Industrial Democracies," "The Political Economy of State Medical Policy," and "Age and Active-Passive Leadership Style."

Each issue has "Articles," "Symposium," "Research Notes," "Controversies," "Review Essay" and "Book Reviews." There are generally nine to ten articles of twenty to forty pages in length. The research notes are much shorter and usually two are published. There are thirty to fifty signed, one-page book reviews per issue. They are grouped under such headings as "American Politics," "International Relations," "Political Theory," etc.

20   ***American Sociological Review.*** DATE FOUNDED: 1936. FREQUENCY: 6/yr. PRICE: $78/yr. institutions, $38/yr. personal, $16/yr. American Sociological Association members. PUBLISHER: American Sociological Association, 1722 N Street, N.W., Washington, D.C. 20036. EDITOR: William Form. ILLUSTRATIONS. INDEX. ADVERTISEMENTS. CIRCULATION: 15,000. MANUSCRIPT SELECTION: Editor, Refereed. MICROFORMS: JAI, MIM, UMI. REPRINTS: UMI. INDEXED/ABSTRACTED: AbAnthro, ABCPolSci, AbSocWor, AdolMentHlthAb, AmBibSlav, AmerH, AnnBibEngLang, ASSIA, CIJE, CommAb, CrimJusAb, CurrCont, EdAdAb, GeoAb, HistAb, IntLabDoc, IntPolSc, LLBA, PAIS, PopInd, PsyAb, RuralRecrTourAb, SageFamStudAb, SagePAA, SageUrbStudAb, SocAb, SOCI, SocSc, SocWAb, SPDA, WomAb, WorAb, WorldAgEconRuralSocAb, WritAmHis. TARGET AUDIENCE: AC, SP.

As with the *American Journal of Sociology*, the *American Sociological Review* is a prime publication in American sociology. It publishes empirical and conceptual work "of interest to the discipline in general, new theoretical developments, results of research ... and methodological innovations." Recent articles of interest to labor and industrial relations are "Bi-Ethnic Labor Markets, Mono-Ethnic Labor Markets, and Socioeconomic Inequality" and "Gender and Promotion."

Each issue contains eight to ten research articles of varying length. Other departments are "Research Notes" and "Comments."

21   ***Annals of the American Academy of Political and Social Science.*** DATE FOUNDED: 1890. FREQUENCY: 6/yr. PRICE: $60/yr.,

$28/yr. American Academy of Political and Social Science members. PUBLISHER: Sage Publication, Inc., 2111 West Hillcrest Drive, Newbury Park, CA 91320. EDITOR: Richard D. Lambert. ILLUS-TRATIONS. INDEX. ADVERTISEMENTS. CIRCULATION: 5,726. MANUSCRIPT SELECTION: Editor. MICROFORMS: UMI, Johnson Associates. BOOK REVIEWS. SPECIAL ISSUES. INDEXED/ABSTRACTED: ABCPolSci, AmBibSlav, AmerH, AnnBibEngLang, BoRvI, BrArchAb, CommAb, CompRev, CurrCont, FutSurv, HistAb, HRA, IEconArt, IntLabDoc, IntPolSc, JEL, KeyEconSci, LLBA, MagInd, PAIS, PeaceResAb, PersLit, RG, SageFamStudAb, SageUrbStudAb, SocAb, SOCI, SocSc, SocWAb, USPSD, WomAb. TARGET AUDIENCE: AC, SP.

The *Annals* is published bi-monthly by the prestigious American Academy of Political and Social Science. Each issue contains articles on some prominent social or politcal problem, written at the invitation of the editors. Also, monographs are published from time to time. Need-less to say, whatever is published in the *Annals* becomes an important reference source. Recent issues have been titled, "The Private Security Industry: Issues and Trends" and "The Ghetto Underclass: Social Science Perspective."

Each issue is a special issue with ten to twelve articles on a designated topic. Articles vary in length but usually are twenty pages. Each issue also has a "Book Department" sub-divided by discipline and geography. Usually fifty or so signed book reviews are included as well as a list of books received.

22   *APEX: Association of Professional, Executive, Clerical and Computer Staff.* DATE FOUNDED: 1908. TITLE CHANGES: *Clerk* (1908-1961). FREQUENCY: 6/yr. PRICE: £7/yr. PUBLISHER: Apex, 22 Worple Rd., London SW19 4DF, England. EDITOR: Neil Hamilton. ILLUSTRATIONS. ADVERTISEMENTS. CIRCULATION: 57,000. MANUSCRIPT SELECTION: Editor. MICROFORMS: LC. SPECIAL ISSUES: Occasional. INDEXED/ABSTRACTED: ASSIA, SciAb. TARGET AUDIENCE: AC, GP, HS. SAMPLE COPIES: Libraries, individuals.

This is a pro-union tabloid which has a decidedly left of center per-spective. Substantial, well written articles are published in each issue. Examples of these are "Education in Turmoil: New Deal for Schools" and "Counting the Heavy Cost of Thatcherism." It includes local, national and international union news in such continuing features as "Union Roundup." New technology, equal rights and multinational business seem to be the major focus. This publication presents an important viewpoint in understanding the international labor movement.

23   ***Applied Economics.*** DATE FOUNDED: 1969. FREQUENCY: m. PRICE: $375/yr. PUBLISHER: Chapman and Hall Ltd., 11 New Fetter Lane, London EC4P 4EE, England. EDITOR: Maurice Peston. ILLUSTRATIONS. INDEX. ADVERTISEMENTS. MANUSCRIPT SELECTION: Editor, Editorial Advisory Board. REPRINTS: ISI. INDEXED/ABSTRACTED: AbHlthCareMgtS, ABIn, BibAg, CREJ, EnerResAb, GeoAb, IEconArt, IntLabDoc, JContQuanMeth, MgtC, PAIS, RiskAb, RuralRecrTourAb, ShipA, SOCI, WorldAgEconRuralSocAb. TARGET AUDIENCE: AC, SP.

Applied Economics' primary purpose is to "encourage the application of economic analysis to specific problems in both the private and public sector." Its major focus is the publication of quantitative studies, "the results of which promise to be of use in the practical field and help to bring economic theory" closer to the real world. Recent titles have included: "Employment, Unemployment, and the Minimum Wage: A Causality Model," and "The Supply of Female Part-Time Labour Over the Life Cycle."

Each issue publishes ten to twelve empirical research articles. They are usually under fifteen pages in length. Most are written by academics from British and other commonwealth countries. Some American scholars are represented.

24   ***Arbitration and the Law: AAA General Counsel's Annual Report.*** DATE FOUNDED: 1981. FREQUENCY: a. PRICE: $50/yr. PUBLISHER: American Arbitration Association, Office of General Counsel, 140 W. 51st Street, New York, NY 10020-1203. EDITORS: Margaret Doyle and Linda M. Miller. INDEX. CIRCULATION: 600. MANUSCRIPT SELECTION: Editors, Editorial Board. TARGET AUDIENCE: AC, SP.

The annual issue of *Arbitration and the Law* publishes fifty-five to sixty case digests in the law of arbitration. It serves as a means of awareness in the field. The cases are in the areas of commercial, labor, international arbitration; alternative dispute resolution; legislation dealing with dispute resolution; and new American Arbitration Association rules. The readership of this journal would be limited to those working specifically in this field or affected by it. The volume contains a general index of subject approach, tables of cases, and a statutory and jurisdictional index.

25   *Arbitration in the Schools*. DATE FOUNDED: 1970. FREQUEN-
       CY: m. PRICE: $90/yr. PUBLISHER: American Arbitration Associa-
       tion, 140 W. 51st St., New York, NY 10020. EDITORS: Roger F.
       Mooney and Robert Wentzler. INDEX. CIRCULATION: 3,800.
       MANUSCRIPT SELECTION: In-house Staff. REPRINTS: Pub-
       lisher. TARGET AUDIENCE: AC, SP.

       This is the only publication that reports arbitration cases in the field of
       education. Its value is especially important to individuals who are
       involved in the dispute settlement of such cases. Preponderance of cases
       deal with the elementary-secondary schools although all levels of
       education are reported. Separate cumulative subject index also includes
       a listing of arbitrators.

       Each issue usually consists of eight pages (punched for maintaining in
       notebook or binder) and thirteen to fifteen decisions summarized. Full
       text of the cases is available, for a fee, from the publisher.

26   *Arbitration Journal: A Dispute Resolution Magazine*. DATE
       FOUNDED: 1937. FREQUENCY: q. PRICE: $40/yr. PUB-
       LISHER: American Arbitration Association, 140 W. 51st St., New
       York, NY 10020. EDITOR: Linda M. Miller. ILLUSTRATIONS.
       INDEX. CIRCULATION: 6,500. MANUSCRIPT SELECTION:
       Refereed. BOOK REVIEWS. INDEXED/ABSTRACTED: ABIn,
       AbsBoRvCurrLegPer, AmerH, BI, BusI, CCLP, CLI, CurrCont,
       HistAb, ILegPer, IntLabDoc, LegCont, LRI, MgtC, PersLit, SOCI,
       TraIndI, WorAb. TARGET AUDIENCE: AC, GP, SP.

       A journal devoted to the publication of articles on alternative dispute
       resolution. Articles written by both academics and attorneys address
       issues from both the scholarly and practical points of view. A typical
       issue covers alternative arbitration used in a medical center, in con-
       sumer arbitration in automobile purchases, and in a large corporation.

       A typical issue contains five to six articles plus the following regular
       features: review of court decisions, recent acquisitions of the Eastman
       Arbitration Library and an opinion page. The book review section
       covers three signed critical reviews of about one page in length.

27   *Arbitration Times: A Quarterly Dispute Resolution Newspaper*.
       DATE FOUNDED: 1974. TITLE CHANGE: *News and Views from
       The American Arbitration Association* (1974-1982). FREQUENCY: q.
       PRICE: Free. PUBLISHER: American Arbitration Association, 140
       W. 51st St., New York, NY 10020. EDITORS: Betty Blaisdell Berry
       and Linda M. Miller. ILLUSTRATIONS. ADVERTISEMENTS.

CIRCULATION: 65,000. MANUSCRIPT SELECTION: In-house Staff. INDEXED: WorAb. TARGET AUDIENCE: AC, GP, SP. SAMPLE ISSUES: Libraries, individuals.

A newspaper format allows for short articles on the most recent developments in the field of alternative dispute resolution. Recent issues cover reports on conferences, items on legislation, court decisions, the international scene and regional news. Regular columns include news about individuals, newly published books, and a calendar of upcoming events. There are many photographs.

28   *Asia Pacific Journal of Management.* DATE FOUNDED: 1983. FREQUENCY: 3/yr. PRICE: $20/yr. PUBLISHER: School of Management, National University of Singapore, Kent Ridge, Singapore 0511. EDITOR: Khin Maung Kyi. ILLUSTRATIONS. INDEX. ADVERTISEMENTS. CIRCULATION: 500. MANUSCRIPT SELECTION: Refereed by International Board. REPRINTS: Publisher. BOOK REVIEWS. SPECIAL ISSUES: Occasional. INDEXED/ABSTRACTED: CurrCont, RevPro, SOCI. TARGET AUDIENCE: AC, SP. SAMPLE COPIES: Libraries, individuals.

This is the only major international journal devoted to the management problems of the Asia Pacific Region. It focuses on comparative management as it is developed and practiced in South, East and Southeast Asia and Oceania. It publishes empirical and analytical studies of both private and public sector management and comparative studies beyond the region. Multidisciplinary and interdisciplinary approaches are encouraged with an international or multicultural perspective in order to broaden existing studies and theories. Authors are drawn from around the world mostly from academic and research institutions.

Each issue contains an average of five scholarly articles which include a review article and a research note. There are two or three lengthy book reviews in each issue of two to three pages with each signed by the reviewer. Regional news and forthcoming conferences are included. Special topical issues are produced on occasion.

29   *BAC Journal.* DATE FOUNDED: 1898. FREQUENCY: m. PRICE: $1.50/yr. PUBLISHER: International Union of Bricklayers and Allied Craftsmen, 815 15th St., N.W., Washington, D.C. 20005. EDITOR: Mary Dresser. ILLUSTRATIONS. CIRCULATION: 85,000. MANUSCRIPT SELECTION: Editor, Editorial Board. REPRINTS: Selective from Editor. SPECIAL ISSUES: Occasional.

TARGET AUDIENCE: SP. SAMPLE COPIES: Libraries, individuals.

Although this is the official journal of the International Union of Bricklayers and Allied Craftsmen, it is more appropriately described as a union newspaper to bring news of concern to people in the masonry trade, i.e. bricklayers, stone masons, plasterers, tile layers, marble masons, cement masons, mosaic and terrazzo workers, painters, cleaners, and caulkers. It supports the point of view of American labor, especially the AFL-CIO. Its writers are skilled craftsmen from the union in the United States and Canada.

An average issue has about fifteen articles. Many of them pertain to union affairs such as setting union priorities, means of increasing the union membership, and legislative activity potentially affecting the union. There are regular features dealing with health information and personal items regarding the membership.

30 *Benefits Today*. DATE FOUNDED: 1984. FREQUENCY: Looseleaf. PRICE: $328/yr. PUBLISHER: Bureau of National Affairs, 1231 25th St., N.W., Washington, D.C. 20037. ILLUSTRATIONS. INDEX. TARGET AUDIENCE: AC, SP.

Benefits Today is another looseleaf service from BNA. In one binder, this service includes reports, analyses, interviews and other practical information for a comprehensive overview to help practitioners create benefits policy. It is updated on a biweekly basis.

31 *Benetax*. DATE FOUNDED: 1985. FREQUENCY: 10-12/yr. (loose-leaf). PRICE: $1250/yr. PUBLISHER: Cullen Egan Dell Australia Pty Ltd., 280 George St., Sydney, NSW, Australia 2000. EDITOR: John V. Egan. INDEX. CIRCULATION: 150. REPRINTS: Publisher. TARGET AUDIENCE: SP.

This loose-leaf service deals with the taxation and motivational issues relating to employee fringe benefits in Australia. As this is a unique service, its use is primarily for specialists in the labor/employer field. Articles which are written by Australian researchers and consultants are selected for inclusion according to their appropriateness to the topic.

A typical issue might include three to five short articles or two in-depth reports. Reports include statistical material and charts. Topics cover such areas as employer benefits between industries and the impact of the fringe benefit tax and non-deductibility on employment costs.

32   *BNA Pension Reporter.* DATE FOUNDED: 1974. FREQUENCY: Looseleaf. PRICE: $460/yr. PUBLISHER: Bureau of National Affairs, 1231 25th St., N.W. Washington, D.C. 20037. ILLUSTRATIONS. INDEX. TARGET AUDIENCE: AC, SP.

The *Pension Reporter* is another looseleaf service from BNA. It provides weekly reports on the latest pension developments in Washington and the states. It gives full text on rulings, legislation and regulatory documents. It is updated weekly and includes three binders.

33   *BNA Policy and Practice Series.* DATE FOUNDED: 1950. FREQUENCY: Looseleaf. PRICE: $757/yr. PUBLISHER: Bureau of National Affairs, 1231 25th St, N.W., Washington, D.C. 20037. ILLUSTRATIONS. INDEX. TARGET AUDIENCE: AC, SP.

Policy and Practices is another looseleaf service from BNA. It is a practical eleven binder service designed to give how-to advice to implement tried practices and suggest cost effective benefits. Titles of binders include *Personnel Management, Compensation* (worker's compensation), *Wages and Hours* (full text, federal labor-related laws), *Fair Employment Practice* (federal and state EEO laws), *Labor Relations* (summaries of federal and state laws), and the *Bulletin to Management* and *Fair Employment Practices Summary of Latest Developments* (both of the latter are newsletters).

All of the services are updated on a biweekly bases. *Bulletin to Management* is a weekly and *Fair Employment* is a biweekly.

34   *British Journal of Industrial Relations.* DATE FOUNDED: 1963. FREQUENCY: 3/yr. PRICE: $47/yr. institutions, $23.50/yr. personal. PUBLISHER: Basil Blackwell Ltd., 108 Cowley Road, Oxford OX4 1JF, England. EDITORS: B.C. Robert, Ray Richardson and David Metcalf. INDEX. ADVERTISEMENTS. CIRCULATION: 2,300. MANUSCRIPT SELECTION: Editors. MICROFORMS: UMI. REPRINTS: Publisher. BOOK REVIEWS. SPECIAL ISSUES. INDEXED/ABSTRACTED: BrHumI, BusI, CurrCont, IntLabDoc, MgtC, MgtMarA, PAIS, SOCI, WorAb. TARGET AUDIENCE: AC, GP, SP. SAMPLE COPIES: Libraries.

A scholarly journal covering research and analysis on every aspect of industrial relations. Although the focus is primarily devoted to issues on Great Britain and the rest of the United Kingdom, it does address issues pertaining to the other industrialized nations. The articles which are chosen by the editors are written by worldwide academicians and researchers. Its coverage is comparable to *Industrial Relations* which focuses more on U.S. employment relationships.

Each issue averages six articles with introductory notes or article summaries at the front of the issue. Symposia on a specific topic are written in some issues. A "Chronicle" or short summary on newsworthy affairs in industrial relations in the United Kingdom during the past four months are noted. Eight to ten books have lengthy signed reviews mostly done by academicians. Reviews average between 500 to 1,000 words. There is a listing of books received but not reviewed.

35   *British Journal of Social Psychology.* DATE FOUNDED: 1962. TITLE CHANGES: *British Journal of Social and Clinical Psychology* (1962-1980). FREQUENCY: q. PRICE: $89/yr. PUBLISHER: British Psychological Society, St. Andrews House, 48 Princess Road East, Leicester LE1 7DR, U.K. EDITOR: A.S.R. Manstead. ILLUSTRATIONS. INDEX. ADVERTISEMENTS. CIRCULATION: 2,300. MANUSCRIPT SELECTION: Editor, Editorial Consultants. MICROFORMS: Swets and Zeitlinger B.V. REPRINTS: ISI. BOOK REVIEWS. INDEXED/ABSTRACTED: AdolMentHlthAb, ASSIA, BibDevMedChildNeur, BioAb, BrHumI, CommAb, CurrCont, ExMed, HiEdCurrAwareBull, IMed, LLBA, PsyAb, RecPubArt, ResHiEdAb, SocAb, SocEdAb, SOCI, SPDA, WomAb. TARGET AUDIENCE: AC, SP.

This vehicle is used by the British Psychological Society for the publication of high quality theory and research. This is truly an international forum for social psychology. Between 1985 and 1987 "126 articles were published in *BJSP*; of these, sixty-five had first authors who were based outside the U.K." It includes both theoretical and empirical papers. Its importance for industrial relations is that it is less rigid than most in its scope of publication and addresses such issues as group dynamics, the psychology of work, and interpersonal relations. More pragmatic field studies which are particularly strong in cross-national problems will be found in the *Journal of Social Psychology*.

Each issue contains substantial articles—usually eight to ten. It also includes editorials, review essays, and a list of manuscripts accepted for publication.

36   *British Journal of Sociology.* DATE FOUNDED: 1950. FREQUENCY: q. PRICE: $60/yr. institutions, $42/yr. personal. PUBLISHER: Routledge, 11 New Fetter Lane, London EC4P 4EE, England. EDITORS: Paul Rock and Ian Roxborough. ILLUSTRATIONS. INDEX. ADVERTISEMENTS. MANUSCRIPT SELECTION: Editor, Editorial Board. MICROFORMS: Publisher, UMI. BOOK REVIEWS. INDEXED/ ABSTRACTED: AdolMentHlthAb, AmerH,

ASSIA, BrHumI, CIJE, CommAb, CurrCont, GeoAb, HiEdCurrA-wareBull, HistAb, IMed, IntLabDoc, LLBA, PAIS, PsyAb, RecPubArt, ResHiEdAb, SocAb, SOCI, SocSc, SocWAb, SPDA, TropDisBull, WomAb, WorAb. TARGET AUDIENCE: AC, SP.

This title is a substantial, well respected journal in the field of sociology. Interdisciplinary in approach, it publishes the research of international academics in empirically, methodologically and conceptually-based articles. Recent titles have included: "Continuities and Change in Skilled Work," "Is Equality of Opportunity a False Idea for Society?" and "Some New Sources of Social Conflict."

Each issue contains an average of six research articles. There is an occasional substantial review article. Book reviews are signed and average ten to fifteen per issue.

37   ***Brookings Papers on Economic Activity.*** DATE FOUNDED: 1970. FREQUENCY: 2/yr. PRICE: $29/yr. institutions, $24/yr. personal. PUBLISHER: Brookings Institution, 1775 Massachusetts Avenue, N.W., Washington, D.C. 20036. EDITORS: William C. Brainard and George L. Perry. ILLUSTRATIONS. INDEX. MANUSCRIPT SELECTION: Editors. MICROFORMS: UMI. INDEXED/AB-STRACTED: BusI, IEconArt, IntLabDoc, MgtC, PAIS, Pred, SocSc. TARGET AUDIENCE: AC, SP.

Brookings Papers on Economic Activity contains articles, reports, and highlights of the discussion from conferences of the Brookings Panel on Economic Activity. It concentrates on the "live" issues of economic performance that confront the maker of public policy and the executive in the private sector. Special attention is paid to recent and current economic developments that are relevant to the contemporary scene,"...especially challenging because they stretch our understanding of economic theory or previous empirical findings." The publication is quantitative and statistical in nature. Recent reports and articles have included: "Back To The Future: European Unemployment Today Viewed from America in 1939," and "Help-Wanted Advertising, Job Vacancies, and Unemployment."

Each issue contains four articles usually fifty to one hundred pages in length. There are also two shorter "Reports." Each article and report is followed by a "Comments and Discussion" section. There is also an "Editors Summary" at the beginning of each issue.

38   ***Brookings Review.*** DATE FOUNDED: 1962. TITLE CHANGES: *Brookings Bulletin* (1962-1982). FREQUENCY: q. PRICE: $15/yr.

PUBLISHER: Brookings Institution, 1775 Massachusetts Avenue, N.W., Washington, D.C. 20036. EDITOR: Martha V. Gottron. ILLUSTRATIONS. INDEX. ADVERTISEMENTS. CIRCULATION: 32,000. MANUSCRIPT SELECTION: Editor. MICROFORMS: UMI. REPRINTS: UMI. BOOK REVIEWS. INDEXED/ABSTRACTED: ABIn, EnerResAb, HospLitI, PAIS, Pred, PROMT, WorBankAb. TARGET AUDIENCE: AC, SP.

The *Brookings Review* is published by the non-profit Brookings Institution. Usually referred to as a liberal think-tank, the *Review* is published to examine issues of domestic and foreign policy. Its purpose is to help resolve "current and emerging policy problems facing the American people." Recent titles of interest have included: "Federalism After Reagan" and "The View from 2020: Transportation in America's Future." Articles are less empirical than expository.

Each issue publishes three to five articles of usually under fifteen pages. There is a section of the Institute's new publications.

39   ***Business History.*** DATE FOUNDED: 1958. FREQUENCY: q. PRICE: $82/yr. institutions, $45/yr. personal. PUBLISHER: Frank Cass & Company, Ltd., Gainsborough House, Gainsborough Road, London E11 IRS, England. EDITORS: Charles Harvey and Geoffrey Jones. ILLUSTRATIONS. INDEX. ADVERTISEMENTS. CIRCULATION: 750. MANUSCRIPT SELECTION: Editors. BOOK REVIEWS. INDEXED/ABSTRACTED: AmerH, BrHumI, BusI, CurrCont, GeoAb, HistAb, MgtC, PAIS, SocAb, SOCI, WritAmHis. TARGET AUDIENCE: AC, SP.

Business History is the British counterpart to the *Business History Review*. It is written by British academics but covers the full spectrum of an international perspective on business history. Recent titles include: "Henry J. Kaiser and the Establishment of an Automobile Industry in Argentina," "Profit Sharing in the Gas Industry" and "Distance to Work in Victorian London."

Each issue publishes four articles, twenty to thirty pages in length. Eighteen to twenty signed book reviews are also published. They are usually two pages in length.

40   ***Business History Review.*** DATE FOUNDED: 1926. TITLE CHANGES: *Bulletin of the Business Historical Society* (1926-1953). FREQUENCY: q. PRICE: $40/yr. institutions, $25/yr. personal. PUBLISHER: Harvard Business School, Soldiers Field, Boston, MA 02163. EDITOR: Richard S. Tedlow. ILLUSTRATIONS. INDEX.

ADVERTISEMENTS. CIRCULATION: 2,000. MANUSCRIPT SELECTION: Editor, Editorial Advisory Board. MICROFORMS: UMI. BOOK REVIEWS. INDEXED/ABSTRACTED: AccI, Am-BibSlav, AmerH, BI, BoRvI, BusI, CurrCont, HistAb, IEconArt, JEL, MarAffBib, MgtC, PAIS, RecPubArt, RefSo, SOCI, SocSc, TraIndI, WorAb, WritAmHis. TARGET AUDIENCE: AC, SP.

Business History Review is published by the Harvard Business School. It is the American counterpart to the British academic journal, *Business History*. Articles are written by American business school faculty on the full range of business and industrial history. Recently published articles include: "Entrepreneurial Failure Reconsidered: The Case of the Interwar British Coal Industry," "Corporatism in Comparative Perspective" and "Big Business, Weimar Democracy and Nazism."

Each issue publishes four articles of thirty pages. There is also a review essay and an archival essay. There is an extensive (usually twenty-five) book review section. Reviews are three to four pages (sometimes longer) and signed. The "Editor's Corner" includes notices of meetings, calls for papers, etc.

41   *Business Lawyer: A Bulletin of the Section of Business Law.* DATE FOUNDED: 1946. FREQUENCY: q. PRICE: $28/yr., $12/yr. American Bar Association members. PUBLISHER: American Bar Association, Section of Business Law, 750 N. Lake Shore Drive, Chicago, IL 60611. EDITOR: George Clemon Freeman, Jr. ILLUSTRATIONS. INDEX. ADVERTISEMENTS. CIRCULATION: 55,000. MANUSCRIPT SELECTION: Editors, Advisory Board. MICROFORMS: MIM, RRI, Temple University. BOOK REVIEWS. SPECIAL ISSUES. INDEXED/ABSTRACTED: AAR, ABIn, AccI, BI, CLI, CurrCont, EnerInfoAb, EnvAb, ILegPer, LawOffInfo, LRI, MgtC, PAIS, SOCI. TARGET AUDIENCE: AC, SP.

The *Business Lawyer* is published by the ABA as a "Journal of business and financial law, with articles on current legal topics and substantive section programs." The section of the ABA publishing this journal is "Business Law," which formerly focused on corporation, banking and business law. Recent titles have included: "A Fifty-year History of the Section of Business Law: 1938-1988," and "The Changing Financial Environment and the Need for Regulatory Realignment." Most articles are written by practicing attorneys.

Each issue publishes ten articles of usually under twenty pages in length. A common feature is "Recent Literature" of about twenty-five annotated bibliographic entries. One or two signed book reviews per issue are usually one page in length.

42   ***Business Month***. DATE FOUNDED: 1893. TITLE CHANGES: *Dun's Review* (1893-1933); (1937-1953); (1967-1969); (1975-1981); *Bradstreet's Weekly* (1933); *Dun and Bradstreet Monthly Review* (1933-1936); *Modern Industry* (1953); *Dun's Review and Modern Industry* (1953-1966); *Dun's* (1970-1974); *Dun's Business Month* (1981-1987). FREQUENCY: m. PRICE: $18/yr. PUBLISHER: Business Month, 488 Madison Avenue, New York, NY 10022. EDITOR: John Van Doorn. ILLUSTRATIONS. INDEX. ADVERTISEMENTS. CIRCULATION: 301,481. MANUSCRIPT SELECTION: Editor. MICROFORMS: UMI, MIM. REPRINTS: Publisher, UMI. INDEXED/ABSTRACTED. ABIn, Access, AccI, BI, BoRvI, BusI, CompConAb, CompLitI, CurrCont, DataProcD, ElecElecAb, EnerInfoAb, EnvAb, KeyEconSci, MagInd, MgtC, OperRes, PAIS, PersLit, PhysAb, Pred, PROMT, RG, SciAb, TraIndI, WorAb. TARGET AUDIENCE: AC, GP, SP.

Written as a comprehensive source of current information for the corporate manager, this publication, much like *Business Week*, *Fortune*, and *Forbes*, covers a wide variety of topics including labor, management, technology, current news, finance, and the economy both national and international. Recent titles have included: "The Snarling Pension Fund Gets Fed" and "The Iatrogenic Minimum Wage."

Each issue has a cover story usually averaging five to ten pages in length. Five articles are additionally published all of varying length. Regular departments include: "Editorials," "Letters," "The Economy," "The Month in Perspective," "Corporate Finance," "Profiles of Corporate Executives," and "Around the World," a news perspective.

43   ***Business Week***. DATE FOUNDED: 1900. TITLE CHANGES: *Magazine of Business*. (1900-1929). FREQUENCY: w. PRICE: $39.95/yr. PUBLISHER: McGraw-Hill Publications Co., 1221 Avenue of the Americas, New York, NY 10020. EDITOR: Stephen B. Shepard. ILLUSTRATIONS. INDEX. ADVERTISEMENTS. CIRCULATION: 852,368. MANUSCRIPT SELECTION: Editors. MICROFORMS: UMI. REPRINTS: UMI. BOOK REVIEWS. INDEXED/ABSTRACTED: ABIn, AccI, BankLitI, BI, BMTA, BoRvI, BusI, ChemAb, CompBus, CompIndUp, CompLitI, CurrLitFamPlan, CurrPackAb, EnerInfoAb, EnvAb, FutSurv, GeoRef, HiEdCurrAwareBull, KeyEconSci, MagInd, MgtC, MgtMarA, MicrocompI,

OceanAb, OperRes, PAIS, PCR2, PersLit, PollAb, RG, ShipA, SRI, TexTechD, TraIndI, WorAb.

Business Week gives "Comprehensive coverage of news and developments affecting the business world. It includes information on computers, finance, labor, industry, marketing, science, technology." Recent articles have included "Are Small Companies in Danger?" "Business Outlook" and "Is the Factory Rebound Real?"

Each issue of this popular press publication is similar in style and content to *Forbes* and *Fortune*. It has articles published under the headings: "Special Reports," "Top of the News," "Government," "Science and Technology," "Marketing," "The Corporation," "Economic Analysis," "Finance," "People," "Information Processing," "Sports Business," and "Personal Business." "Features" includes three or four signed substantial book reviews.

44   *California Management Review.* DATE FOUNDED: 1958. FREQUENCY: q. PRICE: $38/yr. institutions, $28/yr. personal. PUBLISHER: School of Business, 350 Barrows, University of California, Berkeley, CA 94720. EDITOR: David Vogel. ILLUSTRATIONS. INDEX. ADVERTISEMENTS. CIRCULATION: 5,500. MANUSCRIPT SELECTION: Editor, Editorial Board, Reviewers. MICROFORMS: UMI. REPRINTS: Editor. BOOK REVIEWS. INDEXED/ABSTRACTED: ABCPolSci, ABIn, AccDataProAb, AccI, AmerH, ASEANMgtAb, BankLitI, BI, BusI, CompLitI, CurrCont, DataProD, EdAdAb, EmpRelAb, EnerInfoAb, EnvAb, ExMed, FutSurv, HistAb, IEconArt, IntAeroAb, JEL, KeyEconSci, ManI, MgtC, MgtMarA, OperRes, PAIS, PerManAb, PersLit, SOCI, WorAb. TARGET AUDIENCE: AC, SP. SAMPLE COPIES: Libraries, individuals.

California Management Review attempts to serve as a bridge of communication between those who study management and those who practice it. The articles are generally research oriented which have relevancy for the field practitioner. Its primary areas of focus are international competition and competitiveness, strategy and organization, and business and social/public policy. It draws material from many disciplines including economics, psychology, history, political science, sociology, law, philosophy, business administration and education. Writers are mostly academics from the U.S. and Canada although managers and executives contribute as well.

There are an average of nine to ten articles per issue. An abstract of about 100 words for each article is provided in the table of contents.

There is a book review essay with several books reviewed on a specific topic.

45   *California Public Employee Relations (CPER)*. DATE FOUNDED: 1969. FREQUENCY: 7/yr. PRICE: $130/yr. PUBLISHER: Institute of Industrial Relations, University of California, Berkeley, CA 94720. EDITOR: B.V.H. Schneider. INDEX. CIRCULATION: 1,000. BOOK REVIEWS. SPECIAL ISSUES: Occasional. TARGET AUDIENCE: AC, SP. SAMPLE COPIES: Libraries, individuals.

The *California Public Employee Relations* provides scholarly up-to-date, nonadversary information to those involved in employer-employee relations in public employment. Writers are research academics, public sector managers, labor representatives, attorneys and arbitrators. Its major focus is on the problems faced in the efforts to implement and administer collective bargaining systems.

A typical issue contains six to eight articles. Eight to ten books complete with a 200 word abstract are included. Regular features include a column on the status of litigation and summaries of decisions.

46   *Canadian Journal of Economics*. DATE FOUNDED: 1928. TITLE CHANGES: *Contributions to Canadian Economics* (1928-1934); *Canadian Journal of Economics and Political Science* (1935-1967). FREQUENCY: q. PRICE: $65/yr., $40/yr. Canadian Economics Association members. PUBLISHER: University of Toronto Press, Journals Department, 5201 Dufferin Street, Downsview, Ontario M3H 5T8. EDITOR: Robin Boadway. ILLUSTRATIONS. INDEX. ADVERTISEMENTS. CIRCULATION: 3,655. MANUSCRIPT SELECTION: Editor, Board of Editors. MICROFORMS: MIM, UMI. BOOK REVIEWS. SPECIAL ISSUES. INDEXED/ABSTRACTED: ABIn, AmBibSlav, BI, BibAg, CanBusI, CanPerI, CLI, CREJ, CurrCont, ForLangI, GeoAb, IEconArt, ILegPer, IntLabDoc, JEL, KeyEconSci, MgtC, PAIS, RecPubArt, RuralRecrTourAb, SOCI, SocSc, WorAb, WorBankAb, WorldAgEconRuralSocAb. TARGET AUDIENCE: AC, SP.

The *Canadian Journal of Economics/Revue Canadienne d'Economique* is published in French and English by the Canadian Economics Association. It publishes significant contributions to knowledge in all areas of economics, with the exception of extremely narrow papers addressed to small specialist audiences. Recent titles have included: "Organization in Economic Analysis," "Production, Trade, and Migration with Differentiated Skilled Workers," and "The Impact of Progressive Income Tax Rates on Canadian Negotiated Wage Rates."

Each issue has twelve to fifteen articles per issue of usually under twenty pages. Ten or so signed book reviews are published per issue as is a section called "Notices" of upcoming events, conferences, etc.

47   *Canadian Public Administration.* DATE FOUNDED: 1958. FREQUENCY: q. PRICE: $70/yr. PUBLISHER: Institute of Public Administration of Canada, 897 Bay St., Toronto, Ontario M5S 1Z7. EDITOR: V. Seymour Wilson. ILLUSTRATIONS. INDEX. ADVERTISEMENTS. CIRCULATION: 4,000. MANUSCRIPT SELECTION: Editor, Editorial Board, Refereed. MICROFORMS: Micro Media Ltd. REPRINTS: Micro Media Ltd. BOOK REVIEWS. INDEXED/ABSTRACTED: ABCPolSci, AmerH, ASSIA, BI, CanBusI, CanPerI, CMI, CurrCont, EdAdAb, ForLangI, HistAb, HospLitI, ICanLegPerLit, IntPolSc, MgtC, PAIS, PovHumResAb, SagePAA, SOCI. TARGET AUDIENCE: AC, SP.

Canadian Public Administration is the publication of the Institute of Public Administration of Canada. It publishes articles written by administrative practitioners and academics. It is designed for specialists as well as academics and strives not to be too highly technical or specialized in content or methodology. Recent titles have included: "The Merit Principle in the Provincial Governments of Atlantic Canada," "The Changing Shape and Nature of Public Service Employment," and "Motivation, Rewards and Satisfaction in the Canadian Public Service."

Each issue has an average of ten articles. Some are published in French. Ten substantial, signed book reviews are included in each issue.

48   *Career Development Quarterly.* DATE FOUNDED: 1952. TITLE CHANGES: *Vocational Guidance Quarterly* (1952-1986). FREQUENCY: q. PRICE: $20/yr., $7/yr. National Career Development Association members. PUBLISHER: National Career Development Association, 5999 Stevenson Avenue, Alexandria, VA 22304. EDITOR: Paul R. Salomone. ILLUSTRATIONS. INDEX. ADVERTISEMENTS. CIRCULATION: 7,500. MANUSCRIPT SELECTION: Editor, Editorial Board, Refereed. MICROFORMS: UMI. REPRINTS: UMI. BOOK REVIEWS. INDEXED/ABSTRACTED: CIJE, CurrCont, EducI, HiEdAb, HiEdCurrAwareBull, IntLabDoc, PsyAb, Psycscan, SocEdAb, SOCI, SocWAb. TARGET AUDIENCE: AC, SP.

Career Development Quarterly is published by the National Career Development Association. It is a professional journal concerned with research, theory and practice in career development, career counseling, occupational resources, and career education. It focuses on the role of work (paid and unpaid) in peoples' lives, job satisfaction and labor market dynamics. Articles relate conclusions to practical applications. Recent titles have included: "Adult Children of Alcoholics and Chronic Career Indecision" and "The Career Cycle meets the Life Cycle."

Each issue has an average of ten articles. They range from under ten pages in length to over twenty. Most articles are written by American university professors.

49   *Carpenter*. DATE FOUNDED: 1881. FREQUENCY: m. PRICE: $10/yr. PUBLISHER: United Brotherhood of Carpenters and Joiners of America, 101 Constitution Ave., N.W., Washington, D.C. 20001. EDITOR: John S. Rogers. ILLUSTRATIONS. ADVERTISE-MENTS. CIRCULATION: 625,000. MANUSCRIPT SELEC-TION: Editor, Staff. REPRINTS: Editor. BOOK REVIEWS. IN-DEXED/ABSTRACTED: WorAb. TARGET AUDIENCE: SP.

This publication is for the benefit of union members in the trades of carpentry, cabinet making, millwright work, and joinery. The editor and his staff select articles that espouse the union viewpoint and are usually politically liberal.

A typical issue averages six articles dealing with topics on the use of union or nonunion labor, the changing workforce, anti-union tactics, legislative issues, benefits of health care coverage and Social Security. Historical articles on the last Liberty ship and union banners are also included. There are regular features providing an update for members including the "Washington Report" for Americans and the "Ottawa Report" for Canadian members; local union news; a consumer oriented column; "Retirees Notebook" and news about individual members. Occasionally a book review which has relevancy to the trade will receive a one-half page unsigned review.

50   *Catering Industry Employee*. DATE FOUNDED: 1890. TITLE CHANGES: *Mixer & Server* (1890-1929). FREQUENCY: m. PRICE: $5/yr. PUBLISHER: Hotel & Restaurant Employees Interna-tional Union, 1219 28th St., N.W., Washington, D.C. 20007. EDI-TOR: Herman Leavitt. ILLUSTRATIONS. ADVERTISEMENTS. INDEX. TARGET AUDIENCE: SP.

A union publication providing timely information to its membership on national policies and legislation. Interspersed throughout are articles providing consumer and other news features which are of value to hospitality industry workers both in their professional and personal lives. Because of its union affiliation, it does advance labor's perspective on protecting and promoting the right to organize and bargain collectively, to ensure workplace democracy, health and safety, and to encourage fairness in hiring and promotion of the average American worker in this industry. The writers are professional journalists and labor leaders. The majority of subjects relates to the U.S. with a small section on Canadian news written both in English and French.

Typical recent issues contain an average of three articles in addition to regular columns. Topics such as income tax rules, planning in the post-Reagan era, Catholic bishops and employment, local union news and industry news are covered.

51   *Catholic Worker*. DATE FOUNDED: 1933. FREQUENCY: 6/yr. PRICE: $.25/yr. PUBLISHER: The Catholic Worker Movement, 36 East First St., New York, NY 10003. EDITOR: Tim Lambert. ILLUSTRATIONS. INDEX. ADVERTISEMENTS. CIRCULATION: 94,000. MICROFORMS: UMI. BOOK REVIEWS. INDEXED/ABSTRACTED: API, CathPerLitI. TARGET AUDIENCE: AC, GP, SP.

This radical, Catholic newspaper is an outgrowth of the Catholic Worker movement founded by Dorothy Day and Peter Maurin during the Great Depression. The *Catholic Worker* is devoted to social justice with emphasis on voluntary poverty and the practice of works of mercy. It attempts to apply Catholic teaching to social problems. Its articles have supported strikes, picketing and other causes promoted by organized labor. Recent years have seen a focus on the rights of the migrant farm workers.

Each issue runs four to six pages of newsprint. There are several lead articles with brief news summaries. Many of Day's and Maurin's original writings are republished with each issue. There are occasionally signed book reviews. The artwork of Fritz Eichenberg and Rita Corbin make this publication worth a look.

52   *Chartered Secretary*. DATE FOUNDED: 1971. FREQUENCY: m. PRICE: $30/yr. PUBLISHER: Institute of Company Secretaries of India, 'ICSI House,' 22, Institutional Area, Lodi Road, New Delhi 110003, India. EDITOR: V. Balu. ILLUSTRATIONS. INDEX. ADVERTISEMENTS. CIRCULATION: 15,000. MANUSCRIPT SELECTION: Editor, Editorial Advisory Board. BOOK REVIEWS. SPECIAL ISSUES: 2/yr. TARGET AUDIENCE: AC, SP. SAMPLE COPIES: Libraries.

Chartered Secretary is published as a major tool for the dissemination of information in India on all legislation affecting the work of corporate executives. Additional articles cover finance, accounting and management. Although writers may be drawn from corporate executives, academicians, researchers and government officials anywhere, the majority are from India.

The major focus of each issue is threefold. There is a large segment devoted to the digests of the latest decisions on commercial, economic and fiscal legislations decided by various courts and quasi-judicial bodies in India. A second major portion of the journal is reports of recent acts, bills and rules of various economic ministries in India relevant to business and industry. The last portion is a miscellaneous section of short notices of interest to the corporate sector. There are two special issues per year: one deals with the union budget; the second on a topic of interest. There are an average of three one-half page signed book reviews per issue.

53   *Chief Executive*. DATE FOUNDED: 1968. TITLE CHANGES: *Business Administration* (1968-1977); *Chief Executive Magazine* (1977-78). FREQUENCY: 11/yr. PRICE: $60/yr. PUBLISHER: Morgan-Grampian, Morgan-Grampian House, Calderwood St., London SE18 6QH, United Kingdom. EDITOR: Garrod Whatley. ILLUSTRATIONS. ADVERTISEMENTS. CIRCULATION: 21,500. MANUSCRIPT SELECTION: Editor. MICROFORMS: UMI. REPRINTS: Editor. SPECIAL ISSUES. INDEXED/ABSTRACTED: ABIn, AccDataProAb, ASEANMgtAb, BI, MgtC, PROMT, SciAb. TARGET AUDIENCE: AC, SP. SAMPLE COPIES: Libraries, individuals.

Chief Executive is written as a practical aid for senior managers responsible for day-to-day operations of companies. Articles are not academic or theoretical focusing instead on the practical aspects of the management of companies. British in focus but written with usefulness to executives in other English speaking countries. Recent articles include one about a woman CEO, "Woman of Substance" and "Awkward People" about circumventing troublesome employees.

Each issue has seven to ten articles of traditional length for a popular press publication. There are two special issues per year: August, automobiles; and November, business relocation. Other regular features include "Talking Shop," "Motoring" and "Health" among others.

54   *Chronicle of Higher Education*. DATE FOUNDED: 1966. FREQUENCY: w. PRICE: $55/yr. PUBLISHER: Chronicle of Higher

Education, Inc., 1255 23rd Street, N.W., Washington, D.C. 20037. EDITOR: Corbin Gwaltney. ILLUSTRATIONS. INDEX. ADVERTISEMENTS. CIRCULATION: 77,116. MANUSCRIPT SELECTION: Editors. MICROFORMS: UMI. REPRINTS: UMI. BOOK REVIEWS. INDEXED/ABSTRACTED: ArtArchTechAb, BoRvI, EducI, ResHiEdAb, SRI, WomAb. TARGET AUDIENCE: AC, GP, SP.

The *Chronicle of Higher Education* is the newspaper of record for higher education. It includes "News reports and editorials on all facets of higher education in the United States, Canada, and abroad, with reference lists of relevant research, books, seminars, workshops, fellowships and grants, and grants, and targeted toward senior administrative, business and academic officers." Typical articles include: "After a 4-Year Unionization Fight, Faculty Finally Voted at Southern Illinois," and "U.S. Studies Policies at Harvard, UCLA on Admitting Asians."

Each issue runs around fifty pages in length. There is an additional twenty or so pages of faculty positions available around the world and divided by discipline. This is essential reading for the academic.

55 *Collective Bargaining Negotiations and Contracts.* DATE FOUNDED: 1945. FREQUENCY: Loosecleaf. PRICE: $545/yr. PUBLISHER: Bureau of National Affairs, 1231 25th St., N.W., Washington, D.C. 20037. ILLUSTRATIONS. INDEX. TARGET AUDIENCE: AC, SP.

*Collective Bargaining Negotiations and Contract*s is another looseleaf service from BNA. This service is updated on a biweekly basis. It is a source of information for wage and benefits settlements, industry wage patterns, economic conditions and arbitration. There are two reference binders.

56 *Columbia Journal of Law and Social Problems.* DATE FOUNDED: 1965. FREQUENCY: q. PRICE: $30/yr. PUBLISHER: Columbia University, School of Law, 435 W. 116th Street, New York, NY 10027. EDITOR: Ann E. Barlow. ILLUSTRATIONS. INDEX. CIRCULATION: 800. MANUSCRIPT SELECTION: Editor, Editorial Board. MICROFORMS: WSH. INDEXED/ABSTRACTED: ABCPolSci, AdolMentHlthAb, CLI, CurrCont, ILegPer, LegCont, LRI, PAIS, SOCI. TARGET AUDIENCE: AC, SP.

The *Columbia Journal of Law and Social Problems* is a general interest, student written law journal. It accepts no manuscripts from others outside the Columbia University Law School. Its topics are of a wide variety including labor law, labor problems, comparable worth, rights of workers, and management rights and responsibilities. Recent articles have included: "The IND Rewrite and the OMB: Business as Usual at the FDA?" and "Gambling on the Truth: The Use of Purely Statistical Evidence as a Basis for Civil Liability." The focus is very scholarly. It would be of more interest to academics and students than to practitioners in the field.

Each issue publishes only three to five articles. They are usually forty to fifty pages in length. The students occasionally unify an issue around a specific topic.

57   *Communication World.* DATE FOUNDED: 1970. TITLE CHANGES: *Editor's Notebook* (1970-1970); *Reporting* (1970-1970); *IABC Notebook* (1971); *IABC News* (1972-1982). FREQUENCY: 10/yr. PRICE: $48/yr. PUBLISHER: International Association of Business Communicators, 870 Market St., Suite 940, San Francisco, CA 94102. EDITOR: Gloria Gordon. ILLUSTRATIONS. INDEX. ADVERTISEMENTS. CIRCULATION: 12,500. MANUSCRIPT SELECTION: Editor. REPRINTS: Sheridan Press. BOOK REVIEWS. SPECIAL ISSUES. INDEXED/ABSTRACTED: ABIn, MgtC. TARGET AUDIENCE: AC, GP, HS, SP. SAMPLE COPIES: Libraries, individuals.

Communication World is a news magazine for communication and public relations professionals. It is published by the International Association of Business Communicators to provide information about the profession of organizational communication and the IABC, its members, chapters, districts and international affiliates. Recent articles have included "The Changing Face of Corporate Communication" and "How the U.S. Air Force Runs Its Communication Program."

CW is published monthly except in January when a special membership issue is published. Each issue has four to six articles. There are two to three signed book reviews per issue. Other regular features include "Consultants Directory," "Update," "Communicators in Motion," "Spectrum" and "Photographers Portfolio" among others.

58   *Comparative Labor Law Journal.* DATE FOUNDED: 1971. TITLE CHANGES: *Bulletin-International Society for Labor Law and Social Legislation, United States National Committee* (1971-1975); *Comparative Labor Law* (1976-1986). FREQUENCY: q. PRICE: $25/yr. PUBLISHER: University of Pennsylvania, Wharton School, 2203 Steinberg-Dietrich Hall, Philadelphia, PA 19104-6369. EDITOR: Benjamin Aaron. INDEX. ADVERTISEMENTS. CIRCULATION:

500. MANUSCRIPT SELECTION: Editor. BOOK REVIEWS. INDEXED/ABSTRACTED: AbsBoRvCurrLegPer, CLI, ILegPer, IntLabDoc, LRI, MgtC, PAIS. TARGET AUDIENCE: AC, SP.

This journal was formerly published by the UCLA Law School for the International Society for Labor Law and Social Legislation. It is now published by the Wharton School of Business at the University of Pennsylvania for the Society. It is devoted to publishing articles on labor law especially focusing on labor laws in countries other than the U.S. and comparing them with each other. All aspects of labor law are considered in articles written by lawyers from a variety of countries and U.S. academics. Recent topics have included: social security, unemployment, fringe benefits and comparable worth for women.

Each issue publishes four to five articles of varying length but ordinarily under twenty pages. One or two, signed book reviews are included with each issue. Usually there is a central focus for an issue around which the articles cluster. A recent topic was women in the labor market. Recent articles have included "An American Perspective of the German Model of Worker Participation," and "Conditioning Trade on Foreign Labor Law."

59 *Compensation and Benefits Review.* DATE FOUNDED: 1968. TITLE CHANGES: *Compensation Review* (1968-1985). FREQUENCY: 6/yr. PRICE: $64/yr. PUBLISHER: American Management Association, 135 W. 50th Street, New York, N.Y. 10020. EDITOR: Hermine Zagat Levine. ILLUSTRATIONS. INDEX. CIRCULATION: 6,000. MANUSCRIPT SELECTION: Editor, Editorial Advisory Board. MICROFORMS: UMI. REPRINTS: Publisher, ISI, UMI. BOOK REVIEWS. INDEXED/ABSTRACTED: AccDataProAb, ASEANMgtAb, BI, BusI, CurrCont, MgtC, PerManAb, PersLit, SOCI, WorAb. TARGET AUDIENCE: AC, SP. SAMPLE COPIES: Libraries, individuals.

Published by the American Management Association, *Compensation and Benefits Review* is by and for practitioners as well as academics. Recent topics have included: benefits cost containment, employee satisfaction, multiple pay systems, social security benefits and merit pay. Articles are empirical and conceptual with such titles as "Multiple Pay Systems: Are They Worth the Risk," and "Estimating Future Social Security Benefits."

Each issue has four or five twenty to thirty page articles. A regular feature, "Selected Readings" condenses noteworthy articles from the professional or popular press. "In Brief" includes several book reviews written by the staff.

60   *The Conference Board's Management Briefing: Human Resources.*
DATE FOUNDED: 1985. TITLE CHANGES: *Management Brief-
ing. Human Resources* (1985-1986). FREQUENCY: m. PUBLISHER:
The Conference Board, Inc., 845 Third Avenue, New York, NY 10022.
EDITOR: Melissa A. Berman. CIRCULATION: 6,800. MANU-
SCRIPT SELECTION: Editor. TARGET AUDIENCE: AC, SP.

Designed to keep executives up to date on issues in compensation and
benefits, staffing, labor relations, training and development, and quality of worklife, this Conference Board publication, like its counterparts,
Marketing and *Business Finance*, is a popular current news source for
professional managers.

Each issue runs four pages in length. There is usually a lead article.
Recent titles have been "Benefits Policy and Law" and "1988 Labor and
Human Resources Outlook."

61   *Contemporary Policy Issues.* DATE FOUNDED: 1982. FREQUEN-
CY: q. PRICE: $50/yr. institutions, $25/yr. personal. PUBLISHER:
Western Economic Association International, 7400 Center Avenue,
Suite 109, Huntington Beach, CA 92647-3055. EDITOR: Eldon J.
Dvorak. ILLUSTRATIONS. INDEX. CIRCULATION: 3,000.
MANUSCRIPT SELECTION: Editor, Editorial Advisory Board.
MICROFORMS: UMI. INDEXED/ABSTRACTED: CurrCont,
IEconArt, JEL, PAIS, SagePAA, SOCI, WorBankAb. TARGET
AUDIENCE: AC, SP.

Contemporary Policy Issues is the major publication of the Western
Economic Association International. The objectives of this journal of
economic analysis is to focus economic research and analysis on issues
of vital concern to business, government and other decision makers.
Recent articles have included: "Drifting Apart: Canadian and U.S.
Labor Markets," "Costs and Benefits of Exchange Rate Stability," "The
Great Depression Revisited by a New Generation" and "Interstate
Banking and Anti-trust Laws."

Each issue has an average of six to seven articles. Articles are usually
fifteen to twenty pages in length.

62   *Contemporary Sociology: An International Journal of Reviews.*
DATE FOUNDED: 1972. FREQUENCY: 6/yr. PRICE: $72/yr.
institutions, $32/yr. personal, $16/yr. American Sociological Association members. PUBLISHER: American Sociological Association,
1722 N Street, N.W., Washington, D.C. 20036. EDITOR: Ida Harper
Simpson. INDEX. ADVERTISEMENTS. CIRCULATION:

10,000. MANUSCRIPT SELECTION: Editor. MICROFORMS: UMI, JAI. REPRINTS: UMI. BOOK REVIEWS. INDEXED/AB- STRACTED: AdolMentHlthAb, AmBibSlav, BoRvI, LLBA, RefSo, SocAb, SOCI, SPDA, WomAb. TARGET AUDIENCE: AC, SP.

This journal was formerly the book review section of the *American Sociological Review*. Just as its title implies, this is a journal of book reviews. It does have a "Featured Essay" and "Commentary" section with each issue, but it is the book reviews which are the "meat" of the publication.

Each issue divides the reviews into broad subject areas. These areas are essentially the same in each issue. Some of the headings are: "Social Control, Deviance and the Law," "Theory and Methods," "Sociology of Health and Illness" and of interest to labor and industrial relations is "Organizations, Occupations, and Markets." Each section contains ten to twenty signed book reviews. This journal is useful in coping with the information explosion.

63   *Cornell Hotel and Restaurant Administration Quarterly*. DATE FOUNDED: 1960. FREQUENCY: q. PRICE: $30/yr. PUB- LISHER: Cornell Hotel and Restaurant Administration Quarterly, 327 Statler Hall, Cornell University, Ithaca, NY 14853-6901. EDI- TOR: Glenn Withiam. ILLUSTRATIONS. INDEX. ADVERTISE- MENTS. CIRCULATION: 8,000. MICROFORMS: UMI. RE- PRINTS: UMI. BOOK REVIEWS. INDEXED/ABSTRACTED: ABIn, AccI, BI, BibAg, BusI, FoodSciTechAb, HospLitI, PAIS, Rural- RecrTourAb, TraIndI, WorldAgEconRuralSocAb. TARGET AUDI- ENCE: AC, SP.

Published for the industry, this journal is practical, pragmatic and less theoretical in its approach to labor-management issues. It does, how- ever, also have a wider appeal as well. For example, where it is necessary and appropriate to explain the mechanics of a financial analysis or human resources policy, the *Quarterly* provides the details. Recent titles have included: "Older Workers: A Hiring Resource," "Finding and De- veloping Tomorrow's Top Managers," and "Sharing Risks and Deci- sion Making: Recent Trends in the Negotiation of Management Con- tracts."

Each issue has an average of six "full length features" of usually under ten pages. Regular features are "News and Reviews," "Talkback," "Notes," "Statistical Snapshots," "Profiles" and "From the Editor."

64   *Corporation Law Guide*. DATE FOUNDED: 1959. FREQUENCY: bw. PRICE: $285/yr. PUBLISHER: Commerce Clearing House, Inc., 4025 W. Peterson Ave., Chicago, IL 60646. EDITOR: Allen C. Schecter. INDEX. CIRCULATION: 1,500. MANUSCRIPT SELECTION: Editorial Staff. MICROFORMS: Publisher. REPRINTS: Publisher. SPECIAL ISSUES. TARGET AUDIENCE: SP. SAMPLE COPIES: Libraries, individuals.

This is a loose-leaf service published by Commerce Clearing House in the same format as their other titles such as *Congressional Index*, *Tax Reporter*, etc. This title provides wide-angled reporting on state corporation law and practice. It also supplies timely information on federal and state controls. New statutes, regulations, decisions, rulings and interpretations are promptly noted. Editorial comment and analysis put the new rules into perspective for everyday corporation activity. The writers are American lawyers and law-trained generalists.

The bi-weekly issue consists of *Guide* pages for filing into master volume as an update. It is well indexed by topic, by a cumulative index and a listing of current law cases. Volumes are organized by colored tab guides in broad subject areas.

65   *Covered Employment and Wages: Quarterly Report*. DATE FOUNDED: 1978. FREQUENCY: q. PRICE: Free. PUBLISHER: New Mexico Employment Security Department, P.O. Box 1928, Albuquerque, NM 87110. EDITOR: Vince Brunacini. INDEX. CIRCULATION: 235. REPRINTS: Publisher. TARGET AUDIENCE: AC, SP. SAMPLE COPIES: Libraries, individuals.

This is strictly a statistical publication which provides geo-economic and socio-economic data on New Mexico employees to labor, employers, researchers and government agencies among others. It contains only charts, graphs and tables with no analysis.

66   *CSO Statistical Release: Industrial Disputes*. FREQUENCY: q. PUBLISHER: Central Statistics Office, Ardie Road, Dublin 6, Ireland. EDITOR: Michael Kelly. TARGET AUDIENCE: AC, SP.

A statistical publication of the Irish Central Statistics Office, this release gives a general summary of the industrial/labor disputes for the most recent quarter. It provides information by industry, class of workers and geographic areas.

This title is somewhat comparable to a U.S. government publication on work stoppages. A more detailed analysis of industrial disputes appears in each issue of the *Irish Statistical Bulletin*.

67   *Current Contents. Social and Behavioral Sciences*. DATE FOUN-
DED: 1969. TITLE CHANGES: *Current Contents. Behavioral, Social
and Educational Sciences* (1971-1973). MERGER: *Current Contents.
Behavioral, Social and Management Sciences* (1969-1970); *Current Con-
tents. Education* (1969-1970). FREQUENCY: w. PUBLISHER: Insti-
tute for Scientific Information, Inc., 3501 Market Street, Philadelphia,
PA 19104. INDEX. ADVERTISEMENTS. INDEXED/AB-
STRACTED: Compumath, ISciRev, PopInd, SOCI. TARGET
AUDIENCE: AC, SP.

Current Contents. Social and Behavioral Sciences highlights tables of
contents of the world's leading publications covering social and behavioral science. It provides complete bibliographic information for all the
journals it indexes. Regular features include journals from economics,
business, law (including labor law), management and occasionally
industrial relations. Very current information is available. Tables of
contents are usually published within two weeks of receipt.

Each issue usually has a lead article by the publisher, Eugene Garfield
of the Institute for Scientific Information. There are letters to the
editor, a title word index, author index (w/addresses) and a publishers'
address directory in each issue. ISI claims to cover 98,000 journal
articles in the behavioral and social sciences each year.

68   *Current Sociology*. DATE FOUNDED: 1952. FREQUENCY: 3/yr.
PRICE: $75/yr. institutions, $33/yr. personal. PUBLISHER: Sage
Publications Ltd., 28 Banner Street, London ECIY 8QE, England.
EDITOR: William Outhwaite. ILLUSTRATIONS. INDEX. AD-
VERTISEMENTS. MANUSCRIPT SELECTION: Editor, Edito-
rial Board. SPECIAL ISSUES. INDEXED/ABSTRACTED:
ABCPolSci, CurrCont, IntLabDoc, KeyEconSci, LLBA, PAIS,
PsyAb, SocAb, SOCI, SocSc. TARGET AUDIENCE: AC, SP.

Current Sociology provides a forum for communication with a wide
group of sociological professionals. Each issue of this journal is devoted
to a comprehensive "Trend Report" on a topic of interest to an international community of sociologists. The aim is to review new developments, discuss controversies, and to provide extensive bibliographies.
Recent topics have included refugees, labor, migration, cults, religion,
Africa and Afghan refugees.

This journal of the International Sociological Association publishes
five to eight articles of under twenty five pages each. Each issue also has
an extensive bibliography of current publications of interest.

69   *Daedalus: Proceedings of the American Academy of Arts and Sciences.*
DATE FOUNDED: 1846. TITLE CHANGES: *Proceedings of the American Academy of Arts and Sciences* (1846-1958). FREQUENCY: q. PRICE: $16/yr. PUBLISHER: American Academy of Arts and Sciences, 136 Irving Street, Cambridge, MA 02138. EDITOR: Stephen R. Graubard. ILLUSTRATIONS. INDEX. ADVERTISEMENTS. CIRCULATION: 20,000. MANUSCRIPT SELECTION: Editor, Board of Editors. MICROFORMS: Johnson Associates, UMI. REPRINTS: UMI. SPECIAL ISSUES. INDEXED/ABSTRACTED: ABCPolSci, AHCI, AmerH, BioAb, BoRvI, BrArchAb, ChemAb, FutSurv, GeoAb, GeoRef, HistAb, HospLitI, HumI, LLBA, MagInd, MetAb, MLA, PAIS, PsyAb, ResHiEdAb, RILA, SciAb, SocAb, SocWAb, SPDA, WritAmHis.

Daedalus is the journal of the American Academy of Arts and Sciences. Its contents are usually also issued as a volume of the *Proceedings of the American Academy of Arts and Sciences*. Each issue is a special issue focusing on a special topic. Recent issues have been titled: "Futures," "Learning About Women," "Intellect and Imagination," and "Artificial Intelligence." Interdisciplinary in approach, it has appeal to virtually every academic discipline including labor relations.

Each issue publishes an average of ten articles focused on a single theme. The articles generally run under twenty pages in length. A unifying preface begins each issue.

70   *De Economist* (NE). DATE FOUNDED: 1852. FREQUENCY: q. PRICE: Dfl. 120/yr. PUBLISHER: H.E. Stenfert Kroese B.V., P.O. Box 33, 2300 AA Leiden, The Netherlands. EDITOR: S.K. Kuipers. ILLUSTRATIONS. INDEX. ADVERTISEMENTS. CIRCULATION: 1,200. MANUSCRIPT SELECTION: Editor, Board of Editors. MICROFORMS: LC. BOOK REVIEWS. INDEXED/ABSTRACTED: ABIn, BI, ExMed, IEconArt, JEL, KeyEconSci, PAIS, PROMT, RefSo, RiskAb, SOCI. TARGET AUDIENCE: AC, SP.

Not as prestigious as the London School of Economics' *Economica*, *De Economist* is also more parochial in nature. Where *Economica* is very international in nature, *De Economist* only occasionally focuses on issues outside the Netherlands. It does focus on economics, economic history and in some cases statistical analysis. It is good for comparative labor relations studies. Recent titles have included: "Unemployment and Labour Market Flexibility: the United Kingdom" and "World Coal: Economics, Policies and Prospects."

Each issue publishes an average of five articles usually twenty to thirty pages in length. Most authors are Dutch academics. There are ten or so signed book reviews per issue.

71   *Decision Line.* DATE FOUNDED: 1970. FREQUENCY: 5/yr. PRICE: $4/yr. PUBLISHER: Decision Sciences Institute, University Plaza, Atlanta, GA 30303-3083. EDITOR: K. Roscoe Davis. ILLUS-TRATIONS. ADVERTISEMENT. CIRCULATION: 5,000. MANUSCRIPT SELECTION: Editorial Review. REPRINTS: Publisher. BOOK REVIEWS. TARGET AUDIENCE: AC, GP, SP. SAMPLE COPIES: Libraries, individuals.

This newsletter is a supplementary publication for the Decision Sciences Institute. It serves as a means of communication among members of the Institute, provides a forum for discussions, opinions and setting goals. Recent articles have included "NSF Program in Decision, Risk and Management Science," and "Improving Instruction."

This tabloid usually runs ten to fifteen news stories. Regular features include "Names in the News," "Research Round Up", "Regional News" and among others, "Upcoming Institute Meetings."

72   *Decision Sciences.* DATE FOUNDED: 1970. FREQUENCY: q. PRICE: $63/yr. institutions, $48/yr. personal. PUBLISHER: Decision Sciences Institute, 140 Decatur Street, S.E., Atlanta, GA 30303-3083. EDITOR: Robert E. Markland. ILLUSTRATIONS. INDEX. ADVERTISEMENTS. CIRCULATION: 4,000. MANUSCRIPT SELECTION: Editor, Refereed. MICROFORMS: UMI. RE-PRINTS: Publisher. SPECIAL ISSUES: Occasional. INDEXED/ABSTRACTED: AAR, ABIn, AccI, BI, BusI, CompConAb, CurrCont, ElecComA, ElecElecAb, ExMed, IntAbOpRes, ISMEC, JContQuanMeth, MgtC, PhysAb, PollAb, SafSciA, SciAb. TARGET AUDIENCE: AC, SP. SAMPLE COPIES: Libraries, individuals.

This journal is published by the Decision Sciences Institute of Atlanta, Georgia "to promote the development and application of quantitative methodology to functional and behavioral problems of administration by providing a forum for the exchange of ideas, experience and information..." among academics and specialists. Recent articles have included "A Large-Scale Personnel Assignment Model for the Navy," and "An Evaluation of Forecast Error in Master Production Scheduling for Material Requirements Planning Systems."

Each issue has two sections with an average of five articles per section. The first section is "Concepts, Theory, and Techniques." The second is "Applications and Implementations."

73   *Detroit Labor News.* DATE FOUNDED: 1914. FREQUENCY: bw.
       PRICE: $4/yr. institutions, $5.20/yr. personal. PUBLISHER: Metro-
       politan Detroit AFL-CIO, 2550 W. Grand Blvd., Detroit, MI 48204.
       EDITOR: Aldo Vagnozzi. ILLUSTRATIONS. ADVERTISE-
       MENTS. CIRCULATION: 4,500. MANUSCRIPT SELECTION:
       Editor. MICROFORMS: UMI. SPECIAL ISSUES: Occasional.
       TARGET AUDIENCE: AC, GP, HS, SP. SAMPLE COPIES: Li-
       braries, individuals.

       A union newspaper bringing current information to people in the
       Metropolitan Detroit area. It presents the labor position, particularly
       in the AFL-CIO. Topics covered are labor, legislation, and the political
       scene, contract negotiations, and community activities. Its writers are
       professional journalists from the United States.

       A typical issue has an average of twelve articles, a president's column,
       an update on boycotts, bills in the state legislature and a summary of the
       Governor's actions. A special issue was dedicated to Martin Luther
       King on his birthday.

74   *Directors and Boards: The Journal of Corporate Action.* DATE
       FOUNDED: 1976. FREQUENCY: q. PRICE: $115/yr. PUB-
       LISHER: MLR Publishing Co., 229 S. 18th St., Philadelphia, PA
       19103. EDITOR: James Kristie. ILLUSTRATIONS. INDEX.
       ADVERTISEMENTS. CIRCULATION: 5,000. MANUSCRIPT
       SELECTION: Editor. MICROFORMS: UMI. REPRINTS: Pub-
       lisher. SPECIAL ISSUES: Occasional. INDEXED/ABSTRACTED:
       ABIn, AccDataProAb, AccI, ASEANMgtAb, BI, CLI, HospLitI, LRI,
       MgtC, MgtMarA, PAIS, Pred, PROMT, TraIndI. TARGET AUDI-
       ENCE: SP.

       This journal is primarily written by top level business executives who
       are authorities in their fields for other business executives. The focus of
       its content deals with corporate governance, management, government
       relations, finance and human relations. The approach is practical rather
       than theoretical.

       Each quarterly issue has twelve to fifteen articles with roughly one-half
       devoted to a specific topic such as director selection and recruitment or
       director compensation and benefits. There are regular sections such as
       letters from the publisher and readers, "Boardroom Briefs and Mem-
       oirs."

75   *Directory of Faculty Contracts and Bargaining Agents in Institutions
       of Higher Education.* DATE FOUNDED: 1975. FREQUENCY: a.

PRICE: $20/yr. PUBLISHER: National Center for the Study of Collective Bargaining in Higher Education and the Professions, Baruch College, City University of New York, 17 Lexington Ave., Box 322, New York, NY 10010. EDITOR: Joel M. Douglas. ILLUSTRATIONS. INDEX. CIRCULATION: 325. MANUSCRIPT SELECTION: Editor. MICROFORMS: ERIC. TARGET AUDIENCE: AC, SP.

The Directory is the only comprehensive compilation and statistical analysis of faculty contracts and bargaining agents at colleges and universities in the United States and Canada.

76   *Dissent*. DATE FOUNDED: 1954. FREQUENCY: q. PRICE: $25/ yr. institutions, $18/yr. personal. PUBLISHER: Foundation for the Study of Independent Social Ideas, Inc., 521 Fifth Avenue, New York, NY 10017. EDITORS: Irving Howe and Michael Walzer. ILLUSTRATIONS. INDEX. ADVERTISEMENTS. CIRCULATION: 8,500. MANUSCRIPT SELECTION: Editors, Editorial Board. MICROFORMS: UMI, MIM. BOOK REVIEWS. SPECIAL ISSUES. INDEXED/ABSTRACTED: ABCPolSci, AmerH, API, BoRvI, FLI, FutSurv, HistAb, LeftI, LLBA, PAIS, SocAb, SocSc, SocWAb, SPDA. TARGET AUDIENCE: AC, SP.

A socialist magazine of the American Democratic Left which publishes articles by such notables as Frances Fox Piven, Michael Harrington and such radicals as Howard Zinn. Recent topics of this famous publication (although written by academics and available on newstands) have been universities, labor unions, Glastnost, El Salvador, biotechnology, economics, democracy and women. Specific titles of interest to those studying labor/industrial relations are "Unions, Pension Funds and the Economy," "Where Wall and Pennsylvania Interesect; Economics in the Information Age," "A Workable Family Policy" and "Toward Adequate Health Care."

Each issue has ten major articles of usually less than fifteen pages. There are other features: "Comments and Opinions," "Reports from Abroad," shorter articles under "Notebook," and "Cultural Notes." A recent special issue (which are ocassional) focused on "The Democratic Promise." Most issues have a book review section. Book reviews are signed, six to ten when they appear, and are two to three pages in length.

77   *Economic and Industrial Democracy: An International Journal*. DATE FOUNDED: 1980. FREQUENCY: q. PRICE: $94.50/yr. institutions, $37.50/yr. personal. PUBLISHER: Sage Publications Ltd., 28 Banner St., London EC1Y 8QE, U.K. EDITOR: Bengt

Abrahamsson. ILLUSTRATIONS. INDEX. ADVERTISEMENTS. MANUSCRIPT SELECTION: Editors. BOOK REVIEWS. SPECIAL ISSUES. INDEXED/ABSTRACTED: BI, CurrCont, IntBibE, IntLabDoc, MgtC, SocAb, SOCI, WorAb. TARGET AUDIENCE: AC, GP.

This is an academic journal written by Swedish, American and British scholars. Philosophical analysis of industrial relations is present in usually three to five "papers" per issue. Each issue also includes "current information" which is usually two or three shorter pieces with such titles as "Trade Unions and Working Environment Research." Areas covered in lengthier papers are: cooperative movements, rights of workers, workers' management movement, organizational behavior, workers' participation, women's labor issues and humanizing the workplace.

Ten to fifteen signed book reviews are included in each issue. A recent special issue was on "Organizational Democracy in Trade Unions."

78   *Economic History Review.* DATE FOUNDED: 1927. FREQUENCY: q. PRICE: $42/yr. institutions, $20/yr. Economic History Society members. PUBLISHER: Basil Blackwell Ltd., 108 Cowley Road, Oxford OX4 1JF, United Kingdom. EDITORS: R.A. Church and E.A. Wrigley. ILLUSTRATIONS. INDEX. ADVERTISEMENTS. CIRCULATION: 5,000. MANUSCRIPT SELECTION: Editors. MICROFORMS: KTO. BOOK REVIEWS. INDEXED/ABSTRACTED: AHCI, AmerH, BibAg, BrArchAb, BrHumI, CurrCont, GeoAb, HistAb, IEconArt, PAIS, PopInd, RecPubArt, RefSo, SOCI, SocSc, WorAb. TARGET AUDIENCE: AC, SP.

The *Economic History Review* is devoted "principally to furthering the understanding of historical change in an economic and social context since ancient times." Such issues as the political dimensions of economic and social change, the history of economic thought and the development of social ideas are covered. Recent articles have included "The Political Economy of Demoralization: the State and the Coalmining Industry in America and Britain Between the Wars," and "Personal Wealth Distribution in Late Eighteenth Century Britain."

Each issue contains four or five articles and one "Survey and Speculations." Each article and the speculations are usually under twenty-five pages. Each issue also has "Essays in Bibliography and Criticism." There are usually twenty to thirty substantial signed book reviews per issue. Each year a "List of Publications on the Economic and Social History of Great Britain and Ireland" is included. The publication is obviously British in focus.

79   *Economic Outlook USA.* DATE FOUNDED: 1974. FREQUENCY:
q. PRICE: $29/yr. PUBLISHER: Survey Research Center, The University of Michigan, 426 Thompson Street, P.O. Box 1248, Ann Arbor,
MI 48106. EDITOR: F. Thomas Juster. ILLUSTRATIONS. INDEX. MANUCRIPT SELECTION: Editor, Editorial Board.
MICROFORMS: UMI. REPRINTS: UMI. INDEXED/ABSTRACTED: ABIn, BusI, MgtC, PAIS, Pred, PROMT, SageFamStudAb, SocSc, SRI. TARGET AUDIENCE: AC, SP.

Economic Outlook USA is designed to aid private and public decision
makers in achieving a better understanding of the economic and social
environment in which they will be operating. The analysis of this publication incorporates direct measurements of the expectations, attitudes
and plans of both consumers and business firms with the economic and
financial variables traditionally used in forecast models. Recent empirically based articles have included: "AIDS and Public Policy" and "An
International Perspective on the Income and Poverty Status of the U.S.
Aged."

This is a publication of the Survey Research Center of the Institute for
Social Research of the University of Michigan. It usually contains three
or four statistically based articles per issue.

80   *Economica.* DATE FOUNDED: 1921. FREQUENCY: q. PRICE:
$54/yr. institutions, $22/yr. personal. PUBLISHER: London School
of Economics and Political Science, c/o Tieto Ltd., Bank House, 8A
Hill Road, Clevedon, Avon BS21 7HH, England. EDITORS: Frank
Coswell, David de Meza, and Rick van der Ploeg. ILLUSTRATIONS.
INDEX. ADVERTISEMENTS. CIRCULATION: 3,800. MANUSCRIPT SELECTION: Editors, Editorial Board. MICROFORMS:
Johnson Associates, AA. BOOK REVIEWS. INDEXED/ABSTRACTED: ABIn, AmerH, BrHumI, CREJ, ExMed, GeoAb, HistAb, IEconArt, IntLabDoc, JEL, PAIS, RuralRecrTourAb, SocSc,
WorBankAb, WorldAgEconRuralSocAb.

Economica is the premier publication of the prestigious London School
of Economics and Political Science. Its focus is economics, economic
history, statistics and "closely related problems." Articles are written by
academics from a variety of countries. The articles are empirical and
conceptual in style. Recent titles have included: "Where Have Two
Million Trade Union Members Gone?" "Unionized Contracts With
Fixed Wage Rates and State-contingent Employment Levels," and
"What Do Investment Managers Know? An Empirical Study of Practitioners' Predictions."

Each issue has an average of ten articles of under thirty pages each. There is an extensive list of "Books Received." A "Book Reviews" column in each issue usually runs ten to fifteen signed reviews of a page to a page and one-half in length.

81   *Economics and Business.* DATE FOUNDED: 1954. TITLE CHANGES: *Economics Library Selections, Series I: New Books in Economics* (1954-1965); *International Economics Selections Bibliography. Series I: New Books in Economics* (1966-1966); *Economic Selections* (1976-1984). MERGER: *Economics Selections: Series I: New Books in Economics* (1967-1973); *Economic Selections. Series II: Basic Lists in Special Fields* (1967-1967). FREQUENCY: q. PRICE: $122/yr. institutions, $49/yr. personal. PUBLISHER: Gordon and Breach Science Publishers, Inc., 150 Fifth Avenue, New York, NY 10011. EDITOR: H.M. Gitelman. INDEX. MANUSCRIPT SELECTION: Editor. BOOK REVIEWS. INDEXED/ABSTRACTED: CurrCont, SciAb. TARGET AUDIENCE: AC, SP.

Economics and Business is an "international annotated bibliography." The titles reviewed are arranged according to the area of specialization. Areas covered of importance to labor and industrial relations are manpower training, labor force and supply, labor markets, public policy, trade unions, collective bargaining, and labor-mangement relations.

Each issue provides a comprehensive survey of hundreds of new and recent books and monographs in economics and business related subjects. Other features include "Bibliographies; Reference Works; New Journals." Reviews are not signed.

82   *Economist.* DATE FOUNDED: 1843. FREQUENCY: w. PRICE: $98/yr. PUBLISHER: Economist Newspaper Ltd., 25 St. James's Street, London SWIA IHG, England. EDITOR: Andrew Knight. ILLUSTRATIONS. INDEX. ADVERTISEMENTS. CIRCULATION: 170,000. MANUSCRIPT SELECTION: In-house Staff. MICROFORMS: UMI. REPRINTS: UMI. BOOK REVIEWS. INDEXED/ABSTRACTED: BMTA, BoRvD, BoRvI, BrHumI, BusI, CoalA, EnerInfoAb, EnvAb, GeoAb, HiEdCurrAwareBull, IntLabDoc, KeyEconSci, MgtC, MgtMarA, PAIS, Pred, PROMT, ShipA, SocSc, TraIndI, WorTexA. TARGET AUDIENCE: AC, GP, SP.

Ulrich's calls the *Economist* a "Newspaper giving world-wide business and financial news and discussing political events as they affect the economy." It is published in Great Britain and is directed at consumers of the popular press. It also has a creditable reputation among academ-

Bibliography   45

ics as a source of current business and financial news. Its format is not much unlike American popular press magazines such as *Forbes* and *Fortune* or even *Business Week*.

Each issue publishes a number of articles of usually under a page or two in length. They are arranged under such topical headings as "Leaders, World Politics and Current Affairs: America, Asia, International, Europe and Britain," and "Business," "Schools," "Finance," "Science and Technology," "Economic Indicators," and "Letters." There are usually five substantial (one to two pages), signed book reviews per issue.

83   *Economy and Society*. DATE FOUNDED: 1972. FREQUENCY: q. PRICE: $65/yr. PUBLISHER: Routledge Journals, Methuen Inc., 29 W. 35th St., New York, NY 10001. EDITOR: Sami Zubaida. ILLUS-TRATIONS. INDEX. MANUSCRIPT SELECTION: Editor, Editorial Board. MICROFORMS: UMI. REPRINTS: UMI. IN-DEXED/ ABSTRACTED: ASSIA, LLBA, SocAb, SOCI, SPDA, WorBankAb. TARGET AUDIENCE: AC, SP.

This is a British academic journal with a left of center perspective. Its view of economics and society is from a self-proclaimed Marxist viewpoint. Erudite and probably outside the mainstream of traditional scholarship. Recent articles have included: "Analysing the British Miners Strike of 1984-85," "A Political Genealogy of Political Economy" and "Social Theory and Social Policy."

Each issue contains five or six articles usually twenty to thirty pages in length. Other features include briefer review articles (usually one or two) and "Notes on Contributions."

84   *Electrical Union World*. DATE FOUNDED: 1940. FREQUENCY: m. PRICE: Free. PUBLISHER: International Brotherhood of Electrical Workers, Local Union No. 3, 158-11 Jewel Ave., Flushing, NY 11365. EDITOR: Thomas VanArsdale. ILLUSTRATIONS. CIR-CULATION: 50,000. MANUSCRIPT SELECTION: In-house Staff. MICROFORMS: Publisher. SPECIAL ISSUES: Occasional. TARGET AUDIENCE: AC, GP, HS, SP. SAMPLE COPIES: Libraries, individuals.

This is a newspaper tabloid which publishes general labor news, issues confronting labor in government, social events and labor history as it affects this union. It advocates workers' rights and the right of labor unions to represent the interest of working men and women. Its editorial staff which composes the publication are professionals in the field of union work.

Typical issues report of past and future election of officers, information on scholarships available for college students and pictures of recent recipients, U.S. Labor Department rulings affecting farm workers, articles of people who have been active in the trade union movement, and social activities. Advertisements are accepted; several are in the sample issues regarding boycotts on certain products.

85   *Employee Benefits Cases*. DATE FOUNDED: 1980. FREQUENCY: Looseleaf. PRICE: $547/yr. PUBLISHER: Bureau of National Affairs, 1231 25th St., N.W., Washington, D.C. 20037. ILLUSTRATIONS. INDEX. TARGET AUDIENCE: AC, SP.

Employer Benefits Cases is another looseleaf service from BNA. It is a single source for the texts of the latest, precedent setting federal and state employee benefits cases. It is updated weekly; it has one reference binder and past issues are bound for future reference.

86   *Employee Benefits Journal*. DATE FOUNDED: 1975. FREQUENCY: q. PRICE: $35/yr. PUBLISHER: International Foundation of Employee Benefit Plans, 18700 W. Bluemound Rd., P.O. Box 69, Brookfield, WI 53008-0069. EDITOR: Mary E. Brennan. ILLUSTRATIONS. INDEX. CIRCULATION: 34,000. MANUSCRIPT SELECTION: Editor. MICROFORMS: UMI. BOOK REVIEWS. INDEXED/ABSTRACTED: ABIn, BI, BusI, HospLitI, IMed, InsurPerI, MgtC, Pred, PROMT. TARGET AUDIENCE: AC, SP.

Published by the foundation for its membership, this journal covers topics such as health and welfare plans; pensions and pension plans; pertinent federal and state legislation; and managing benefit plans. The *Employee Benefits Journal* is written from a decidedly management perspective.

Each issue contains six to eight substantive articles such as "Continuation of Health Benefits for Employees: Snake in the Grass to Employers," and "Cost Containment Advantages of Managed Dental Care." Ten to fifteen unsigned book reviews are included in each issue.

87   *Employee Relations*. DATE FOUNDED: 1979. FREQUENCY: 6/yr. PRICE: $359.95/yr. PUBLISHER: MCB University Press Ltd., 62 Toller Lane, Bradford BD8 9BY, England. EDITOR: Mick Marchington. INDEX. MANUSCRIPT SELECTION: Editor, Editorial Advisory Board, Refereed. REPRINTS: Publisher. BOOK RE-

VIEWS. SPECIAL ISSUES. INDEXED/ABSTRACTED: ABIn, CIJE, IntLabDoc, MgtC, MgtMarA. TARGET AUDIENCE: AC, SP.

The focus of this British publication is on relationships whether it be between management and employees, between union members and management or between managerial employees. Articles are written by both management and employees. It is comprehensive in its coverage: developments in collective bargaining, equal opportunities in employment, health and safety at work, and shop steward training. It presents the material in a straight-forward manner so that readers may assimilate and assess the experiences of their peers. The special issues provide a critical overview of high interest areas.

A typical issue has approximately six articles usually enhanced by charts, diagrams, or figures. There is a separate section which reports on the latest news, analyzes new developments in the field and provides book reviews of interest to the readers. The reviews which are written by academics are signed and about a page in length.

88   *Employee Relations Law Journal.* DATE FOUNDED: 1975. FREQUENCY: q. PRICE: $135/yr. PUBLISHER: Executive Enterprise Publications Co., Inc., 22 W. 21st Street, New York, NY 10010-6904. EDITOR: William J. Kilberg. ILLUSTRATIONS. INDEX. ADVERTISEMENTS. CIRCULATION: 2,200. MANUSCRIPT SELECTION: Editor, Editorial Advisory Board. MICROFORMS: UMI, WSH. REPRINTS: UMI. BOOK REVIEWS. INDEXED/ABSTRACTED: ABIn, BankLitI, BI, BusI, CLI, CurrCont, HospLitI, ICommLegPer, ILegPer, LegCont, LRI, MgtC, PersLit, SageFamStudAb, TraIndI. TARGET AUDIENCE: AC, SP.

The *Employee Relations Law Journal* publishes articles in the areas of labor-management relations, equal employment opportunity, employee benefits and pension plans, and occupational health and safety. Recent articles have included "Reducing the Risk of Negligence in Hiring," "Avoiding Liability in Employee Handbooks" and "When Hospitals Limit Organizing Activity."

Each issue has an average of ten articles of varying length. There is a "Bookshelf" of five or so unsigned book reviews.

89   *Employee Relations Weekly.* DATE FOUNDED: 1983. FREQUENCY: Looseleaf. PRICE: $560/yr. PUBLISHER: Bureau of National Affairs, 1231 25th St., N.W., Washington, D.C. 20037. ILLUSTRATIONS. INDEX. TARGET AUDIENCE: AC, SP.

Employee Relations Weekly is another looseleaf service from BNA. This service covers developments in a changing workplace by reporting on: hiring policies, pension and health care plans, compensation programs, dispute resolution, productivity programs, training efforts, pay equity and labor negotiations. *ERW* is updated weekly and is housed in two storage binders.

90   *Employer.* DATE FOUNDED: 1971. FREQUENCY: 6/yr. PUBLISHER: New Zealand Employers Federation, P.O. Box 1786, Wellington, New Zealand. EDITOR: Karen Lloyd. CIRCULATION: 15,000. MANUSCRIPT SELECTION: Editor, Directors. REPRINTS: Publisher. SPECIAL ISSUES: Occasional. INDEXED/ ABSTRACTED: INZPer. TARGET AUDIENCE: AC, SP. SAMPLE COPIES: Libraries, individuals.

The aim of this publication is to provide information to the private sector employers on those issues which affect them and efforts which are being undertaken on their behalf by the Federation. It is an advocate for the provision of genuine, productive and unsubsidized jobs in the private sector and espouses the employers' perspective. The majority of the writers are academics, researchers and managers from New Zealand.

A typical issue has an average of eight articles of up-to-date analysis of the industrial scene and current legislation as it affects the employer.

91   *Employment Bulletin* (R.I.). DATE FOUNDED: 1955. FREQUENCY: m. PRICE: Free. PUBLISHER: R.I. Dept. of Employment Security, Division of Research & Program Standards, 24 Mason St., Providence, RI 02903. CIRCULATION: 2,000. MICROFORMS: Publisher. REPRINTS: Publisher. SAMPLE COPIES: Libraries, individuals.

Published and written by state government researchers, the *Employment Bulletin* is a statistical compilation of employment and unemployment data for the State of Rhode Island by the Department of Employment Security in cooperation with the U.S. Department of Labor, Bureau of Labor Statistics.

There are two articles per issue with a variety of statistical tabulations, charts and graphs.

92   *Employment Guide.* DATE FOUNDED: 1986. FREQUENCY: Looseleaf. PRICE: $248/yr. PUBLISHER: Bureau of National Af-

fairs, 1231 25th St., N.W., Washington, D.C. 20037. ILLUSTRA-
TIONS. INDEX. TARGET AUDIENCE: AC, SP.

Employment Guide is another looseleaf service from BNA. In a regularly
updated guide and biweekly newsletter, *Employment Guide* covers:
hiring to retirement, wages and salaries, employee benefits, rules and
discipline, safety and health, dealing with unions, and employment laws
and regulations. This service is designed for managers. It is housed in
one binder.

93   *Employment Initiatives.*   DATE FOUNDED: 1982. TITLE
CHANGES: *Initiatives* (1982-87). FREQUENCY: 6/yr. PRICE: $44/
yr. PUBLISHER: Longman Group UK Ltd., 6th Floor, Westgate
House, The High, Harlow, Essex CM19 5AA, United Kingdom.
EDITOR: Colin Ball. ILLUSTRATIONS. INDEX. ADVERTISE-
MENTS. CIRCULATION: 1,000. MANUSCRIPT SELECTION:
Editor. BOOK REVIEWS. TARGET AUDIENCE: AC, GP, SP.
SAMPLE COPIES: Libraries, individuals.

Initiatives is the journal of the Centre for Employment Initiatives. The
Centre is an independent, non-profit organization providing technical
assistance, research and development, and information services to organizations involved in combatting and responding to unemployment.
Topics covered have included community development, trade unions,
long-term and youth unemployment, community cooperatives, and
collaborative approaches to unemployment in general. Mainly British
in focus, but useful in other countries experiencing any level of unemployment. This is a publication designed to share practical information.

Four or five articles are published per issue. Three to four signed book
reviews are published in each issue. Other features include "Notice
Board" and "What's Happening Now."

94   *Employment Relations Today.* DATE FOUNDED: 1974. TITLE
CHANGES: *EEO Today* (1974-1983). FREQUENCY: q. PRICE:
$120/yr. PUBLISHER: Executive Enterprises Publication Co., 22
West 21st St., New York, NY 10010-6904. EDITOR: Jean Stephen-
son. ILLUSTRATIONS. INDEX. ADVERTISEMENTS. CIRCU-
LATION: 1,915. MANUSCRIPT SELECTION: Editor, Editorial
Advisory Board. MICROFORMS: UMI. INDEXED/AB-
STRACTED: ABIn, BI, BusI, MgtC, WorAb. TARGET AUDI-
ENCE: AC, SP.

This is a major journal in the employee relations area. The focus is
human resource management, equal employment opportunity, unions,

mediation, legal and legislative action related to the personnel field. Typical articles have included, "The Reemergence of Unions," and "Dealing With Sexual Harassment in the Work Place."

Each issue has eight to ten substantive articles of varying length. Regular features include "Key Court Action," "Washington Scene," "Employment Relations Programs" and a regular information sharing column, "Questions and Answers."

95   *Entertainment Worker.*   DATE FOUNDED: 1986. TITLE CHANGE: *In Focus* (nd). FREQUENCY: q. PUBLISHER: K. OPHEL, Box 2, Trades Hall, Carlton South 3053 Victoria, Australia. EDITOR: C. Livingstone. ILLUSTRATIONS. CIRCULATION: 13,000. MANUSCRIPT SELECTION: Editor. SPECIAL ISSUES: Occasional. INDEXED/ABSTRACTED: AustNatBib. TARGET AUDIENCE: SP. SAMPLE COPIES: Libraries.

This is the official publication of the Australian entertainment industry. It advocates issues important to the technical and related workers rather than that of performers or employers. A major quarterly journal, the articles published include such titles as: "Australia's Media Crisis" and "New Policy for Overseas Artists". Generally it is written by staff with an occasional piece by an academic.

It contains five to six major articles per issue with twelve to fifteen briefs. The journal publishes special issues as "the need arises."

96   *Equal Opportunities Review.*   DATE FOUNDED: 1985. FRE-QUENCY: 6/yr. PRICE: £78/yr. PUBLISHER: Industrial Relations Services, 18-20 Highbury Place, London N5 1QP, England. EDI-TORS: Gary Bowker and Michael Rubenstein. ILLUSTRATIONS. INDEX. MANUSCRIPT SELECTION: Editors. REPRINTS: Publisher. SPECIAL ISSUES. TARGET AUDIENCE: AC, SP.

Equal Opportunities Review is a British publication which provides analysis on current and forthcoming anti-discrimination legislation (exclusively in Great Britain), surveys on the practice and problems from both the public and private sector, guidance on developing equal opportunity policies and procedures and full reports and commentary on case law.

Each issue has several features. The news section has twelve to fifteen short items of current interest. There is a "Features" section in which issues are discussed in greater depth. Recent topics have been AIDS in the workplace and equalizing of the retirement age between men and women. Other regular sections are the profiling of a person prominent in the field, a discussion of documents recently released in the equal opportunity area, and lastly, a substantial section regarding recent legal judgments.

97   *ETU News*. DATE FOUNDED: 1912. TITLE CHANGES: *Electrical Trades Journal* (1912-1954). FREQUENCY: q. PRICE: $2.50/yr. PUBLISHER: Electrical Trades Union of Australia, 302-306 Elizabeth Street, Sydney, N.S.W. 2010, Australia. EDITOR: T.A. Johnson. ILLUSTRATIONS. ADVERTISEMENTS. CIRCULATION: 80,026. MANUSCRIPT SELECTION: Editor. SPECIAL ISSUES: Occasional. INDEXED/ABSTRACTED: APAIS. TARGET AUDIENCE: SP. SAMPLE COPIES: Individuals.

ETU News is the official organ of the Electrical Trades Union and is sent to members throughout Australia. It reflects the union position with regard to collective bargaining, industrial relations and occupational safety. The articles are of broad interest and not just for electricians.

The publication is written by officers of the union for a sizeable membership. It includes a "Dates and Events" calendar which seems quite well done. Typical articles include: "National Wage Case—The Principles" and "The Incredible Shrinking Dollar."

98   *European Industrial Relations Review*. DATE FOUNDED: 1974. FREQUENCY: m. PRICE: £165/yr. PUBLISHER: Industrial Relations Services, 18-20 Highbury Place, London N5 1QP, England. INDEX. CIRCULATION: 1,500. MANUSCRIPT SELECTION: Editor. REPRINTS: Publisher, UMI. SPECIAL ISSUES: Occasional. INDEXED/ABSTRACTED: IntLabDoc, KeyEconSci, MgtC, MgtMarA. TARGET AUDIENCE: AC, SP.

This British publication is directed toward the managers and executives in the field of industrial relations from the European Economic Community. There are special correspondents reporting on issues from their countries. The coverage is objective.

The first section has short items from the EEC countries. In a sample issue, many dealt with pay-related issues. The second section has longer articles. In a recent issue the feature section covered legislation on long-term French unemployment and social security reforms in France. From Ireland, an article on the "shared learning experience" originating in Norway and applied to Irish companies proves to be highly successful. Features on employment, labor laws, pensions and retirement are other topics which are presented from specific countries.

There is a table of statistics, such as the consumer price indices for twenty countries.

99   *European Journal of Operational Research.* DATE FOUNDED: 1977. FREQUENCY: 15/yr. PRICE: Dfl. 1075/yr. institutions, Dfl. 200/yr. personal. PUBLISHER: Elsevier Science Publishers B.V. (North Holland), P.O. Box 1991, 1000 B2 Amsterdam, The Netherlands. EDITORS: Alan Mercer, C. Bernhard Tilanus, Hans-Jurgen Zimmerman. ILLUSTRATIONS. INDEX. ADVERTISEMENTS. CIRCULATION: 1,500. MANUSCRIPT SELECTION: Editors. MICROFORMS: Publisher. REPRINTS: Publisher. BOOK REVIEWS. SPECIAL ISSUES: 4/yr. INDEXED/ABSTRACTED: ABIn, CoalA, CompConLit, ElecComA, ElecElecAb, EnerResA, EngI, EngIBioengAb, EngIEnerAb, ExMed, IntAbOpRes, ISMEC, MathR, MgtC, PhysAb, PollAb, SafSciA, ShipA. TARGET AUDIENCE: AC, SP. SAMPLE COPIES: Libraries, individuals.

This international scholarly journal, which is sponsored by the Association of European Operational Research Societies, publishes high-quality original papers that contribute to the practice of decision-making. The major focus of its articles involves the application of scientific methods to the managment of complex systems of people, machinery, materials, money and information. Articles are written by academicians and researchers both from "within Europe and beyond Europe."

Each issue contains a leading review covering the developments of an operations research topic over the last five years. There is also a section of letters and technical notes. There is a book review section which contains approximately ten signed reviews per issue which have been published within the previous year. Each review averages 600 words. There are usually four special issues per year devoted to a single topic.

100   *European Management Journal.* DATE FOUNDED: 1982. FREQUENCY: q. PRICE: £80/yr. PUBLISHER: Basil Blackwood Ltd., 108 Cowley Rd., Oxford OX4 1JF, England. EDITOR: Paul Stonham. ADVERTISEMENTS. CIRCULATION: 5,000. MANUSCRIPT SELECTION: Editor. REPRINTS: Publisher. BOOK REVIEWS. INDEXED/ABSTRACTED: MgtMarA. TARGET AUDIENCE: AC, SP. SAMPLE COPIES: Libraries, individuals.

A scholarly, objective journal, *European Management Journal* provides needed practical and scholarly information for senior managers in the manufacturing arena. The articles cover a range of topics from the European Economic Community to microchips. As the focus is primarily on Europe and its relationship with the rest of the world, the majority of writers are European academics.

A typical issue contains ten to twelve articles. In a recent issue, many of the articles were concerned with the human element in management ranging from one's employees to competing in cross cultural environments. There is a lengthy critical book review section. Each issue contains an average of sixteen one-page signed reviews.

101   *Evaluation Review*. DATE FOUNDED: 1977. TITLE CHANGES: *Evaluation Quarterly* (1977-1979). FREQUENCY: 6/yr. PRICE: $96/yr. institutions, $36/yr. personal. PUBLISHER: Sage Publications, Inc., 2111 West Hillcrest Drive, Newbury Park, CA 91320. EDITORS: Richard A. Berk and Howard E. Freeman. ILLUSTRATIONS. INDEX. ADVERTISEMENTS. MANUSCRIPT SELECTION: Editors, Refereed. MICROFORMS: UMI. INDEXED/ABSTRACTED: AbHlthCareMgtS, AdolMentHlthAb, CIJE, CLI, CrimJusAb, CurrCont, CurrIStat, CurrLitFamPlan, HRA, HRIS, LRI, PAIS, PsyAb, SageFamStudAb, SagePAA, SocAb, SOCI, SocSc, SPDA. TARGET AUDIENCE: AC, SP.

Evaluation Review "is the forum for researchers, planners, and policy makers engaged in the development, implementation, and utilization of studies aimed at the betterment of the human condition." Topics covered in the published research are: income security, manpower, child development, health, education, mental health, criminal justice, and the physical and social environments. Recent titles have included: "Measuring Validity Using Coworker Samples," and "Reliable Assessment Data in Multisite Programs."

Each issue includes four to six articles of twenty to thirty pages in length. Other features occasionally include review essays, "research briefs" and "craft reports" which are focused on innovative research techniques.

102   *Execu-Time*. DATE FOUNDED: 1970. FREQUENCY: bi-m. PRICE: $65/yr. PUBLISHER: Timelet Corp., 26940 North Longwood Road, Lake Forest, IL 60045-1071. EDITOR: Lauren R. Januz. CIRCULATION: 10,000. MANUSCRIPT SELECTION: Editor. TARGET AUDIENCE: SP.

Execu-Time is a time management newsletter for the in-the-field practitioner. Articles, usually brief, are designed to help promote "effective use of executive time." Recent articles have included, "Freezing Time Drains," "Effectiveness Models" and "Memo Style Letters."

Each issue contains seven to ten articles. All articles are very brief and focus on time efficiency.

103   *Facts*. DATE FOUNDED: 1977. FREQUENCY: 6/yr. PRICE: Free. PUBLISHER: Canadian Union of Public Employees, 21 Florence St., Ottawa, Ontario, K2P OW6. EDITOR: Ed Finn. ILLUSTRA-TIONS. INDEX. CIRCULATION: 40,000. MANUSCRIPT SE-LECTION: Editors. TARGET AUDIENCE: GP, SP. SAMPLE COPIES: Libraries, individuals.

A pro-labor publication aimed at providing information on social issues and labor research. The majority of writers are Canadian academicians, researchers, or practitioners. Canadian Union of Public Employees publishes both the *Facts* and the *Public Employee*. The *Facts* encompasses more articles than the latter but they are aimed at the same union clientele. Articles in the *Facts* are geared toward Canadians but are global enough to be of interest to Americans.

A recent issue contained articles on workplace surveillance, shiftwork problems, information in the post-industrial age, and drug testing.

104   *Facts and Figures*. DATE FOUNDED: 1958. FREQUENCY: q. PRICE: Free. PUBLISHER: New Mexico Employment Security Department, P.O. Box 1925, Albuquerque, NM 87110. EDITOR: Vince Brunacini. CIRCULATION: 50. REPRINTS: Publisher. TARGET AUDIENCE: AC, GP, SP. SAMPLE COPIES: Libraries, individuals.

Compiled and written by New Mexico state government researchers, *Facts and Figures* is strictly statistical in nature. It provides geo-economic data to labor, employers, researchers and government agencies.

Strictly employment data for New Mexico, each issue runs approximately thirty to fifty pages. It includes tables, graphs and charts.

105   *Fair Labor Standard Handbook for States, Local Government and Schools*. DATE FOUNDED: 1985. FREQUENCY: m. PRICE: $165/yr. PUBLISHER: Thompson Publishing Group, 1725 K Street, N.W., Suite 200, Washington, D.C. 20006. EDITOR: Kathleen M. Dunten. INDEX. CIRCULATION: 10,000. MANUSCRIPT SE-LECTION: Editor. REPRINTS: Publisher. TARGET AUDI-ENCE: AC, SP.

The *Fair Labor Standards Handbook for States, Local Governments and Schools* was designed to help public employees of each of those sectors implement the Fair Labor Standards Act. The Act extended coverage to public employees in 1985. This is a "loose-leaf like" service where the basic two-volume set is updated on a monthly basis.

Current Developments is a monthly newsletter also issued as part of the service. It usually averages five to six pages. Topics covered are news items of interest to those implementing the Fair Labor Standards Act.

106   *Far Eastern Economic Review.* DATE FOUNDED: 1946. FRE-
QUENCY: w. PRICE: $98/yr. PUBLISHER: Review Publishing Co., Ltd., G.P.O. Box 160, Hong Kong. EDITOR: Derek Davies. ILLUS-
TRATIONS. INDEX. ADVERTISEMENTS. CIRCULATION: 65,000. MANUSCRIPT SELECTION: Editor. MICROFORMS: Bell and Howell, RPI. BOOK REVIEWS. INDEXED/AB-
STRACTED: HRRep, IntLabDoc, KeyEconSci, MgtC, PAIS, RefSo, RuralRecrTourAb, ShipA, SocSc, WorldAgEconRuralSocAb. TAR-
GET AUDIENCE: AC, GP, SP.

Far Eastern Economic Review reports and interprets finance, stock market and investment trends in thirty Asian countries as well as giving industrial and other business news. Recent articles in this popular magazine format publication of importance to labor relations include: "Manila Hopes to Revive Its Stagnant Mining Industry," "Thailand Union Leaders Unite," "Only the Black Economy is Keeping Burma Afloat" and "Workers Protest at Steel Plant's New Owners."

Each issue contains about fifteen articles of under ten pages in this *Business Week* look alike. There are several signed, substantial book reviews in each issue. Other features include: "Regional Affairs," "Arts and Society," "Business Affairs," "Exchange Rates," and among others, "Stockmarkets."

107   *Federal Managers Quarterly.* DATE FOUNDED: 1983. FRE-
QUENCY: q. PRICE: $12/yr. PUBLISHER: Federal Managers Asso-
ciation, 1000 16th Street, N.W., Suite 701, Washington, DC 20036. EDITOR: David W. Sanasack. ILLUSTRATIONS. INDEX. AD-
VERTISEMENTS. CIRCULATION: 25,000. MANUSCRIPT SELECTION: Editor. REPRINTS: Publisher. SPECIAL ISSUES: Annually. INDEXED/ABSTRACTED: PersLit, SagePAA. TAR-
GET AUDIENCE: AC, GP, SP. SAMPLE COPIES: Libraries, indi-
viduals.

As the official publication of the Federal Managers Association, the *Federal Managers Quarterly* provides information on management, personnel, and leadership issues that impact on the nation's federal em-

ployees. Recent titles have included "Finding the Best Conflict Resolution Strategy," "Managing to Payroll" and "Purdue University: People and Industry." It also promotes federal employers' position on legislation.

Each issue has three or four articles under each of the following headings: "Features," "Professional Development" and "Departments." Each issue also has several major focus articles such as "49th Annual Convention and Management Seminar" and "The Constitution's Bicentennial."

108   *Forbes*. DATE FOUNDED: 1917. FREQUENCY: b-w. PRICE: $45/yr. PUBLISHER: Forbes, Inc., 60 Fifth Ave., New York, NY 10011. EDITOR: James W. Michaels. ILLUSTRATIONS. INDEX. ADVERTISEMENTS. CIRCULATION: 735,000. MANUSCRIPT SELECTION: Editors. MICROFORMS: UMI, MIM. REPRINTS: UMI. INDEXED/ABSTRACTED: ABIn, AccI, BankLit, BI, BusI, CADCAMA, ChemAb, ChemIndN, CoalA, CompBus, CompLitI, DataProcD, EnerI, EnerInfoAb, EnvAb, KeyEconSci, MagInd, MgtC, Pred, PROMT, RehabLit, RG, SRI, TraIndI. TARGET AUDIENCE: AC, GP, SP.

Forbes, like *Business Week* and *Fortune*, is one of the leading U.S. business magazines. Popular and journalistic in style, recent typical articles have included "Charles Wang and His Thundering Nerds," and "Carver Mead's Powerful Vision." But its real strength, apart from the feature articles, are company profiles which are particularly important.

Each issue has a cover story, ten company history-based articles, and features titled "Industries," "International," "On the Docket," "Taxing Matters," "Investing," "Faces Behind the Figures" and among several others, "Marketing" and "Science and Technology."

109   *Fortune*. DATE FOUNDED: 1930. FREQUENCY: b-w. PRICE: $47.97/yr. PUBLISHER: Time Inc., Time and Life Building, Rockefeller Center, New York, NY 10020-1393. EDITOR: Marshall Loeb. ILLUSTRATIONS. INDEX. ADVERTISEMENTS. CIRCULATION: 724,822. MANUSCRIPT SELECTION: Editor. MICROFORMS: UMI, Bell and Howell, MIM. REPRINTS: UMI. BOOK REVIEWS. SPECIAL ISSUES. INDEXED/ABSTRACTED: ABIn, AccI, AmBibSlav, BI, BMTA, BusI, CADCAMA, ChemIndN, CoalA, CompBus, CompIndUp, EnerInfoAb, EnerResAb, EnvAb, ExMed, FuelEnerAb, GeoRef, HospLitI, IntAeroAb, IntLabDoc, IPapChem, KeyEconSci, MagInd, MgtC, MgtMarA, OceanAb, OperRes, PAIS, PCR2, PollAb, Pred, PROMT, Re-

sourceCenI, RG, SciAb, SelWaterResAb, SRI, TexTechD, TraIndI, WorAb, WorBankAb. TARGET AUDIENCE: AC, GP, SP.

Fortune is a popular business magazine in the mold of *Business Week* and even more similar to *Forbes*. It is written for the professional needing current information on business and economics. Recent articles have included: "The World According to the American Association of Retired People," and "The Slow Death of E.F. Hutton."

Each issue, written by in-house staffers, usually runs several cover stories of varying length. Regular features include: "The Economy," "Technology," "Corporate Performance," "Money and Markets," and "Politics and Policy." *Fortune* does include occasional, signed book reviews.

110   *Free Labour World.* DATE FOUNDED: 1951. FREQUENCY: sm. PRICE: 750 Belgian francs. PUBLISHER: International Confederation of Free Trade Unions, rue Montagne aux Herbes Potageres 37, 1000 Brussels, Belgium. EDITOR: Ian Graham. ILLUSTRATIONS. CIRCULATION: 13,000. MANUSCRIPT SELECTION: Editor. REPRINTS: Publisher. INDEXED/ABSTRACTED: HRRep, PAIS. TARGET AUDIENCE: GP, SP. SAMPLE COPIES: Libraries, individuals.

Each issue of *Free Labour World* is published separately in four different languages: English, French, German and Spanish. Focus is the world trade union movement with broad geographic coverage.

Four to five articles per issue with many newsbriefs are written by in-house staff with an occasional guest writer. Typical articles are: "International Support for Turkish Union Rights Campaign" and "South Africa Embargo Violations."

111   *Futures.* DATE FOUNDED: 1968. FREQUENCY: 6/yr. PRICE: £119/yr. institutions, £34/yr. personal. PUBLISHER: Butterworth Scientific Ltd., P.O. Box 63, Westbury House, Bury Street, Guildford GU2 5BH, United Kingdom. EDITOR: Colin Blackman. ILLUSTRATIONS. INDEX. ADVERTISEMENTS. MANUSCRIPT SELECTION: Editor, Advisory Board. MICROFORMS: UMI. BOOK REVIEWS. INDEXED/ABSTRACTED: ABCPolSci, ABIn, CISAb, CoalA, CurrCont, EnerInfoAb, EngI, EngIBioengAb, EngIEnerAb, EnvAb, FutSurv, IntLabDoc, MgtC, RefSo, RuralRecrTourAb, SocAb, SOCI, SocSc, SPDA, WorldAgEconRuralSocAb.

Futures is billed as a journal of forecasting and planning. It is written by strategic planners, sociologists, social, and science policy specialists from a wide array of countries. Recent topics covered have been unemployment, the middle class, robotics, forecasts for the 1990's, the Soviet future, and secondary schools. Recent titles have been "The Bonsai Trees of Japanese Industry" and "Employment Puzzle: Job Creation or Job Diversion?" Most articles are empirically based.

Each issue has an average of four articles usually under twenty pages in length. Under the heading "Review," there are usually four additional short articles. In addition to fifteen to twenty signed book reviews per section, there are columns of "Publications Received," "News" and "Meetings."

112   *Government Executive.* DATE FOUNDED: 1969. FREQUENCY: m. PRICE: $48/yr. PUBLISHER: National Journal, Inc., 1730 M Street, N.W., 11th floor, Washington, D.C. 20036. EDITOR: Timothy B. Clark. ILLUSTRATIONS. INDEX. ADVERTISEMENTS. CIRCULATION: 72,377. MANUSCRIPT SELECTION: Editor. MICROFORMS: UMI. REPRINTS: UMI. BOOK REVIEWS. INDEXED/ABSTRACTED: ABIn, BI, MgtC, PersLit, SagePAA. TARGET AUDIENCE: AC, GP, SP.

This popular format magazine is published for the government executive. Its articles are directed at understanding the business of government for those who run its departments, agencies, and bureaus. It could be useful for those executives in state and local governments as well. Recent articles have included: "Halfway For Hatch Act Reform," "Are Bureaucrats Lazy?," "Is Government Too Big?" and "Implications for Management."

Each issue publishes an average of eight articles of ten pages or less. Regular departments include: "Letters," "Executive Memo," "People" and among others, "Calendar." There are several signed book reviews per issue.

113   *Government Finance Review.* DATE FOUNDED: 1926. TITLE CHANGES: *Comptroller* (1926-1933); *Municipal Finance* (1933-1971). MERGER: *Government Financial Management Resources in Review* (1978-1984); *Governmental Finance* (1972-1984). FREQUENCY: 6/yr. PRICE: $30/yr. PUBLISHER: Government Finance Officers Association, 1750 K Street, N.W., Suite 200, Washington, D.C. 20006. EDITOR: Barbara Weiss. ILLUSTRATIONS. INDEX. ADVERTISEMENTS. CIRCULATION: 11,000. MANUSCRIPT SELECTION: Editors. MICROFORMS: UMI. REPRINTS: UMI. BOOK REVIEWS. INDEXED/ABSTRACTED: ABCPolSci, BusI, MgtC, PAIS, PROMT, SagePAA. TARGET AUDIENCE: AC, SP.

Government Finance Review is published by the Government Finance Officers Association of the United States and Canada. *GFR* seeks "to reflect a broad spectrum of thought and practice in finance and financial management for state and local governments." Recent articles of interest have included: "The Wellness Approach to Reducing Employee Illness," "Ethics and the Public Finance Function," and "Financing Programs for Local Government."

Each issue publishes an average of five articles usually under ten pages in length. There is a calendar of events, "Fiscal and Economic Indicators" and "From the Library" which is an annotated list of books received at the GFOA. There are usually five or so signed book reviews in each issue as well.

114   *Graduate Management Research*. DATE FOUNDED: 1983. FREQUENCY: Irregular. PRICE: $30.59/yr. PUBLISHER: Cranfield Press, Cranfield Institute of Technology, Cranfield, Bedford MK43 0AL, England. EDITOR: N. Craig Smith. ILLUSTRATIONS. ADVERTISEMENTS. CIRCULATION: 500. MANUSCRIPT SELECTION: Editor, Refereed. BOOK REVIEWS. SPECIAL ISSUES: Occasional. TARGET AUDIENCE: AC. SAMPLE COPIES: Libraries, individuals.

This publication conveys the ideas, issues, and problems in the management research process. It advocates that better management research will result if there is a better understanding of the research process and the problems involved. Because of this viewpoint, this journal is unique. It has particular appeal to Ph.D. candidates in management areas. The authors are mainly United Kingdom academics.

A typical issue has four relatively lengthy articles, a listing of recently completed management theses and dissertations from British institutions, letters, short news items and forthcoming conferences. There is also a book review section with short annotations. A recent special issue is devoted to meaning and method in management research.

115   *Graphic Communicator: The Newspaper of the Graphic Communications Union*. DATE FOUNDED: 1978. TITLE CHANGES: *Union Tabloid* (1978-1983). FREQUENCY: 9/yr. PRICE: $5/yr. PUBLISHER: Graphic Communications International Union, 1900 L Street, N.W., Washington, D.C. 20036. EDITOR: James J. Norton. ILLUSTRATIONS. ADVERTISEMENTS. CIRCULATION: 200,000. MANUSCRIPT SELECTION: Editor. MICROFORMS: UMI. TARGET AUDIENCE: GP, SP. SAMPLE COPIES: Libraries limited.

A current awareness tabloid published by the Graphic Communications International Union for the benefit of all of its members. It brings to its membership over 100 short articles, newsy in nature.

It educates and informs the members about the activities and programs of the union, new technology, training opportunities, and feed back from the membership. It also includes extensive coverage of state and federal legislative news.

116 *Group & Organization Studies.* DATE FOUNDED: 1976. FREQUENCY: q. PRICE: $82/yr. institutions, $36/yr. personal. PUBLISHER: Sage Publications, Inc., 2111 West Hillcrest Drive, Newbury Park, CA 91320. EDITOR: Laurie Larwood. ILLUSTRATIONS. INDEX. ADVERTISEMENTS. MANUSCRIPT SELECTION: Editor, Editorial Review Board. MICROFORMS: UMI. REPRINTS: UMI. BOOK REVIEWS. INDEXED/ABSTRACTED: ABIn, AdolMentHlthAb, BI, CIJE, CINAHL, HRA, LLBA, MgtC, PersLit, PsyAb, Psycscan, SageFamStudAb, SagePAA, SocAb, SPDA. TARGET AUDIENCE: AC.

This journal hopes to attract cross-cultural research directed at an international audience of group facilitators, trainers, educators, consultants and managers in organizations. It publishes databased, research articles dealing with such subjects as leadership, management development, group processes, communication in organizations, consultation, and organizational development.

Each issue has six to eight articles. Recent articles were twenty to thirty pages in length and included titles such as "Organizational Restructuring: the Impact on Role Perceptions, Work Relationships, and Satisfaction" and a symposium article "When a Woman is the Boss: Dilemmas in Taking Charge."

117 *Guidance and Assessment Review.* DATE FOUNDED: 1985. FREQUENCY: 6/yr. PRICE: $50/yr. PUBLISHER: British Psychological Society, St. Andrews House, 48 Princess Road East, Leicester LE1 7DR, England. EDITOR: Charles E. Rethell-Fox. ADVERTISEMENTS. CIRCULATION: 250. MANUSCRIPT SELECTION: Editor, Consultant. BOOK REVIEWS. TARGET AUDIENCE: AC, SP. SAMPLE COPIES: Libraries, individuals.

This journal publishes practical information for professionals involved in the assessment of people and systems in the workplace. It provides information on new materials and developments, and offers a forum for practical ideas and experiences. The majority of writers are British academics and researchers.

There are usually three articles per issue. They are written in a concise format with headings and identification of major points. Occasionally a signed book review of 250 words may be included.

118   *Guide to Recently Published Material in Industrial Relations*. DATE FOUNDED: 1974. FREQUENCY: q. PRICE: £6/yr. PUBLISHER: Workers' Educational Association, 9 Upper Berkeley Street, London W1H 8BY, England. EDITOR: Mel Doyle. CIRCULATION: 500. MANUSCRIPT SELECTION: Editorial Committee. REPRINTS: Publisher. TARGET AUDIENCE: AC, SP. SAMPLE COPIES: Libraries.

This journal is an annotated listing of books, pamphlets, journal articles and British government publications in English. It is the only bibliographical listing on industrial relations in the United Kingdom.

119   *Harvard Business Review*. DATE FOUNDED: 1922. FREQUENCY: 6/yr. PRICE: $49/yr. PUBLISHER: Graduate School of Business Administration, Harvard University, Soldiers Field Road, Boston, MA 02163. EDITOR: Theodore Levitt. ILLUSTRATIONS. INDEX. ADVERTISEMENTS. CIRCULATION: 210,000. MANUSCRIPT SELECTION: Editor, Editorial Board. MICROFORMS: UMI. REPRINTS: Publisher. INDEXED/ABSTRACTED: AbHlthCareMgtS, ABIn, AccDataProcAb, AccI, ASEANMgtAb, BankLitI, BI, BMTA, BoRvI, BusI, CADCAMA, CoalA, CompBus, CompConAb, CompLitI, CompRev, CurrCont, ElecElecAb, EnerInfoAb, EnerResAb, EnvAb, ExMed, FutSurv, HiEdCurrAwareBull, HospLitI, IntAeroAb, IntLabDoc, KeyEconSci, LawOffInfo, MagInd, MgtC, MgtMarA, OperRes, PAIS, PCR2, PerManAb, PersLit, PhysAb, PROMT, PsyAb, RehabLit, RG, RiskAb, SciAb, ShipA, SOCI, TraIndI, WorAb, WorBankAb. TARGET AUDIENCE: AC, GP, SP.

As its masthead claims, *HBR* is "the magazine of the thoughtful manager." It is published by the Graduate School of Business Administration at Harvard University and its pragmatic articles are designed to help practitioners better understand theories, concepts and new ideas in management. Its articles are generally written by American business school academics or practitioners of renown. Typical articles of use in labor/industrial relations have included: "Experiments in Employment—a British Cure," "The Same Old Principles in the New Manufacturing," and "Information Technology and Tomorrow's Manager."

Each issue contains eight to ten articles of approximately ten pages each. There is one of those "famous" "HBR Case Studies" (of a management problem), special reports, "Ideas for Action" and "Getting Things Done." There is also a "For the Manager's Bookshelf" section in each issue with one or two book reviews. Each is signed and one to two pages in length.

120   *Harvard Civil Rights - Civil Liberties Law Review*. DATE FOUNDED: 1966. FREQUENCY: 2/yr. PRICE: $20/yr. PUBLISHER: Harvard University Law School, Hastings Hall Publications Center, Cambridge, MA 02138. EDITOR: A. Mechele Dickerson. INDEX. ADVERTISEMENTS. CIRCULATION: 1,500. MANUSCRIPT SELECTION: Editor. MICROFORMS: UMI, WSH. REPRINTS: WSH, UMI. BOOK REVIEWS. INDEXED/ABSTRACTED: CIJE, CLI, CrimJusAb, CurrCont, HRA, ILegPer, LegCont, LRI, PAIS, SageUrbStudAb, SOCI. TARGET AUDIENCE: AC, SP.

This journal is published by the Harvard University Law School. Many of its issues cover labor law and the rights of workers. A recent special issue was devoted solely to a "Symposium on Civil Rights and Civil Liberties in the Workplace." Recent articles have included "Labor-Management Cooperation and the Law: Perspective from Year Two of the Laws Project," "Cooperation vs. Competition at Eastern Airlines," and "Lie Detectors in Employment."

Each issue contains four to seven articles of varying but substantive length. There are special issues as noted and other features include "Comments" and a review essay. There are two or three lengthy, signed book reviews per issue.

121   *Hawkins Merit Systems Protection Board Digest Service*. DATE FOUNDED: 1984. FREQUENCY: m. PRICE: $270/yr. PUBLISHER: Hawkins Publishing Co., Inc., 1207 B Central Avenue, P.O. Box 480, Mayo, MD 21106. EDITOR: Carl R. Eyler. INDEX. CIRCULATION: 100. MANUSCRIPT SELECTION: Editor. SUPPLEMENTS: 12/yr. TARGET AUDIENCE: AC, SP.

This publication gives references to the current and past decisions of the Merit Systems Protection Board. It is a one volume, loose-leaf service which includes citations and analyses of Federal and U.S. Supreme Court decisions relating to the Civil Service Reform Act of 1978.

All parts are arranged either alphabetically or numerically. The service is divided into seven sections: general index, table of cases, docket citator, decision citators, definitions, words and phrases, regulations of the Board, and a topic digest.

122   ***Health and Safety Information Bulletin.*** DATE FOUNDED: 1976. FREQUENCY: m. PRICE: £76/yr. PUBLISHER: Industrial Relations Services, 18-20 Highbury Place, London N5 1QP, England. EDITORS: Phil James and John Manos. INDEX. CIRCULATION: 4,000. MANUSCRIPT SELECTION: Editors. REPRINTS: Publisher, UMI. SPECIAL ISSUES: Occasional. INDEXED/AB-STRACTED: BrCerA, LabHazBull. TARGET AUDIENCE: AC, SP.

This title is the fourth part of the *Industrial Relations Review and Report.* It provides current information on news on the health and safety front in the field of industrial relations in the United Kingdom. Much of the information which is prepared in conjunction with legal experts deals with the enforcement of major court cases and legislation. The contents would be most practical for safety specialists and managers dealing with safety responsibilities.

The most important documents issued by the British Health and Safety Commission are published along with background articles. Decision of major cases in the courts are detailed. A recent issue has a lengthy piece on no-smoking policies in the workplace, guidelines for providing safety in the construction industry, and a short news column providing information on health and safety hazards in the workplace.

123   ***Hofstra Labor Law Journal.*** DATE FOUNDED: 1983. TITLE CHANGES: *Hofstra Labor Law Forum* (1983-1983). FREQUENCY: 2/yr. PRICE: $12/yr. PUBLISHER: School of Law, Hofstra University, Hempstead, NY 11550. ILLUSTRATIONS. INDEX. MANUSCRIPT SELECTION: Editor. BOOK REVIEWS. INDEXED/ ABSTRACTED: ILegPer. TARGET AUDIENCE: AC, SP.

The *Hofstra Labor Law Journal,* unlike the *Comparative Labor Law Journal* which focuses on a variety of different countries, publishes articles primarily concerned with U.S. labor law and labor relations. Recent titles have included: "Current Issues in Union Democracy," and "Membership Rights in Union Referenda to Ratify Collective Bargaining Agreements." Most articles are written by Hofstra law students, faculty and other labor law specialists.

Each issue contains four to six research articles of usually under twenty pages in length. There are occasional, signed book reviews of varying length.

124   *Hong Kong Manager (K'obsueb Kuan Li)*. DATE FOUNDED:
       1965. FREQUENCY: 6/yr. PRICE: $52/yr. PUBLISHER: Hong
       Kong Manager, c/o The Hong Kong Management Association, 14/F
       Fairmont House, 8 Cotton Tree Drive, Central Hong Kong. ILLUS-
       TRATIONS. ADVERTISEMENTS. CIRCULATION: 7,000.
       MANUSCRIPT SELECTION: Editorial Board. REPRINTS: Pub-
       lisher. TARGET AUDIENCE: AC, GP, SP. SAMPLE COPIES:
       Libraries.

       Hong Kong Manager is a bilingual journal which focuses on widening the
       knowledge of the dynamic changes in the business world and highlight-
       ing its impact on Hong Kong. The writers are academics and senior
       business managers from Hong Kong and worldwide whose writings are
       objective. A typical issue has an average of three articles in both English
       and Chinese.

125   *Human Relations*. DATE FOUNDED: 1947. FREQUENCY: m.
       PRICE: $255/yr. PUBLISHER: Plenum Publishing Corporation, 233
       Spring Street, New York, NY 10013. EDITOR: Michael Foster.
       ILLUSTRATIONS. INDEX. MANUSCRIPT SELECTION: Edi-
       tor, Editorial Board. INDEXED/ABSTRACTED: AbAnthro,
       AbCrimPen, ABIn, ABSCAN, AbSocWor, AdolMentHlthAb, An-
       throI, ASSIA, BI, BrHumI, ChildDevAb, CINAHL, CommAb,
       CurrCont, EdAdAb, IntLabDoc, LLBA, MentHlthAb, MgtC, MLA,
       PAIS, PeaceResAb, PersLit, PsyAb, Psycscan, SocAb, SocEdAb,
       SOCI, SocSc, SocWAb, SPDA, WomAb, WorAb. TARGET AUDI-
       ENCE: AC, SP.

       This is an interdisciplinary journal in which academics from a variety of
       fields and countries are encouraged to share in the linking of theory and
       practice in the study of human problems. Authors are encouraged to
       present "theoretical developments, new methods, or review articles, as
       well as reports of empirical research which may include both qualitative
       and quantitative data." This journal is particularly in search of innova-
       tive approaches to problems.

       Recent articles have included "Effects of Assimilation of Work Expe-
       rience on Growth Satisfaction" and "Relations Among Lateness, Ab-
       sence, and Turnover: Is There a Progression of Withdrawal." Four
       substantive articles per issue of varying length are written by academics
       for students, academics and specialists.

126   *Human Resource*. DATE FOUNDED: 1968. TITLE CHANGES:
       Canadian Training Methods (1968-1979); *CTM, the Human Element*
       (1979-1984). FREQUENCY: 6/yr. PRICE: $12/yr. PUBLISHER:

Grant Walker, 1252 Lawrence Ave., Suite 206, Don Mills, Ontario M3A 1C3. EDITOR: Cindy Woods. ILLUSTRATIONS. INDEX. ADVERTISEMENTS. CIRCULATION: 10,000. MANUSCRIPT SELECTION: Editor, Editorial Board. MICROFORMS: Publisher. REPRINTS: Publisher. BOOK REVIEWS. SPECIAL ISSUES: 1/yr. INDEXED/ABSTRACTED: CanBusI. TARGET AUDIENCE: SP.

This publication is Canada's only national publication serving training personnel and resource management people. *Human Resource* and *Human Resource Management* both address similar issues. The latter title, a United States journal, views issues from both theoretical and practical bases; *Human Resource* addresses concerns for the practitioners. Authors are both Canadian academics and business managers.

There are a number of regular features in each issue including training ideas, computers in training, industry news, employee assistance programs, new product and service review, and events calendar. There are typically five feature articles per issue and three to four book reviews of 200-225 words each. There is a separate review of videos in the same format. An annual Human Resource Directory in the August/September issue provides a guide to professional services; courses, seminars, workshops; equipment supplies and facilities; and a complete listing of suppliers.

127   *Human Resource Management.* DATE FOUNDED: 1961. TITLE CHANGES: *Management of Personnel Quarterly* (1961-1971). FREQUENCY: q. PRICE: $52/yr. PUBLISHER: John Wiley & Sons, Inc., 605 Third Ave., New York, NY 10158. EDITOR: Noel M. Tichy. ILLUSTRATIONS. INDEX. ADVERTISEMENTS. CIRCULATION: 3,000. MANUSCRIPT SELECTION: Editors, Refereed. REPRINTS: Publisher, UMI. BOOK REVIEWS. SPECIAL ISSUES: 1/yr. INDEXED/ABSTRACTED: ABIn, AccDataProAb, ASEANMgtAb, BI, BusI, EdAdAb, HospLitI, MgtC, MgtMarA, PAIS, PerManAb, PersLit, TraIndI. TARGET AUDIENCE: AC, SP. SAMPLE COPIES: Libraries, individuals.

Human Resource Management's aim is to serve as a link between academicians, theorists, and practitioners in the field. It communicates the state of the art concepts, theories, and practice of strategic import to both scholars and executives. Authors are predominantly U.S. academics and researchers; the remainder are executives.

Topics range from societal and international trends which impact human resources management to strategic selection, development, appraisal and reward of a firm's human resources. Practical aspects discussed are such issues as pragmatic guidelines to improve and shape practices in a global environment.

There are six to seven articles in each issue. There are also three to five signed book reviews of between three to five pages. There is a listing of books recently received.

128   ***Human Resource Planning: HR.*** DATE FOUNDED: 1978. FRE-QUENCY: q. PRICE: $48/yr. PUBLISHER: Human Resource Plan-ning Society, 228 East 45th Street, New York, NY 10017. EDITOR: Randall S. Schuler. ILLUSTRATIONS. INDEX. ADVERTISE-MENTS. CIRCULATION: 1,500. MANUSCRIPT SELECTION: Editor, Editorial Review Board, Refereed. MICROFORMS: UMI. BOOK REVIEWS. INDEXED/ABSTRACTED: ABIn, BusI, ManRes, MgtC, PerManAb, PersLit. TARGET AUDIENCE: AC, SP.

Human Resource Planning is published by the Human Resource Plan-ning Society. Its focus is to allow for an open forum dedicated to the exchange of information among professionals working in the field. New and innovative concepts, research results and applications are heavily emphasized. The audience and the authors are academicians, personnel and human resource managers, and consultants. Original articles take the form of literature reviews, models and/or theories, reports of empirical research results, or case studies.

Each issue contains lengthy articles of ten to twenty-five pages with an executive summary (abstract) of 200 words. Short notes of less than ten pages are also included. Book reviews and descriptions of recent publications of interest are included in selected issues. None were available for review.

129   ***ICFTU Economic and Social Bulletin.*** DATE FOUNDED: 1953. FREQUENCY: q. PRICE: 250 Belgian francs. PUBLISHER: Inter-national Confederation of Free Trade Unions, 37 rue Montagne aux Herbes Potageres, 1000 Brussels, Belgium. EDITOR: Renate Peltzer. CIRCULATION: 1,400. REPRINTS: Publisher. TARGET AUDI-ENCE: AC, GP, SP. SAMPLE COPIES: Libraries, individuals.

The *Economic and Social Bulletin* appears quarterly in English, French, German and Spanish and reports on economic and social questions emanating from national, regional or international trade union sources. It regularly reproduces official ICFTU documents as well as statements submitted to the United Nations and its specialized agencies and to other bodies or conferences.

Each issue is made up of eight to ten "Articles" which include documents of substantial length. A typical title might be "Annual Survey of Violations of Trade Union Rights" or "Trade Union Programme for Caribbean Economic Transformation." A clue to ICFTU's political perspective might be its motto "Bread, Peace and Freedom."

130   *ILR Report.* DATE FOUNDED: 1960. TITLE CHANGES: *Industrial & Labor Relations Report* (1960-1982). FREQUENCY: 2/yr. PRICE: Free. PUBLISHER: New York State School of Industrial and Labor Relations, Cornell University, Ithaca, NY 14851-0952. EDITOR: Mary T. Cullen. ILLUSTRATIONS. CIRCULATION: 3,500. MANUSCRIPT SELECTION: Editor. REPRINTS: Editor. BOOK REVIEWS. INDEXED/ABSTRACTED: MgtC, PAIS. TARGET AUDIENCE: AC, GP, SP.

A single topic currently in the news is the focus of each issue. As such, *ILR* provides several points of view on key issues which are on the leading edge of change in the field of industrial and labor relations. U.S. lawyers, arbitrators, and business executives of a moderate or liberal persuasian are invited by the editor to write on a specific topic. Although articles are written primarily by practitioners, there is a blend suitable for the workplace and substantial enough for the classroom.

Recent issues each contain five to six articles dealing with such topics as flexible pay systems, smoking, drugs and the healthy employee, and innovations in the office environment. Each issue also contains a profile or interview with a person in the field and short, unsigned reviews of books recently published by the Industrial & Labor Relations Press as well as new books by faculty of the New York State School of Industrial and Labor Relations.

131   *Imprint: Official Journal of the New Zealand Printing and Related Trades Industrial Union of Workers.* DATE FOUNDED: 1945. FREQUENCY: 11/yr. PUBLISHER: National Secretary, P.O. Box 6413, Te Aro, Wellington, New Zealand. EDITOR: J.L. Webb. ILLUSTRATIONS. ADVERTISEMENTS. CIRCULATION: 14,000. MANUSCRIPT SELECTION: Editor. REPRINTS: Publisher. TARGET AUDIENCE: SP. SPECIAL COPIES: Libraries, individuals.

This tabloid is designed to disseminate news to the trade union membership. It is newsy, chatty and geographically limited. Ten to fifteen articles of some substance are included in each issue.

It includes legislative information, a union directory and innovations in printing. An example of an article is the recently published "Policy on the Handling of Camera Ready Copy."

132 **Indian Journal of Industrial Relations.** DATE FOUNDED: 1965. FREQUENCY: q. PRICE: $44/yr. PUBLISHER: Shri Ram Centre For Industrial Relations and Human Resources, 4E/16, Jhandewalan Extension, New Dehli 110005, India. EDITOR: J.S. Sodhi. INDEX. ADVERTISEMENTS. CIRCULATION: 800. MANUSCRIPT SELECTION: Editor, Refereed. BOOK REVIEWS. INDEXED/ ABSTRACTED: ASSIA, IndPsyAb, IntLabDoc, PsyAb, RuralRecrTourAb, SOCI, WorAb, WorldAgEconRuralSocAb. TARGET AUDIENCE: AC, SP.

The *Indian Journal of Industrial Relations* is published by the Shri Ram Centre for Industrial Relations and Human Resources in New Dehli. Its main focus is industrial relations, human resource management and rural labor development. Recent articles have included: "Liberalist Economic Thought on the Role of Unions in Inflation," "Productivity Culture in Japan," and "Labour-Managment Cooperation and Conflict in the Indian Steel Industry."

Each issue publishes eight substantive articles of under thirty pages per issue. Three or four, one-page, signed book reviews are published in each issue.

133 **Industrial and Labor Relations Review.** DATE FOUNDED: 1947. FREQUENCY: q. PRICE: $30/yr. institutions, $18/yr. personal. PUBLISHER: New York State School of Industrial and Labor Relations, Cornell University, Ithaca, NY 14851-0952. EDITOR: John F. Burton, Jr. ILLUSTRATIONS. INDEX. ADVERTISEMENTS. CIRCULATION: 4,100. MANUSCRIPT SELECTION: Editor, Editorial Board, Refereed. MICROFORMS: UMI, WSH. REPRINTS: UMI. BOOK REVIEWS. INDEXED/ABSTRACTED: ABCPolSci, ABIn, AbsBoRvCurrLegPer, AmerH, ASSIA, BI, BoRvI, BusI, CIJE, CLI, CLOA, CREJ, CurrCont, EngI, EngIBioengAb, EngIEnerAb, HistAb, HRA, IEconArt, ILegPer, IntBibSoc, IntLabDoc, IntPolSc, IPerArtRelatLaw, JEL, KeyEconSci, LRI, MgtC, PAIS, PerManAb, PovHumResAb, PsyAb, SageUrbStudAb, SocAb, SOCI, SocSc, SPDA, TraIndI, WomAb, WorAb. TARGET AUDIENCE: AC, SP.

Industrial and Labor Relations Review is the premier journal in the area of industrial and labor relations. It is published by the prestigious New York State School of Industrial and Labor Relations. Recent articles have included: "Returns to Seniority in Union and Nonunion Jobs: A

New Look at the Evidence," "Do Job Opportunities Decline with Age," and "Labor Market Conditions and the Re-employment of Displaced Workers."

Each issue publishes eight to ten articles, empirical as well as conceptual in nature. The length of articles is usually fifteen to twenty pages. There is always an extensive "Research in Progress" section. Signed book reviews are organized under the following headings: "Labor-Management Relations," "Health and Safety," "Labor Markets," "International and Comparative Relations," "Human Resources," "Personnel and Organizational Behavior," "Historical Studies and Information Sources."

134   *Industrial Law Journal.* DATE FOUNDED: 1972. FREQUENCY: q. PRICE: £19.50/yr. PUBLISHER: Sweet and Maxwell, Ltd., 11 New Fetter Lane, London EC4P 4EE, England. EDITOR: Paul Davies. INDEX. ADVERTISEMENTS. CIRCULATION: 2,000. MANUSCRIPT SELECTION: Editor. BOOK REVIEWS. INDEXED/ ABSTRACTED: ASSIA, CLI, ILegPer, IndSAPer, IntLabDoc, LRI. TARGET AUDIENCE: AC, SP.

Sweet and Maxwell publishes this academic quarterly journal for the Industrial Law Society. The focus is British and the audience is academics and researchers in practicing legal professions (lawyers, judges, etc.) interested in labor law.

In addition to well documented articles such as "The Government's Philosophy Towards Reform of Social Security," each quarterly contains columns on recent legislation and recent cases. Book reviews are one page in length and signed with three to four per issue.

135   *Industrial Participation.*   DATE FOUNDED: 1894. TITLE CHANGES: *Labour Co-Partnership* (1894-1906); *Co-Partnership* (1907-1971). FREQUENCY: q. PRICE: £8/yr. PUBLISHER: Industrial Participation Association, 85 Tooley St., London SE1 2QZ, England. EDITOR: Gerald Solomon. ILLUSTRATIONS. ADVERTISEMENTS. CIRCULATION: 2,000. MANUSCRIPT SELECTION: Editor. MICROFORMS: Publisher. REPRINTS: Publisher. BOOK REVIEWS. SPECIAL ISSUES: Occasional. INDEXED/ ABSTRACTED: AccDataProAb, BrHumI, IntLabDoc, MgtMarA. TARGET AUDIENCE: SP.

Industrial Participation is a journal of "information and comment on current trends and practice" with substantial articles written by business leaders, members of Parliament and academics. Its orientation is toward management. Recent articles included "Profit Sharing—The Road to

Full Employment?" and "Employees and Unions—Now and Tomorrow." There are 250-500 unsigned book reviews in each issue.

136   *Industrial Relations*. DATE FOUNDED: 1961. FREQUENCY: 3/ yr. PRICE: $27.50/yr. institutions, $15/yr. personal. PUBLISHER: Institute of Industrial Relations, University of California, Berkeley, CA 94720. EDITORS: Michael Reich and Jonathan Leonard. ILLUSTRATIONS. INDEX. ADVERTISEMENTS. CIRCULATION: 2,500. MANUSCRIPT SELECTION: Editors, Board of Reviewers. MICROFORMS: UMI. REPRINTS: UMI. INDEXED/ABSTRACTED: ABIn, AccDataProcAb, BI, BusI, CLI, IEconArt, IntLabDoc, JEL, LRI, MgtC, PAIS, PerManAb, SocAb, SOCI, SPDA, TraIndI, WomAb, WorAb. TARGET AUDIENCE: AC, SP. SAMPLE COPIES: Libraries, individual.

Published under the auspices of the Institute of Industrial Relations at the University of California at Berkeley, *Industrial Relations* publishes articles on all aspects of the employment relationship. Recent titles include "Income Inequality: An Inter-Industry Analysis," "The Changing Importance of Lifetime Jobs, 1892-1978," "Wages, Non-wage Compensation, and Municipal Unions," and "The Impact of Internal Union Politics on the 1981 UMWA Strike."

Each issue contains on average seven articles of twenty plus pages. An occasional symposium such as "Australian Industrial Relations in Transition" is also published. Each issue has shorter articles, "Research Notes."

137   *Industrial Relations Europe*. DATE FOUNDED: 1972. TITLE CHANGES: *Industrial Relations Europe Newsletter* (1973). FREQUENCY: m. PRICE: $185/yr. PUBLISHER: ECS, The Wyatt Company SA, Ave. Roger Vandendriessche 8 (Box 3), 1150 Brussels, Belgium. EDITOR: Mike Groushko. MANUSCRIPT SELECTION: Editor. REPRINTS: Editor. BOOK REVIEWS. SPECIAL ISSUES: Approximately 6/yr. TARGET AUDIENCE: AC, SP. SAMPLE COPIES: Libraries, individuals.

This reporting service relates European industrial relations development to a specialized business audience in western Europe. Its writers are academics, business professionals and journalists specializing in business affairs.

Each issue contains about forty short articles. The issue is introduced by a general piece; the remainder of the issue contains reports from the participating countries. On occasion, an appropriate book might be reviewed in less than one-half page.

138   *Industrial Relations Journal.* DATE FOUNDED: 1970. FREQUENCY: q. PRICE: $107.75/yr. institutions, $81.50/yr. personal. PUBLISHER: Basil Blackwell Ltd., 108 Cowley Road., Oxford OX4 IJF, England. EDITOR: Brian Towers. ILLUSTRATIONS. INDEX. ADVERTISEMENTS. CIRCULATION: 1,100. MANUSCRIPT SELECTION: Editor, Editorial Board. MICROFORMS: UMI. BOOK REVIEWS. INDEXED/ABSTRACTED: ElecComA, IntLabDoc, ISMEC, MgtC, MgtMarA, PollAb, SafSciA, ShipA, WorAb. TARGET AUDIENCE: AC, SP.

The *Industrial Relations Journal* is an important source of information but more parochial than the London School of Economics' *British Journal of Industrial Relations.* The latter includes articles focusing on international as well as United Kingdom industrial relations. The *IRJ* focuses on the labor relations scene mainly in the United Kingdom, Australia and other European countries. It is written by British academics for "practitioners and practice oriented academics." Recent issues have focused on British trade unions, management, strikes, pensions and personnel management.

Each issue contains abstracts in English and French for each of the scholarly articles published, usually ten to under fifteen pages in length. Four to six, signed book reviews per issue are published. Other regular features include a commentary on recent legal developments in labor relations, research notes and editorials.

139   *Industrial Relations Law Journal.* DATE FOUNDED: 1976. FREQUENCY: q. PRICE: $36/yr. institutions, $30/yr. personal. PUBLISHER: University of California Press, 2120 Berkeley Way, Berkeley, CA 94720. EDITOR: Students of Boalt Hall School of Law. INDEX. ADVERTISEMENTS. CIRCULATION: 1,000. MANUSCRIPT SELECTION: Editors. MICROFORMS: UMI. BOOK REVIEWS. INDEXED/ABSTRACTED: ABIn, AbsBoRvCurrLegPer, BI, CrimJusAb, CurrCont, ILegPer, LegCont, LRI, MgtC, PAIS, SOCI. TARGET AUDIENCE: AC, SP. SAMPLE COPIES: Libraries.

IRLJ covers the full range of labor and employment law. Major topics covered are employment discrimination, "traditional" labor law, public sector employment issues, employee benefits law, "and the emerging doctrines of wrongful termination." It is written by academic researchers.

Each issue includes three to five articles. A variety of formats are used "from traditional scholarly articles and student authored comments, to the book review essay and short, focused 'forum' articles."

140   *Industrial Relations Law Reports.* DATE FOUNDED: 1972. FREQUENCY: m. PRICE: £160/yr. PUBLISHER: Industrial Relations Services, 18-20 Highbury Place, London N5 1QP, England. EDITOR: Michael Rubenstein. INDEX. CIRCULATION: 3,500. MICROFORMS: UMI. REPRINTS: Publisher, UMI. SPECIAL ISSUES: Occasional. TARGET AUDIENCE: AC, SP.

This British journal is devoted to providing the text of all major industrial relations cases heard by the House of Lords and various tribunals and courts. There is a unique casemark system of indexing which allows one to determine the key issues and serves as a referencing system. There is an introductory summary page which presents the highlights of each case.

141   *Industrial Relations Legal Information Bulletin.* DATE FOUNDED: 1971. FREQUENCY: bw. PRICE: £105/yr. PUBLISHER: Industrial Relations Services, 18-20 Highbury Place, London N5 1QP, England. EDITOR: Edward Benson. INDEX. CIRCULATION: 2,000. MANUSCRIPT SELECTION: Editor. REPRINTS: Publisher, UMI. SPECIAL ISSUES: Occasional. INDEXED/ABSTRACTED: BrCerA, IntPkgA, MgtMarA. TARGET AUDIENCE: AC, SP.

Limited to the United Kingdom, this journal publishes recent information dealing with the legal aspects of labor and industrial relations. Its major purposes are to: explain the practical implications of employment law developments; provide authoritative and independent analysis of recent employment decisions of the courts and of new legislation; supply guidance on an area of major concern, e.g. unfair dismissal; and report on activities of statutory enforcement agencies in the industrial relations field. It is an integral part of *Industrial Relations Review and Report.*

142   *Industrial Relations Review and Report.* DATE FOUNDED: 1971. FREQUENCY: sm. PRICE: £190/yr. PUBLISHER: Industrial Relations Services, 18-20 Highbury Place, London N5 1QP, England. EDITOR: David Martin. ILLUSTRATIONS. INDEX. CIRCULATION: 4,500. MICROFORMS: UMI. REPRINTS: Publisher, UMI. INDEXED/ABSTRACTED: IntPkgA, MgtMarA. TARGET AUDIENCE: AC, SP.

This British publication provides objective coverage of all major legislation affecting personnel and industrial relations in the United Kingdom. It incorporates several other bulletins within its covers: *Industrial Relations Legal Information Bulletin, Health and Safety Information Bulletin*, and *Pay and Benefits Bulletin.*

Each issue contains two to four lengthy articles dealing with a topic, a news section with short items and a section reporting on appropriate activities in the House of Commons.

143   *Industrial Worker.* DATE FOUNDED: 1909. FREQUENCY: m. PRICE: $8/yr. institutions, $4/yr. personal. PUBLISHER: Industrial Workers of the World, 3435 N. Sheffield Ave., Chicago, IL 60657. EDITOR: Carlos Cortez. ILLUSTRATIONS. CIRCULATION: 8,000. MANUSCRIPT SELECTION: Editor. BOOK REVIEWS. SPECIAL ISSUES. INDEXED/ABSTRACTED: API. TARGET AUDIENCE: AC, GP, HS, SP. SAMPLE COPIES: Libraries, individuals.

This tabloid is the news organ of the Industrial Workers of the World (The IWW's). It reports on world labor news, covers labor history and is dedicated to "revolutionary, industrial unionism." Its focus is rank and file worker struggles. Recent articles have been titled "U.S. Rehearses Nicaraguan Invasion," "Class Struggle: East and West" and "South Africa: Workers Still Fighting."

There are approximately twenty-four articles per issue and several signed book reviews of one-half page length. A column titled "Books for Union People" is also included.

144   *Industry and Development.* DATE FOUNDED: 1958. TITLE CHANGES: *Industrialization and Productivity* (1958-1975). FREQUENCY: q. PUBLISHER: United Nations Industrial Development Organization, P.O. Box 300, A-1400 Vienna, Austria. ILLUSTRATIONS. INDEX. MANUSCRIPT SELECTION: Supervisory Panel. BOOK REVIEWS. INDEXED/ABSTRACTED: CREJ, IEconArt, KeyEconSci, PAIS. TARGET AUDIENCE: AC, SP.

A UNIDO publication, *Industry and Development* hopes to provide a link between practitioners and theorists working on economic and related aspects of industrialization. Recent articles published in this journal of applied economics include: "Industrial Policy in Developing Countries: The Foreign Exchange Cost of Exports," and "Comparative Advantage, External Finance and the Vulnerability of Industrialization."

Each issue has five or six articles of twenty to forty pages. Five substantial, signed book reviews are also included.

145   *Insider's Report: A Special Bulletin for Leaders of Concerned Educators Against Forced Unionism.* DATE FOUNDED: 1976. TITLE CHANGES: *Recaps* (1976-1983). FREQUENCY: 3/yr. PRICE: Free. PUBLISHER: Concerned Educators Against Forced Unionism, 8001 Braddock Rd., Springfield, VA 22160. EDITOR: Jo Seker. CIRCULATION: 30,000. MANUSCRIPT SELECTION: Editor. REPRINTS: Publisher. TARGET AUDIENCE: AC, GP, HS. SAMPLE COPIES: Libraries, individuals.

An anti-union newsletter advocating that "no one should be forced to join a union as a condition of employment." Brief recent articles have included "Coercive Unionism Legislation Kept at Bay," "Study Shows Bargaining Hampers School Reform," and "Union Officials Keeping 79% to 90% of Forced Dues Illegally."

This is a "Right to Work" publication with four short articles per issue. Short news briefs are also included.

146   *Interchange.* DATE FOUNDED: 1901. TITLE CHANGES: *Railway Clerk* (1901-1969); *Railway Clerk Interchange* (1970-1985). FREQUENCY: 9/yr. PRICE: $5/yr. PUBLISHER: Brotherhood of Railway, Airline and Steamship Clerks, Freight Handlers, Express and Station Employees, 3 Research Place, Rockville, MD 20850. EDITOR: R.I. Kilroy. ILLUSTRATIONS. INDEX. CIRCULATION: 184,000. MANUSCRIPT SELECTION: Editor. SPECIAL ISSUES: Occasional. INDEXED/ABSTRACTED: WorAb. TARGET AUDIENCE: SP. SAMPLE COPIES: Libraries, individuals.

Interchange is published by a labor union. It explores those issues of concern to its members from a pro-labor point of view. Issues relating to collective bargaining, legislative goals, and trends affecting the transportation industry are the major focus of the magazine. Writers are journalists and researchers who are drawn from the U.S. labor movement. Supplements are occasionally published particularly at the time of a national congressional election.

A typical recent issue contained an article dealing with drug testing in the workplace and articles on union contract negotiations, training, and union support. There are several regular features such as a legislative report, union and national news, and a section reporting news on retirees.

147   *Interfaces.* DATE FOUNDED: 1954. TITLE CHANGES: *Bulletin of the Institute of Management Sciences* (1954-1970); *Institute of Management Sciences. Bulletin* (1970-1971). FREQUENCY: 6/yr. PRICE: $25/yr., $17/yr. The Institute of Management Sciences and Operations Research Society of America members. PUBLISHER: The Institute of Management Sciences and the Operations Research Society of America, 290 Westminster Street, Providence, RI 02903. EDITOR: Frederic H. Murphy. ILLUSTRATIONS. INDEX. ADVERTISEMENTS. CIRCULATION: 10,000. MANUSCRIPT SELECTION: Editors. MICROFORMS: UMI. REPRINTS: UMI. BOOK REVIEWS. SPECIAL ISSUES. INDEX/ABSTRACTED: ABIn, BI, BMTA, BusI, CompConAb, CompRev, CurrCont, DataProcD, ElecElecAb, ErgAb, ExMed, IntAbOpRes, IntAeroAb, JContQuanMeth, MgtC, PerManAb, PhysAb, PsyAb, SOCI, WorAb. TARGET AUDIENCE: AC, SP. SAMPLE COPIES: Libraries, individuals.

Interfaces is the journal of the Institute of Management Sciences and the Operations Research Society of America. It hopes to improve communication between managers and professionals in MS/OR in commerce, industry, government, or education. Recent articles have included: "Manager's Guide for Evaluating Competitive Analysis Techniques," "Information Technology, Integration, and Organizational Change," and "Success Strategies for Businesses That Perform Poorly."

Each issue contains ten articles of varying length, usually under fifteen pages. Book reviews are published, usually five or six per issue. They are signed and substantial. Other features include a calendar of meetings, "Applications Reviews," and letters to the editor.

148   ***International Encylopedia for Labour Law and Industrial Relations.*** DATE FOUNDED: 1977. FREQUENCY: Looseleaf. PUBLISHER: Kluwer Law and Taxation Publishers, Deventer, The Netherlands. EDITOR: Prof. Dr. R. Blanpain. INDEX. TARGET AUDIENCE: AC, SP.

The *International Encyclopedia for Labour Law and Industrial Relations* is a multi-volume looseleaf service. It is a comprehensive, up-to-date service focusing on labor law and industrial relations in "over 70 countries."

The service is divided into five parts. International monographs analyze the labor laws and regulations enacted by international institutions such as the ILO and the OECD. National monographs and national case law focuses on individual countries. A Codex of the growing number of "international instruments" promoting labor standards is third. International case law is covered in section four and section five is national labor legislation. This is an excellent serial publication for comparative labor law and industrial and labor relations.

149   *International Journal of Manpower.* DATE FOUNDED: 1980. MERGER: *Quality of Working Life* (1980-1986). FREQUENCY: 5/yr. PRICE: $359.95/yr. PUBLISHER: MCB University Press Ltd., 62 Toller Lane, Bradford BD8 9BY, England. EDITOR: David Ashton. ILLUSTRATIONS. INDEX. ADVERTISEMENTS. CIRCULA-TION: 350. MANUSCRIPT SELECTION: Editor, Advisory Board. REPRINTS: Publisher. SPECIAL ISSUES: 1 or 2/yr. INDEXED/ABSTRACTED: ABIn, AccDataProAb, BI, CIJE, IntLabDoc, KeyEconSci, MgtC, MgtMarA, WorAb. TARGET AUDIENCE: AC, SP. SAMPLE COPIES: Libraries, individuals.

The aim of the *International Journal of Manpower* is to cover all of the key issues in the development of manpower planning and economics. It is equally as relevant to those concerned with local issues as to the international scene. It publishes the newest thinking and practices on all topics in the area of manpower planning. It covers theoretical issues only as they apply to real problems.

A typical issue contains an average of five objective and scholarly articles. There are usually one to two special issues per year which highlight in depth a specific key area. The journal has also initiated an annual *Quality of Working Life* abstracting service as an integral portion. This series provides lengthy abstracts of journal and book literature.

150   *International Journal of Project Management.* DATE FOUNDED: 1983. FREQUENCY: q. PRICE: £108/yr. PUBLISHER: Butter-worth Scientific Ltd., P.O. Box 63, Westbury House, Bury St., Guild-ford, Surrey GU2 5BH, U.K. EDITOR: Angela Jamieson. ILLUS-TRATIONS. INDEX. ADVERTISEMENTS. MANUSCRIPT SELECTION: Editor, Refereed. REPRINTS: Publisher. BOOK REVIEWS. SPECIAL ISSUES. INDEXED/ABSTRACTED: MgtC. TARGET AUDIENCE: AC, SP. SAMPLE COPIES: Librar-ies, individuals.

This journal is published in cooperation with the International Project Managers Association (INTERNET). This journal is written by proj-ect managers as well as academics and interested industrial engineers for project managers. Articles deal with technique, applications and re-sources. Typical article titles are: "Development of Project Manage-ment in Brazil... Historical Overview" and "Matrix Approach to Project

Planning Design and Management." Calendar of events and Association news are included as a regular feature.

151 *International Journal of Quality and Reliability Management*. DATE FOUNDED: 1984. FREQUENCY: q. PRICE: $179.95/yr. PUBLISHER: MCB University Press Ltd., 62 Toller Lane, Bradford, W. Yorkshire BD8 9BY, England. EDITORS: Alf Keller and Barrie Dale. INDEX. ADVERTISEMENTS. MANUSCRIPT SELECTION: Editorial Board, Refereed. REPRINTS: Publisher. BOOK REVIEWS. TARGET AUDIENCE: AC, SP. SAMPLE COPIES: Libraries, individuals.

This is a fairly new journal which focuses on maintaining quality and improving reliability in industrial organizations. Its objectives are to describe new techniques and systems, to provide a forum for the exchange of ideas and to serve as an updating service. The audience is a mix of executives, senior management, academicians and practitioners in such fields as manufacturing, energy and oil production, construction and defense. The scope is international with writers being well-respected in the areas which make up the readership. Manuscripts are reviewed anonymously before final selection for inclusion.

A typical issue contains four to six scholarly articles covering such topics as health and quality circles, Soviet standards of quality and the use of computers for fire and gas detection systems. Also included is a signed "Report Review" of research. A sample issue contains a report of research which was carried out in the machine tool industry and its implications on an international basis. The book review section has a one-half page signed review by the editor.

152 *International Journal of Sociology and Social Policy*.   DATE FOUNDED: 1976. TITLE CHANGES: *Scottish Journal of Sociology* (1976-1980). FREQUENCY: 3/yr. PRICE $254.95/yr. PUBLISHER: Barmarick Publications, Enholmes Hall, Patrington, Hull, N. Humberside HU12 OPR, England. EDITOR: Barrie O. Paetman. ILLUSTRATIONS. INDEX. ADVERTISEMENTS. CIRCULATION: 200. MANUSCRIPT SELECTION: Editor, Editorial Board. BOOK REVIEWS. SPECIAL ISSUES. INDEXED/ABSTRACTED: ASSIA, LLBA, SocAb, SPDA. TARGET AUDIENCE: AC, SP.

International Journal of Sociology and Social Policy is the forum for the publication of applied research. Recent articles, empirically based, are "Understanding Unemployment: The Need for a Social Perspective" and "Trade Unions and the State Since 1945: Corporatism and Hegemony." One special issue focused on "Quitting Time: The End of Work."

Topics included are: full employment, labor history, unemployment, productivity, technology, human relations, reducing work time and the quality of life.

Each issue runs five to seven articles of varying length. An occasional special issue is published. "Publications Received" is a regularly run feature of recently published books of interest.

153   *International Labor and Working Class History.* DATE FOUNDED: 1972. TITLE CHANGES: *Newsletter. European Labor and Working Class History* (1972-1975). FREQUENCY: 2/yr. PRICE: $20/yr. institutions, $12/yr. personal. PUBLISHER: University of Illinois Press, 54 E. Gregory Drive, Champaign, IL 61820. EDITOR: David Montgomery. ADVERTISEMENTS. CIRCULATION: 800. MANUSCRIPT SELECTION: Editor, Editorial Board. BOOK REVIEWS. SPECIAL ISSUES: Occasional. INDEXED/ABSTRACTED: AmerH, HistAb, RecPubArt, WritAmHis. TARGET AUDIENCE: AC, SP. SAMPLE COPIES: Libraries.

This scholarly journal focuses on the research being undertaken in the area of the working class culture, the politics relating to it, and the labor movement. It also includes news and reviews which are designed to allow the interchange of ideas and research among historians of the working class from different countries. Authors are mainly international scholars and occasionally labor activists.

Most issues have a similar format. There is a section called "Scholarly Controversies" in which a panel of three or four scholars address important debates appearing in contemporary historiography. Another major section publishes "Review Essays" about current research in the field. A strong feature is the in-depth, signed book reviews. There is an average of ten per issue, each consisting of three to four pages. A section on "Reports and Correspondence" provides a two to three page summary of recent scholarly conferences. Finally there is a regular feature of pertinent upcoming events, conferences or publications.

154   *International Labour Documentation.* DATE FOUNDED: 1949. TITLE CHANGES: *ILO Library Daily Reference List* (1949-1953). FREQUENCY: m. PRICE: $42.75/yr. PUBLISHER: ILO Publications, International Labour Office, CH-1211 Geneva 22, Switzerland. INDEX. CIRCULATION: 1,400. MICROFORMS: Publisher. INDEXED/ABSTRACTED: HRRep, PopInd. TARGET AUDIENCE: AC, SP. SAMPLE COPIES: Libraries, individuals.

International Labour Documentation is a current-awareness and abstracting service of materials received at the International Labour Office Library. It includes ILO publications, commercially produced books, journal articles, conference reports, and technical documents. The complete citation is given, the abstract incorporates the description from the *ILO Thesaurus*. There is a table of contents plus a detailed subject index in English, French and Spanish.

155   *International Labour Review*. DATE FOUNDED: 1921. TITLE CHANGES: *Daily Summary* (nd); *Daily Intelligence* (1921-1921). MERGER: *Notes Bibliographiques* (1921-1922); *Industry and Labour Information* (1922-1940); *Industry and Labour* (1940-1948). FREQUENCY: 6/yr. PRICE: $42/yr. PUBLISHER: International Labour Office, CH-1211 Geneva 22, Switzerland. EDITOR: T. Lines. ILLUSTRATIONS. INDEX. ADVERTISEMENTS. CIRCULATION: 9,500. MANUSCRIPT SELECTION: Editor. MICROFORMS: UMI. REPRINTS: UMI. BOOK REVIEWS. INDEXED/ABSTRACTED: AbHyg, ABIn, ASSIA, BI, BibAg, BoRvI, BusI, CIJE, CLOA, CREJ, CurrCont, FutSurv, HRRep, HumI, IEconArt, IntLabDoc, JEL, KeyEconSci, MedCareRev, MgtC, MgtMarA, PAIS, PerManAb, PersLit, PopInd, RehabLit, RuralRecrTourAb, SOCI, SocSc, SocWAb, TropDisBull, WomAb, WorAb, WorBankAb, WorldAgEconRuralSocAb. TARGET AUDIENCE: AC, SP.

The *International Labour Review* is published by the International Labour Office (ILO) with the purpose of contributing to a wider understanding of questions of labor, social policy, and administration related to the programs of the ILO. Articles published are based on recent ILO and other research into economic and social topics of international interest affecting labor. Recently published examples are: "Multinational Union-Management Consultation in Europe: Resurgence in the 1980's," "Social Security and Part-time Employment," and "Evaluating the American Job Creation Experience."

Each issue contains an average of seven articles, twenty to thirty pages in length. There is usually an extensively annotated list of ILO publications (sometimes as many as twenty or more) in each issue.

156   *International President's Bulletin*. DATE FOUNDED: 1937. TITLE CHANGES: *Brotherhood of Railway & Airline Clerks Bulletin* (1967-1967). FREQUENCY: q. PUBLISHER: Brotherhood of Railway, Airline & Steamship Clerks, Freight Handlers, Express & Station Employees (BRAC), 3 Research Place, Rockville, MD 20850. EDITOR: R.I. Kilroy. ILLUSTRATIONS. CIRCULATION: 4,100. MANUSCRIPT SELECTION: Editor. BOOK REVIEWS. IN-

DEXED/ABSTRACTED: WorAb. TARGET AUDIENCE: AC, SP. SAMPLE COPIES: Libraries, individuals.

Published by a labor union for its members in the transportation industry, the magazine covers all aspects of union activity including collective bargaining agreements, court cases, awards from the National Railroad Adjustment Board, and pertinent legislation. The articles are written by journalists and researchers drawn from the labor movement. Although the title indicates an international focus, a sample issue dealt mostly with matters concerning American workers. Members are kept informed on current issues by the union newsletter, *Leadership Action Line*.

A typical issue may have four or five major articles of one to three pages each plus regular features dealing with grievances, labor cases, and legislation. Lengthy, signed book reviews are sometimes included.

157   *International Review of Administrative Services*. DATE FOUNDED: 1928. MERGER: *Revue Internationale des Sciences Administrative* (1928-1956); *Progress in Public Administration* (1953-1956). PRICE: $82.50/yr. institutions, $45/yr. personal. PUBLISHER: International Institute of Administrative Sciences, 1 rue Defacqz, Bte.11, 1050 Brussels, Belgium. EDITOR: James Sundquist. ILLUSTRATIONS. INDEX. ADVERTISEMENTS. CIRCULATION: 6,000. MANUSCRIPT SELECTION: Editor, Editorial Committee. BOOK REVIEWS. SPECIAL ISSUES. INDEXED/ABSTRACTED: ABCPolSci, ASSIA, ForLangI, IntLabDoc, KeyEconSci, MgtC, PAIS, PeaceResAb. TARGET AUDIENCE: AC, SP.

The International Institute of Administrative Sciences (IIAS) publishes the *International Review of Administrative Services*. The IIAS aims to promote the development of the administrative sciences, the better operation of public administrative agencies, the improvement of administrative techniques, and the progress of international administration. Recent issues in the *IRAS* have included: "Management Techniques in the United Kingdom Public Sector" and "The Management Role and Productivity Increases in the Italian Public Administration."

Each issue contains five to seven substantive articles of between fifteen to thirty pages. A recent special issue was titled "Symposium on Public Management and Accountability." Other features include an annotated bibliography of recently published monographs of importance to public administrators.

158   *International Review of Social History*. DATE FOUNDED: 1937.
TITLE CHANGES: *Bulletin of the International Institute for Social
History* (1937-1955). FREQUENCY: 3/yr. PRICE: Dfl. 85/yr. PUB-
LISHER: Royal Van Gorcum, POB 43, 9400 AA Assen, The Nether-
lands. EDITOR: Marcel van der Linden. ILLUSTRATIONS. IN-
DEX. ADVERTISEMENTS. CIRCULATION: 1,400. MANU-
SCRIPT SELECTION: Editor. MICROFORMS: UMI. BOOK RE-
VIEWS. SPECIAL ISSUES. INDEXED/ABSTRACTED: AHCI,
AmerH, CurrCont, HistAb, RecPubArt, SOCI, SocSc, SocWAb,
WorAb. TARGET AUDIENCE: AC, SP.

An academic journal published under the sponsorship of the International Institut Voor Sociate Geschiedenis, Amsterdam, for the publication of research from scholars of a variety of nationalities. Recent
articles have included several on labor history, among them: "The
International Secretariat of National Trade Union Centres, 1901-
1913," "Employers, Unions and American Exceptionalism: A Comparative View" and "British Working-Class Attitudes to Social Reform,
1880-1930."

Each issue includes several articles of as many as 100 pages. Also
included are "News of the Profession," resumes of contributors, and a
substantial bibliography of recent publications of interest.

159   *International Social Science Journal*. DATE FOUNDED: 1949.
TITLE CHANGES: *International Social Science Bulletin* (1949-1958).
FREQUENCY: q. PRICE: $50.50/yr. institutions, $28/yr. personal.
PUBLISHER: Basil Blackwell Ltd., 108 Cowley Road, Oxford OX4
1JF, UK. EDITOR: Ali Kazancigil. ILLUSTRATIONS. INDEX.
ADVERTISEMENTS. CIRCULATION: 4,500. MANUSCRIPT
SELECTION: Editor. MICROFORMS: UMI, MIM. REPRINTS:
UMI. BOOK REVIEWS. INDEX/ABSTRACTED: AbAnthro,
ABCPolSci, AmerH, AnthroI, ASSIA, CIJE, CurrCont, ExMed,
FutSurv, GeoAb, GeoRef, HiEdCurrAwareBull, HistAb, IEconArt,
IntLabDoc, LLBA, MLA, PAIS, PsyAb, RuralRecrTourAb, SageFam-
StudAb, SagePAA, SocAb, SOCI, SocSc, SocWAb, WomAb, World-
AgEconRuralSocAb. TARGET AUDIENCE: AC, SP.

The *International Social Science Journal* is a UNESCO publication which
is also released in Chinese, Spanish, French and Arabic. It aims to
publish articles of a substantive and theoretical nature which will
promote scholarly debate on social science related issues of importance
to the international community. Titles of recent articles include: "Latin
American Industrialization," "Growth and Development Policies: A
Global Perspective," and "The Rural World and Peasant Studies."

Each issue of the journal is focused by a unifying theme. The most recent was "Modernity and Identity: A Symposium." Usually eight to ten articles of ten to fifteen pages in length are published. There is also a section of "Discussions" about current topics and occasionally a bibliography of recent UNESCO publications.

160   *International Social Security Review.* DATE FOUNDED: 1948. TITLE CHANGES: *Bulletin of the International Social Security Association* (1948-1966). FREQUENCY: q. PRICE: SwF. 50. PUBLISHER: International Social Security Association, Case Postale 1, CH-1211 Geneva 22, Switzerland. ILLUSTRATIONS. INDEX. ADVERTISEMENTS. CIRCULATION: 5,000. MANUSCRIPT SELECTION: Editor. BOOK REVIEWS. INDEXED/ABSTRACTED: AbHyg, ASSIA, CISAb, CLOA, ExMed, IntLabDoc, MedCareRev, PAIS, TropDisBull. TARGET AUDIENCE: AC, SP.

The main publication of the ISSA is the *International Social Security Review* which also publishes the *World Bibliography of Social Security*, *Current Research in Social Security*, and the series *Studies and Research*. The *Review* is published in four languages and is the only international quarterly dealing with Social Security. Recent research articles have included: "Unemployment Insurance, Social Protection and Employment Policy: An International Comparison" and "Unemployment Compensation and Employment in Industrialised Market-economy Countries."

Five to six major articles per issue of ten to twenty pages comprise the main part. Each issue also has several articles each under the headings "Social Security News," "International News" and "ISSA News."

161   *IPM Manpower Journal.* DATE FOUNDED: 1973. TITLE CHANGES: *People and Profits* (1973-1982). FREQUENCY: m. PRICE: R45. PUBLISHER: Institute of Personnel Management, P.O. Box 31390, Braamfontein 2017, South Africa. EDITOR: Mrs. B.J. Spence. ILLUSTRATIONS. MANUSCRIPT SELECTION: Editor, Publications Board. REPRINTS: Publisher. SPECIAL ISSUES: Occasional. INDEXED/ABSTRACTED: IndSAPer. TARGET AUDIENCE: AC, SP. SAMPLE COPIES: Libraries.

This journal provides practical up-to-date information and opinions for personnel executives and human resource managers. Each issue has a theme. Articles are written by authorities who are usually academics, practitioners, or consultants in the personnel field. The journal is written in both English and Dutch mainly by and for South Africans.

Recent issues have focused on organization development, social responsibility, education crisis, and computers in personnel work. A typical monthly issue contains seven to ten articles. Occasionally signed book reviews of one-third page are included. A section is devoted to activities of the Institute.

162   *IRRA Newsletter: Industrial Relations Research Association Series Newsletter.* DATE FOUNDED: 1959. FREQUENCY: q. PRICE: Membership. PUBLISHER: Industrial Relations Research Association, 7226 Social Science Building, University of Wisconsin, Madison, WI 53706. EDITOR: Michael E. Borus. ADVERTISEMENTS. MANUSCRIPT SELECTION: Editor. TARGET AUDIENCE: AC, SP.

Published in conjunction with the Institute of Management and Labor Relations at Rutgers, the *IRRA Newsletter* is mainly a vehicle for the dissemination of Association and local chapter news. Each issue varies in length and includes a calendar of events, a description of activities at the fifty-nine *IRRA* chapters nationwide, "positions available" and very brief news stories of interest to association members.

163   *IS: Industrial Society Magazine.* DATE FOUNDED: 1918. TITLE CHANGES: *Industrial Welfare* (1918-1929; 1932-1965); *Industrial Welfare and Personnel Management* (1929-1932); *Industrial Society* (1965-1987). FREQUENCY: q. PRICE: £15/yr. PUBLISHER: Industrial Society, Peter Runge House, 3 Carlton House Terrace, London SW1Y 5DG, England. EDITOR: Anna Smith. ILLUSTRATIONS. INDEX. ADVERTISEMENTS. CIRCULATION: 13,500. MANUSCRIPT SELECTION: Editor. MICROFORMS: World Microfilms. BOOK REVIEWS. INDEXED/ABSTRACTED: AccDataProAb, ASEANMgtAb, BI, CISAb, MgtC, PerManAb, SciAb, WorAb. TARGET AUDIENCE: AC, GP, HS, SP. SAMPLE COPIES: Libraries, individuals.

The Industrial Society which publishes this practical and informative journal deals with the management of people in industrial settings. It promotes the increase of efficiency, productivity, and profitability of goods and services created by employees. Its focus is primarily British as are its writers who are usually drawn from managerial ranks.

There are twelve to fifteen concise, practical articles per issue plus regular features such as the most pertinent news, a commentary, a question and answer page on management and employment law, and a section devoted to education and industry. The Society fosters education and runs training courses and conferences as well as works with students in high schools. There is a book review section which reviews six titles dealing with management. The 250 word signed reviews are usually prepared by management executives. There are also one or two work-related videos included.

164   *ITF Newsletter.* DATE FOUNDED: 1905. FREQUENCY: m. PUBLISHER: International Transport Workers' Federation, 133 Great Suffolk St., London SEI IPD, England. EDITOR: David Cockcroft. ILLUSTRATIONS. INDEX. CIRCULATION: 3,000. MANUSCRIPT SELECTION: Editor. TARGET AUDIENCE: SP. SAMPLE COPIES: Libraries, individuals.

This is a tabloid publication focusing on international transport and general trade union issues. It is published not only in English but French, German, Swedish, and Spanish as well. Typical articles (all of which originate with ITF staffers) include "Save Shipping Industry Call in Germany" and "Unions Query Ferry Design Safety." Some articles focus on general trade unionism ("Union Unity.")

165   *Japan Labor Bulletin.* DATE FOUNDED: 1959. FREQUENCY: m. PRICE: 3,600 Japanese Yen. PUBLISHER: Japan Institute of Labour, Chutaikin Building, 7-6, Shibakoen 1-Chome, Minato-Ku, Tokyo, 105 Japan. ILLUSTRATIONS. INDEX. ADVERTISEMENTS. CIRCULATION: 2,200. MANUSCRIPT SELECTION: Editorial Board. SPECIAL ISSUES: 4/yr. INDEXED/ABSTRACTED: CISAb, IntLabDoc, WorAb. TARGET AUDIENCE: AC. SAMPLE COPIES: Libraries, individuals.

The *Japan Labor Bulletin* aims to promote a better understanding of industrial relations with the rest of the world by providing background information. It is prepared by Japanese academicians and researchers.

The *Bulletin* is divided roughly into two parts. One part covers current developments; the other half provides analysis of some specific facet of industrial relations in Japan. The contents for each issue follow the same categories: general survey, working conditions and the labor market, labor disputes and trade unions, international relations, public policy and special topics. A directory of major trade unions in Japan appears as a separate insert in the May issue; labor statistics appear as an insert in the November issue.

166   *Jewish Labor Committee. Review.* DATE FOUNDED: 1934. TITLE CHANGES: *JLC News* (1934-1985). FREQUENCY: 6/yr. PUBLISHER: Jewish Labor Committee, 25 E. 21st St., New York, NY

10010. EDITOR: Martin Lafan. CIRCULATION: 3,000. MANU-SCRIPT SELECTION: Staff. REPRINTS: Publisher. TARGET AUDIENCE: AC, SP. SAMPLE COPIES: Libraries, individuals.

The *Review* has brief but worthwhile articles dealing with activities of the Jewish Labor Committee. It is published by the ATRAN Center for Jewish Culture. Typical recent articles include, "JLC Rallies Support Against Industrial Homework" and "JLC Intensifies Campaign on Plant Closings."

Special features occur occasionally. One recent topic dealt with U.S. and West German Unionists. Another short piece is titled "Holocaust Studies Implemented in Schools."

167   *Job Safety and Health*. DATE FOUNDED: 1977. FREQUENCY: Looseleaf. PRICE: $356/yr. PUBLISHER: Bureau of National Affairs, 1231 25th St., N.W., Washington, D.C. 20037. ILLUSTRATIONS. INDEX. TARGET AUDIENCE: AC, SP.

Job Safety and Health is another looseleaf service from BNA. Every other week, this "how-to" bulletin gives information about compliance with safety and health standards, variance options, technical rules, and promoting safety awareness. It is updated biweekly and housed in a binder.

168   *John Herling's Labor Letter*. DATE FOUNDED: 1934. TITLE CHANGES: *Chester Wright's Labor Letter* (1934-1950). FREQUENCY: w (bw in August). PRICE: $60/yr. PUBLISHER: John Herling, 1411 K St., N.W., Washington, D.C. 20005. EDITOR: John Herling. MANUSCRIPT SELECTION: Editor. REPRINTS: Publisher. TARGET AUDIENCE: AC, SP. SAMPLE COPIES: Libraries, individuals.

The format of this publication is similar to that of *I.F. Stone's Weekly* with a focus on labor. The *Letter* covers news of workers, labor organizations, topics of interest to labor such as legislation, economic conditions, civil rights, women's and family issues. It is pro-labor and supports "democratic, forward looking unions."

Material from research studies, government agencies and other sources are often quoted. There are usually four to five articles per issue.

169   *JOM. Journal of Occupational Medicine*. DATE FOUNDED: 1959. TITLE CHANGES: *Journal of Occupational Medicine* (1959-1967). FREQUENCY: m. PRICE: $85/yr. institutions, $60/yr. personal.

PUBLISHER: Williams and Wilkins, 428 East Preston Street, Baltimore, MD 21202. EDITOR: Lloyd B. Tepper, M.D. ILLUSTRATIONS. INDEX. ADVERTISEMENTS. CIRCULATION: 8,000. MANUSCRIPT SELECTION: Editor, Editorial Board. MICROFORMS: UMI. REPRINTS: UMI. INDEXED/ABSTRACTED: AbHyg, BI, BioAb, ChemAb, CISAb, CoalA, CurrCont, EnerInfoAb, EnerResAb, EnvAb, ErgAb, ExMed, HospLitI, IDentLit, IMed, IntAeroAb, ISciRev, LabHazBull, Leadscan, NoiPolPubA, NuclearSciAb, SCI, TraIndI, TropDisBull. TARGET AUDIENCE: AC, SP.

Journal of Occupational Medicine is published by the American College of Occupational Medicine for practicing physicians and academics. Like *AAOHN Journal,* its focus is a practical examination of issues important to occupational health and safety. Recent titles of interest include: "Management Roles for Physicians: Training Residents for Reality," "Occupational Motor Vehicle Injury Morbidity among Municipal Employees," and "Counting Recognized Occupational Deaths in the United States."

Each issue publishes ten clinically based research articles of usually under ten pages. Regular features include "Occupational Medicine Forum," "Selected Reviews from the Literature" and "People, Events, and a Calendar."

170   *Journal of Applied Behavioral Science.* DATE FOUNDED: 1965. FREQUENCY: q. PRICE: $75/yr. institutions, $35/yr. personal. PUBLISHER: JAI Press Inc., 55 Old Post Road, No.2, P.O. Box 1678, Greenwich, CT 06836-1678. EDITOR: Louis A. Zurcher, Jr. ILLUSTRATIONS. INDEX. ADVERTISEMENTS. CIRCULATION: 3,000. MANUSCRIPT SELECTION: Editors, Refereed. MICROFORMS: JAI, UMI. SPECIAL ISSUES. INDEXED/ABSTRACTED: ABCPolSci, ABIn, ASSIA, CINAHL, CurrCont, EdAdAb, EducI, HospLitI, LLBA, MgtC, PerManAb, PersLit, PsyAb, Psycscan, SageFamStudAb, SagePAA, SocAb, SOCI, SocSc, SocWAb, SPDA, WorAb. TARGET AUDIENCE: AC, SP.

Journal of Applied Behavior Science is the publication of the NTL Institute for Applied Behavioral Science. It publishes empirical research, theoretical, conceptual and practical articles in the behavioral sciences. Its balance between practice and theory has resulted in the following typical articles: "Developing Cooperative Labor-Management Relations in Unionized Factories," "Dealing With Work Stress and Strain" and "Individual Strategies for Coping With Stress During Organizational Transitions."

Each issue has seven to ten articles of less than twenty-five pages in length. There is an occasional call for papers and special issues.

171 *Journal of Applied Psychology*. DATE FOUNDED: 1917. FREQUENCY: q. PRICE: $120/yr. institutions, $60/yr. personal, $30/yr. American Psychological Association members. PUBLISHER: American Psychological Association, 1200 17th Street, NW, Washington, DC 20036. EDITOR: Robert M. Guion. ILLUSTRATIONS. INDEX. ADVERTISEMENTS. CIRCULATION: 6,000. MANUSCRIPT SELECTION: Editor, Consulting Editors, Refereed. MICROFORMS: UMI, MIM, Johnson Associates, Princeton Microfilms. REPRINTS: UMI. INDEXED/ABSTRACTED: ABIn, Adol-MentHlthAb, ASSIA, BI, BioAb, CINAHL, CommAb, CrimJusAb, CurrCont, EdAdAb, EducI, ErgAb, ExMed, IMed, INI, IntAeroAb, IntLabDoc, MgtC, PersLit, PsyAb, Psycscan, ResHiEdAb, RiskAb, SOCI, SocSc, SocWAb, WomAb. TARGET AUDIENCE: AC, SP.

The *Journal of Applied Psychology* focuses on all areas of applied psychology except clinical psychology. The journal considers quantitative investigations of interest to psychologists doing research or working in such settings as universities, industry, government, urban affairs, corrections, health, education, transportation and consumer affairs. Little in the way of theoretical articles is published here. Typical titles have been: "Supervision-Subordinate Similarities," "Japanese Management Progress: Mobility Into Middle Management," and "Compensation Satisfaction: Its Measurement and Dimensionality."

Each issue publishes twenty articles (8 1/2 x 11 size paper) of under ten pages. Ten shorter articles are also published. There is usually one substantially longer, empirically based research article called a "monograph" in each issue. There is also a section of announcements, and calendar of upcoming meetings in each issue.

172 *Journal of Business Administration*. DATE FOUNDED: 1969. FREQUENCY: 2/yr. PRICE: Can. $16/yr. PUBLISHER: Faculty of Commerce and Business Administration, The University of British Columbia, Vancouver, British Columbia V6T 1Y8. EDITOR: Peter N. Nemetz. INDEX. ADVERTISEMENTS. CIRCULATION: 500. MANUSCRIPT SELECTION: Refereed. MICROFORMS: UMI. REPRINTS: Publisher. SPECIAL ISSUES: Occasional. INDEXED/ABSTRACTED: ABIn, CanBusI, ElecComA, ISMEC, MgtC, PollAb. TARGET AUDIENCE: AC, SP. SAMPLE COPIES: Libraries, individuals.

An objective scholarly publication which provides an international focus on business administration. The primary areas deal with business administration, policy analysis, applied economics and operations research. The majority of authors are academics from around the world.

A typical issue has an average of ten lengthy articles. A recent issue focuses on the Pacific basin. Several articles deal with trade, investment and development in this area of the world with several focusing on Japan. Numerous charts, tables and figures amplify the text. Extensive references are also included.

173   *Journal of Business Administration.* DATE FOUNDED: 1975. TITLE CHANGES: *Journal of Management, Business and Economics* (1975-1986). FREQUENCY: q. PRICE: $25/yr. PUBLISHER: Institute of Business Administration, University of Dhaka, Bangladesh. EDITOR: Dr. Anwar Hossain. INDEX. ADVERTISEMENTS. MANUSCRIPT SELECTION: Refereed. REPRINTS: Editor. BOOK REVIEWS. TARGET AUDIENCE: AC, SP. SAMPLE COPIES: Libraries.

The *Journal of Business Administration* seeks to provide a forum for research, empirical and philosophical topics on "critical issues" of national, regional and international interest. The research published focuses on business administration and various management and developmental issues. The *Journal* is published to "augment the teaching and training activities of the Institute." It is written by international academics and specialists.

Each issue contains an average of six articles of varying length. It includes usually two or three signed book reviews two to three pages long.

174   *Journal of Business Ethics: JBE.* DATE FOUNDED: 1982. FREQUENCY: m. PRICE: $208.50/yr. institutions, $72/yr. personal, $60/yr. Society for Business Ethics members. PUBLISHER: Kluwer Academic Publishers Group, P.O. Box 322, 3300 AH Dordrecht, The Netherlands. EDITOR: Deborah C. Poff. ILLUSTRATIONS. INDEX. ADVERTISEMENTS. MANUSCRIPT SELECTION: Editor, Editorial Board. MICROFORMS: UMI. BOOK REVIEWS. INDEXED/ABSTRACTED: AccDataProAb, BI, CommAb, CurrCont, MgtC, MgtMarA, PAIS, PhilI, RiskAb, SOCI, TraIndI. TARGET AUDIENCE: AC, SP.

The *Journal of Business Ethics* publishes original scholarly articles dealing with a wide interpretation of both business and ethics. The majority of authors are academicians. The examples of specific areas which are covered in an objective manner are systems of production, consumption, marketing, labor relations and organizational behavior analyzed from a moral viewpoint.

A sample issue has an average of ten articles including a 100-200 word abstract. Titles of recent articles are "Teaching Business Ethics," "Political Consequences of Ethical Investing: The Case of South Africa," and "The Challenge of Preparing Ethically Responsible Managers: Closing the Rhetoric-Reality Gap." Three or four books are reviewed. Reviews which are signed are critical and lengthy.

175   *Journal of Collective Negotiations in the Public Sector.* DATE FOUNDED: 1972. FREQUENCY: q. PRICE: $75/yr. institutions, $27/yr. personal. PUBLISHER: Baywood Publishing Co., 120 Marine St., Farmingdale, NY 11735. EDITOR: Harry Kershen. ILLUSTRATIONS. INDEX. ADVERTISEMENTS. CIRCULATION: 1,000. MANUSCRIPT SELECTION: Editor, Editorial Board. BOOK REVIEWS. INDEXED/ABSTRACTED: ABIn, BI, CIJE, CLI, CurrCont, EdAdAb, HospLitI, LRI, MgtC, PAIS, PersLit, RG, SOCI, WorAb. TARGET AUDIENCE: AC, GP, SP. SAMPLE COPIES: Libraries.

The *Journal of Collective Negotiations in the Public Sector* "serves as a forum for the interchange of ideas and information among the international community of individuals concerned with the negotiation process." Articles emphasize practical ideas that will guide readers toward usable techniques for the negotiations process and contract administration, or that will recommend constructive approaches for dealing with public sector labor relations.

Each issue publishes an average of six articles of usually twenty pages. Articles are written by practitioners in the field as well as academics.

176   *Journal of Conflict Resolution.* DATE FOUNDED: 1957. TITLE CHANGES: *Conflict Resolution* (1957-1957). FREQUENCY: q. PRICE: $110/yr. institutions, $38/yr. personal. PUBLISHER: Sage Publications, Inc., 2111 West Hillcrest Drive, Newbury Park, CA 91320. EDITOR: Bruce M. Russett. ILLUSTRATIONS. INDEX. ADVERTISEMENTS. MANUSCRIPT SELECTION: Editor, Editorial Board, Refereed. MICROFORMS: UMI. REPRINTS: UMI. BOOK REVIEWS. INDEXED/ABSTRACTED: ABCPolSci, AbSocWor, AmBibSlav, AmerH, ContPgEd, CurrCont, EdAdAb, EthnStudBib, HistAb, HRA, IEconArt, IntPolSc, JEL, PAIS, PeaceResAb, Pred, PROMT, PsyAb, Psycscan, SagePAA, SageUrbStudAb,

SocAb, SocEdAb, SOCI, SocSc, SocWAb, USPSD. TARGET AUDI-
ENCE: AC, SP.

The *Journal of Conflict Resolution* is an "interdisciplinary journal of social
scientific theory and research on human conflict." Its major focus is
international conflict but it has published articles on intergroup conflict
as well as research on conflict between nations. It publishes pragmatic
information as well as basic research. Recent titles which might be of
interest to those in labor/industrial relations are: "Patterns of Crisis
Management" and "Value Differences in Conflict Resolution."

Each issue usually has nine articles of under thirty pages each. Some
issues occasionally have short research notes as well.

177   ***Journal of Economic Behavior and Organization.*** DATE
FOUNDED: 1980. FREQUENCY: q. PRICE: $410/yr. PUB-
LISHER: Elsevier Science Publishers B.V., P.O.B. 211, 1000 AE
Amsterdam, The Netherlands. EDITOR: Richard Day. ILLUSTRA-
TIONS. INDEX. ADVERTISEMENTS. MANUSCRIPT SELEC-
TION: Editors. MICROFORMS: Elsevier Sequoia, RPI. BOOK
REVIEWS. INDEXED/ABSTRACTED: BI, CREJ, CurrCont,
IEconArt, MathR, MgtC, RiskAb, SOCI. TARGET AUDIENCE:
AC, SP.

The *Journal of Economic Behavior and Organization* "is devoted to theoretical and empirical research concerning economic decision, organization and behavior. Its specific purpose is to foster an improved understanding of how human cognitive, computational and informational
characteristics influence the working of economic organizations and
market economics." Recent articles have included: "The Transactional
Structure of the Firm: A Comparative Survey," "Caring and Family
Income," and "The Life Cycle of Worker-Owned Firms in Market
Economies: A Theoretical Analysis."

Each issue contains an average of six articles. Articles usually run twenty
to forty pages in length. Three book reviews, substantial and signed, are
published with each issue.

178   ***Journal of Economic History.*** DATE FOUNDED: 1941. MERGER:
Tasks of Economic History (1941-1950). FREQUENCY: q. PRICE: $40/
yr. institutions, membership rates for Economic History Association
members. PUBLISHER: Cambridge University Press, 32 E. 57th
Street, New York, NY 10022. EDITORS: Paul Hohenberg and
Thomas Weiss. ILLUSTRATIONS. INDEX. ADVERTISE-
MENTS. CIRCULATION: 3,500. MANUSCRIPT SELECTION:

Editors, Editorial Board. MICROFORMS: MIM, UMI. REPRINTS: UMI. BOOK REVIEWS. INDEXED/ABSTRACTED: AHCI, AmBibSlav, AmerH, BibAg, BoRvI, CurrCont, GeoAb, HistAb, HumI, IEconArt, JEL, PAIS, PopInd, RecPubArt, RuralRecrTourAb, SocAb, SOCI, SocSc, WomAb, WorAb, WorldAgEconRuralSocAb, WritAmHis. TARGET AUDIENCE: AC, SP.

The *Journal of Economic History* is published under the sponsorship of the Economic History Association and Rensselaer Polytechnic Institute to promote research in the area of economic history and other related aspects of either history or economics. Recently published titles include: "Inventive Activity in Early Industrial America," "Ocean Freight Rates and Productivity" and "Strike Success and Union Ideology: The United States and France, 1880-1914."

Each issue publishes four to eight research articles of varying length, usually twenty to thirty pages. There is a notes and discussion section. There is an extensive book review section, all signed. They average one page and are arranged around topics such as Latin America, the United States, China and other geographical locations and historical periods such as "Medieval and Early Modern."

179 *Journal of Economic Perspectives: A Journal of the American Economic Association*. DATE FOUNDED: 1987. FREQUENCY: q. PRICE $125/yr. institutions, $72/yr. personal, $38.50-$53.90/yr. American Economics Association members. PUBLISHER: American Economic Association, 1313 21st Avenue So., Suite 809, Nashville, TN 37212-2786. EDITOR: Joseph E. Stiglitz. ILLUSTRATIONS. INDEX. ADVERTISEMENTS. MANUSCRIPT SELECTION: Editor, Associate Editors. TARGET AUDIENCE: AC, SP.

The *Journal of Economic Perspectives* is one of the three major publications of the American Economic Association. The other two are the *American Economic Review* and the *Journal of Economic Literature*. Empirical as well as conceptual articles are published here. Examples of recently published titles are: "The Rise and Fall of Unions: The Public Sector and the Private," "Symposium on Public and Private Unionization" and "A Seller's (and Buyer's) Guide to the Job Market for Beginning Academic Economists."

Each issue publishes symposia results (two or three), two articles (usually over thirty pages in length), and five or six shorter "Features." There is a notes section calling for papers, information for members and upcoming meetings. *Perspectives* also publishes correspondence.

180   *Journal of Economic Psychology.* DATE FOUNDED: 1981. FRE-
QUENCY: q. PRICE: Dfl. 261.00/yr. PUBLISHER: Elsevier Science
Publishers B.V., P.O. Box 1991, 1000 BZ Amsterdam, The Nether-
lands. EDITOR: W. Fred van Raay. ILLUSTRATIONS. INDEX.
ADVERTISEMENTS. MANUSCRIPT SELECTION: Editor,
Editorial Board. MICROFORMS: RPI, Elsevier Sequoia S.A. BOOK
REVIEWS. SPECIAL ISSUES. INDEXED/ABSTRACTED:
CREJ, HRIS, MgtC, PsyAb, SOCI. TARGET AUDIENCE: AC, SP.

The *Journal of Economic Psychology* is an international journal published
under the auspices of the International Association for Research in
Economic Psychology. It publishes empirical and theoretical research
focusing on "The psychological mechanisms that underlie consumption and other economic behavior. It deals with preferences, choices,
decisions and factors influencing these, as well as the consequences of
decisions and choices with respect to the satisfaction of needs." Recent
titles published are: "Diary Reports on Daily Economic Decisions of
Happy versus Unhappy Couples" and "Risk and Income Distribution."

Each issue publishes seven to eight research articles of twenty to thirty
pages in length. An average of four book reviews are published per issue.
They are signed and usually several pages long. Special issues are
published occasionally.

181   *Journal of Employment Counseling.* DATE FOUNDED: 1964.
FREQUENCY: q. PRICE: $11/yr., $5/yr. American Association for
Counseling and Development members. PUBLISHER: American
Association for Counseling and Development, 5999 Stevenson Ave-
nue, Alexandria, VA 22304. EDITOR: Robert Drummond. ILLUS-
TRATIONS. INDEX. ADVERTISEMENTS. CIRCULATION:
2,440. MANUSCRIPT SELECTION: Editor, Editorial Board.
MICROFORMS: UMI. REPRINTS: UMI. BOOK REVIEWS.
INDEXED/ABSTRACTED: ASSIA, CIJE, CurrCont, IntLabDoc,
MgtC, PsyAb, SageFamStudAb, SOCI. TARGET AUDIENCE: AC,
SP.

The *Journal of Employment Counseling* seeks articles illuminating theory
or practice in employment counseling, reporting professional experi-
mentation or research, and exploring current client vocational problems or the professional concerns of counselors. Recent articles have
included: "The Experience of Underemployment," "The Effect of Job
Level and Amount of Information on the Evaluation of Male and
Female Job Applicants," and "Job Satisfaction of Primary-Care Workers Who Assist the Elderly."

Each issue regularly publishes five to six articles of under twenty-five pages. There is usually one substantial, signed book review per issue.

182   *Journal of European Industrial Training*. DATE FOUNDED: 1975. TITLE CHANGES: *Human Resource Development* (1980-1981) Am. Edition. MERGER: *Industrial Training International* (1975-1976); *Journal of European Training* (1975-1976). FREQUENCY: 8/yr. PRICE: $389.95/yr. PUBLISHER: MCB University Press Limited, 62 Toller Lane, Bradford, West Yorkshire BD8 9BY, England. EDITOR: Dr. Roger Bennett. ILLUSTRATIONS. INDEX. ADVERTISEMENTS. MANUSCRIPT SELECTION: Editor, Editorial Advisory Board. BOOK REVIEWS. SPECIAL ISSUES: 3/yr. INDEXED/ABSTRACTED: ABIn, AccDataProAb, ASEANMgtAb, BI, CIJE, CurrCont, HiEdCurrAwareBull, IntLabDoc, MgtC, MgtMarA, ResHiEdAb, SagePAA, WorAb. TARGET AUDIENCE: AC.

This journal is designed to keep the training professional/practitioner in touch with current trends and new ideas. It is aimed at training managers, personnel specialists, and teachers and researchers of personnel management. Topics covered in *JEIT* include personnel training techniques, new developments and their application, management education and development, and personnel training effectiveness.

Each issue contains an average of six articles of ten to fifteen pages in length. Regular features in the serial include unsigned book and film reviews, conference diaries and reports, and current news.

183   *Journal of Human Resources*. DATE FOUNDED: 1966. FREQUENCY: q. PRICE: $47/yr. institutions, $25/yr. individuals. PUBLISHER: Journal Division, University of Wisconsin Press, 114 No. Murray St., Madison, WI 53715. EDITOR: Jan Levine Thal. ILLUSTRATIONS. INDEX. ADVERTISEMENTS. CIRCULATION: 3,000. MANUSCRIPT SELECTION: Editors. MICROFORMS: MIM, UMI. BOOK REVIEWS. SPECIAL ISSUES. INDEXED/ABSTRACTED: AbHlthCareMgtS, ABIn, AdolMentHlthAb, ASSIA, BI, BibAg, CIJE, CINAHL, CLOA, CurrCont, EdAbAd, EngI, IEconArt, IMed, IntBibE, JEL, MedCarRev, MgtC, PAIS, PerManAb, PersLit, RiskAb, RuralRecrTourAb, SOCI, SocSc, SocWAb, WomAb, WorAb, WorldAgEconRuralSocAb. TARGET AUDIENCE: AC, SP. SAMPLE COPIES: Libraries.

This academic journal with a statistical/empirical approach is sponsored by the Industrial Relations Research Institute and the Institute for Research on Poverty at the University of Wisconsin. Scholarly articles examine the "role of education and training in enhancing production skills, employment opportunities, and income, as well as manpower, health and welfare policies as they relate to the labor market and to economic and social development." Two recent articles include, "Employer's Discriminatory Behavior and the Estimation of Wage Discriminiation" and "The Definition and Measurement of Poverty."

Each issue contains five to six articles. There are also two to three lengthy, signed book reviews.

184   *Journal of Industrial Economics*. DATE FOUNDED: 1952. FRE-QUENCY: q. PRICE: $85/yr. institutions, $35/yr. personal. PUB-LISHER: Basil Blackwell Ltd., 108 Cowley Road, Oxford OX4 IJF, United Kingdom. EDITOR: Stephen W. Davies. ILLUSTRA-TIONS. INDEX. ADVERTISEMENTS. CIRCULATION: 1,850. MANUSCRIPT SELECTION: Editor, Editorial Board. MICRO-FORMS: UMI, MIM. REPRINTS: UMI. INDEXED/AB-STRACTED: ABIn, ASSIA, BI, BrHumI, BusI, CREJ, CurrCont, EnerI, EnerInfoAb, EnerResAb, EnvAb, GeoAb, IEconArt, KeyEcon-Sci, MgtC, MgtMarA, OperRes, PAIS, Pred, PROMT, RiskAb, SOCI, WorAb, WorBankAb. TARGET AUDIENCE: AC, SP.

The *Journal of Industrial Economics* promotes the analysis of modern industry, particularly the behavior of firms and the functioning of markets. More specifically it seeks to bring the tools of modern economic analysis to bear on the analysis of real problems of industrial economics. Recent topics have included: case studies of firms, the changing structure of industry, pricing, public policy, monopolies, regulation, changes in productivity and international competitiveness.

Each issue contains an average of five articles of under thirty pages. There are also several short articles as well, usually under ten pages.

185   *Journal of Industrial Relations*. DATE FOUNDED: 1959. FRE-QUENCY: q. PRICE: $45/yr. PUBLISHER: Industrial Relations Society of Australia, GPO Box 4479, Sydney, NSW 2001, Australia. EDITOR: John Niland. ILLUSTRATIONS. INDEX. ADVER-TISEMENTS. CIRCULATION: 4,000. MANUSCRIPT SELEC-TION: Editor, Editorial Board. BOOK REVIEWS. INDEXED/ABSTRACTED: APAIS, ASSIA, CREJ, IntLabDoc, LLBA, SocAb, SPDA, WorAb. TARGET AUDIENCE: AC, SP.

The *Journal of Industrial Relations* is the Australian counterpart to the American publications, *Industrial Relations* (Berkeley) and the *Industrial and Labor Relations Review* (Cornell). It covers the broad spectrum of industrial relations including topics such as management, trade unions, and government relations. It is written primarily by Australian academics and professionals in the field. Recent titles have included: "Job Mobility and Earnings: An Internal Labour Market Analysis," "Trade Unions and the Law," and "The Impact of Redundancy on Subsequent Labour Market Experience." This is truly a journal of international stature and scope.

Each issue has six research articles of varying length but usually under twenty pages. Ten to fifteen signed book reviews are published in each issue and are usually one page in length. A recent issue has five "year in review" topics on wages, legislation, unionism, legal decision, and management all in Australia.

186   *Journal of Labor Economics.* DATE FOUNDED: 1983. FREQUENCY: q. PRICE: $70/yr. institutions, $35/yr. personal. PUBLISHER: University of Chicago Press, 5801 South Ellis Avenue, Chicago, IL 60637. EDITOR: Edward P. Lazear. ILLUSTRATIONS. INDEX. ADVERTISEMENTS. CIRCULATION: 1,500. MANUSCRIPT SELECTION: Editors. MICROFORMS: UMI. BOOK REVIEWS. SPECIAL ISSUES. INDEXED/ABSTRACTED: CREJ, CurrCont, IEconArt, JEL. TARGET AUDIENCE: AC, SP.

This journal is published by the University of Chicago Press in association with the Economics Research Center/National Opinion Research Center. It is written generally by American academics with a research focus on "the supply and demand for labor services, compensation, labor markets, the distribution of income, labor demographics, unions and collective bargaining, and applied policy issues in labor economics." Recent articles include, "Multiunit Bargaining in Oligopolistic Industries," and "Sex-Related Wage Differentials and Women's Interrupted Labor Careers."

Each issue contains five to seven scholarly articles of twenty pages or more. Occasional special issue is published.

187   *Journal of Labor Research.* DATE FOUNDED: 1980. FREQUENCY: q. PRICE: $65/yr. institutions, $30/yr. individuals. PUBLISHER: Dept. of Economics, George Mason University, 4400 University Drive, Fairfax, VA 22030. EDITOR: James T. Bennett. ILLUSTRATIONS. INDEX. ADVERTISEMENTS. CIRCULATION: 2,000. MANUSCRIPT SELECTION: Editor, Refereed. MICROFORMS: UMI. REPRINTS: UMI. BOOK REVIEWS. SPECIAL ISSUES. INDEXED/ABSTRACTED: BI, CurrCont,

HRA, IntBibE, JEL, MgtC, PAIS, SOCI, WorAB. TARGET AUDI-
ENCE: AC, SP. SAMPLE COPIES: Libraries.

This journal was initiated to "enhance understanding of the political
economic and social objectives and impacts of labor unions." It is
written by U.S. economists and academics about the U.S. labor situation and is empirical and statistical in nature. Recent articles are:
"Grievance Initiation: A Literature Survey and Suggestions for Future
Research," and "Unionism and Voter Turnout."

Each issue has five to seven scholarly articles. There are as few as three
and as many as ten signed book reviews per issue.

188   *Journal of Management*. DATE FOUNDED: 1975. FREQUEN-
CY: q. PRICE: $49/yr. institutions, $34/yr. personal. PUBLISHER:
Southern Management Association, Department of Management,
College of Business Administration, Texas A & M University, College
Station, TX 77843. EDITOR: David D. VanFleet. ILLUSTRA-
TIONS. ADVERTISEMENTS. CIRCULATION: 1,400. MANU-
SCRIPT SELECTION: Editorial Board, Refereed. MICROFORMS:
UMI. REPRINTS: Authors. SPECIAL ISSUES. INDEXED/AB-
STRACTED: ABIn, ABSCAN, CIJE, CurrCont, HRA, JNE, MgtC,
MgtMarA, MgtRes, OperRes, PAIS, PerManAb, PsyAb, SocAb,
SOCI, SPDA, WorAb. TARGET AUDIENCE: AC, SP.

Journal of Management is an international publication containing original research articles that are interdisciplinary, theoretical or empirical
and related to the study of management and organizations. One issue
per year is published as "Yearly Review of Management." This special
issue examines in detail specific areas of management over a recurring
two to three year cycle. Authors are usually U.S. academicians and
researchers.

A typical issue has nine to ten articles each with a brief abstract. Some
issues contain a topical symposium with several related articles.

189   *Journal of Management Development*. DATE FOUNDED: 1982.
FREQUENCY: 5/yr. PRICE: $287.95/yr. PUBLISHER: MCB Uni-
versity Press Limited, 62 Toller Lane, Bradford, West Yorkshire BD8
9BY, England. EDITOR: Charles Margerison. ILLUSTRATIONS.
INDEX. MANUSCRIPT SELECTION: Editor, Editorial Advisory
Board. REPRINTS: Editor. INDEXED/ABSTRACTED: ABIn,
AccDataProAb, ASEANMgtAb, CurrCont, MgtC, MgtMarA, PsyAb.
TARGET AUDIENCE: AC, SP.

This journal is designed for the manager/practitioner as well as the academic. Topics include: experiential learning methods, new technology of managerial development, team building, productivity, self appraisal as well as case studies on management development. Recent articles have included "Training Managers for the Coal Industry," and "Management Development and Strategic Management Change." Articles are written by an international array of academic and management specialists.

Each issue contains an average of six articles. Their length runs ten to fifteen pages. Special issues have included "Action Learning" and "Multicultural Management Development."

190   *Journal of Management Studies*. DATE FOUNDED: 1964. FREQUENCY: 6/yr. PRICE: $168/yr. institutions, $74.35/yr. individuals. PUBLISHER: Basil Blackwell, Ltd., 108 Cowley Road, Oxford OX4 1JF, U.K. EDITORS: Karen Legge and Geoff Lockett. ILLUSTRATIONS. ADVERTISEMENTS. MANUSCRIPT SELECTION: Editors. MICROFORMS: UMI. BOOK REVIEWS. INDEXED/ABSTRACTED: AbHlthCareMgtS, ABIn, AccDataProAb, ASEANMgtAb, BI, BusI, CompConAb, CurrCont, EdAdAb, ElecElecAb, IntAbOperRes, IntLabDoc, KeyEconSci, MgtC, MgtMarA, OperRes, PersLit, PhysAb, WorAb. TARGET AUDIENCE: AC, SP.

An academic empirical journal published under the auspices of the Manchester (England) Business School. It is written by British and other commonwealth scholars. Primary focus is management studies but there is some emphasis on the interaction with labor. Recent articles have included: "Participation Under Conditions of Conflict," and "The Influence of Organization Structure on the Utility of an Entrepreneurial Top Management Style."

Each issue includes four to six scholarly articles. One issue includes seven lengthy, signed book reviews. Another issue has none.

191   *Journal of Occupational Psychology: An International Journal of Industrial and Organizational Psychology*. DATE FOUNDED: 1922. TITLE CHANGES: *Journal of the National Institute of Industrial Psychology* (1922-1931); *Human Factor* (1931-1937); *Occupational Psychology* (1937-1973). FREQUENCY: q. PRICE: $89/yr. PUBLISHER: British Psychological Society, St. Andrews House, 48 Princess Road East, Leicester LE1 7DR, United Kingdom. EDITOR: David Guest. ILLUSTRATIONS. INDEX. ADVERTISEMENTS. CIRCULATION: 2,100. MANUSCRIPT SELECTION: Editor, Editorial Board, Refereed. MICROFORMS: Swets & Zeitlinger.

REPRINTS: ISI. BOOK REVIEWS. SPECIAL ISSUES. IN-
DEXED/ ABSTRACTED: ABIn, AccDataProAb, ASSIA, BI, BioAb,
BMTA, BrEdI, BrHumI, CINAHL, CISAb, CurrCont, ErgAb, IMed,
IntLabDoc, LLBA, MgtC, NoiPolPubA, PersLit, PsyAb, Psycscan,
ResHiEdAb, SciAb, ShipA, SocAb, SOCI, TraIndI, WorAb. TAR-
GET AUDIENCE: AC.

The purpose of the *Journal of Occupational Psychology* is to increase
understanding of people in the workplace. The areas which are covered
are industrial, organizational, vocational and personnel psychology as
well as occupational counselling and behavioral aspects of industrial relations, ergonomics, human factors and industrial sociology. The
articles are empirical research papers, critical surveys of the field, or
theoretical contributions. The authors are international academics and
researchers.

There are six to eight articles per issue. Some issues include signed book
reviews. A recent special issue focuses on technological change and
innovation. Recent articles have included "Psychology of Work and
Employment" and "Robotics: A Challenge for Occupational Psychology."

192   *Journal of Pension Planning and Compliance*. DATE FOUNDED:
1974. TITLE CHANGES: *Pension and Profit-Sharing Tax Journal*
(1974-1977). FREQUENCY: q. PRICE: $105/yr. PUBLISHER:
Panel Publishers, Inc., 14 Plaza Road, Greenvale, NY 11548. EDI-
TOR: Bruce J. McNeil. ILLUSTRATIONS. INDEX. ADVERTISE-
MENTS. MANUSCRIPT SELECTION: Editor, Editorial Board.
MICROFORMS: UMI. INDEXED/ABSTRACTED: ABIn, AccI,
BI, CLI, ILegPer, LegCont, LRI, MgtC, PAIS, TraIndI. TARGET
AUDIENCE: AC, SP.

The *Journal of Pension Planning and Compliance* publishes articles which
provide practical information and ideas. It covers matters of importance
to professionals who deal with the tax, legal, and business planning
aspects of pensions and related benefits in their practices. Recent
articles have included: "Simplified Employee Pension Plans (SEPs):
Past, Present and Future," "Determination of Highly Compensated
Employee Status" and "Recent Developments in Welfare Benefits."

Each issue has five major articles of varying length. Other features
include "Current Financial Developments" and "Washington Update."

193   *Journal of Policy Analysis and Management: the Journal of the Association for Public Policy Analysis and Management.* DATE FOUNDED: 1981. MERGER: *Policy Analysis* (1975-1981); *Public Policy* (1940-1981). FREQUENCY: q. PRICE: $60/yr. institutions, $44/yr. personal. PUBLISHER: Wiley Journals, 605 Third Ave., New York, NY 10158. EDITOR: David L. Weimer. ILLUSTRATIONS. INDEX. ADVERTISEMENTS. CIRCULATION: 2,700. MANU-SCRIPT SELECTION: Editors, Editorial Board. MICROFORMS: UMI, RPI. BOOK REVIEWS. INDEXED/ABSTRACTED: ABCPolSci, AbHlthCareMgtS, AmBibSlav, AmerH, BI, CurrCont, EnerInfoAb, EnerResAb, EnvAb, HistAb, HospLitI, IEconArt, JEL, MedCareRev, MgtC, PAIS, RecPubArt, SagePAA, SageUrbStudAb, SocAb, SOCI, SocSc, SocWAb, SPDA, UrbAffAb. TARGET AUDI-ENCE: AC, SP.

Published for APPAM—The Association for Public Policy Analysis and Management—*JPAM* is written "by the professional, for the professional, to better evaluate and use the tools..." to find policies that work. Recent subjects of research articles have dealt with deregulation and its impact on specific industries, ethics in decision making and development of policy analysis and management. Recent articles have included "Supply Creates Demands: An Organizational Process View of Administrative Expansion" and "The Minimum Wage and the Poor: End of a Relationship."

Each issue contains seven to ten articles of ten to twenty-five pages in length. Other features are "Insights" (shorter articles), "Curriculum and Case Notes," "Word from the Front" and "Working Papers." There is a "Book Reviews" section of ten to twenty signed book reviews.

194   *Journal of Political Economy.* DATE FOUNDED: 1892. FRE-QUENCY: 6/yr. PRICE: $65/yr. institutions, $35/yr. personal. PUB-LISHER: University of Chicago Press, 5720 S. Woodlawn Avenue, Chicago, IL 60637. EDITOR: Sam Peltzman. ILLUSTRATIONS. INDEX. ADVERTISEMENTS. CIRCULATION: 7,300. MANU-SCRIPT SELECTION: Editor, Refereed. MICROFORMS: UMI, KTO, MIM, Johnson Associates. REPRINTS: UMI, ISI. BOOK REVIEWS. INDEXED/ABSTRACTED: ABCPolSci, ABIn, AmerH, BankLitI, BI, BoRvD, BoRvI, CREJ, CurrCont, EnerInfoAb, EnerResAb, EnvAb, GeoAb, HistAb, IEconArt, IntLabDoc, JEL, KeyEconSci, MgtC, PAIS, RuralRecrTourAb, SocAb, SOCI, SocSc, WomAb, WorldAgEconRuralSocAb. TARGET AUDIENCE: AC, SP.

If the *Review of Radical Political Economics* is socialist in perspective, the

Journal of Political Economy is less ideologically confined in its analyses of economic issues. It publishes empirical research articles on such topics as pricing, unemployment, inflation, the stock market, and agricultural commerce. Surely a wide spectrum of interest is also reflected in the following recently titled articles: "The Economics of Fait Accompli," "Women's Labor Supply and Marital Choice," and "Welfare Effects of British Free Trade."

Each issue publishes an average of ten articles, usually twenty to thirty pages in length. There is an occasional review article and a comments section. There are usually one or two signed book reviews of several pages.

195   *Journal of Public Economics.* DATE FOUNDED: 1972. FREQUENCY: 3/yr. PRICE: SwF. 720/yr. institutions, SwF. 26/yr. personal. PUBLISHER: Elsevier Science Publishers B.V., P.O. Box 1991, 1000 BZ Amsterdam, The Netherlands. EDITORS: A.B. Atkinson and N.H. Stern. ILLUSTRATIONS. INDEX. ADVERTISEMENTS. MANUSCRIPT SELECTION: Editors, Editorial Board. MICROFORMS: RPI, Elsevier Sequoia S.A. INDEXED/ABSTRACTED: ABIn, ASSIA, BI, CREJ, CurrCont, ExMed, IEconArt, JEL, MgtC, PAIS, SagePAA, SageUrbStudAb, WorBankAb. TARGET AUDIENCE: AC, SP.

The aim of the *Journal of Public Economics* is to encourage original scientific contributions to the problems of public sector economics, with particular emphasis on the application of modern economic theory and methods of quantitative analysis. Recent articles have included: "A Welfare Analysis of the Walrasion Mechanism with Transfers," and "A Residence Time Model of Housing Markets."

Each issue publishes seven research articles averaging twenty pages in length. Contributors are from a variety of countries. Academic in aim and scope, it is written for academics by academics.

196   *Journal of Social History.* DATE FOUNDED: 1967. FREQUENCY: q. PRICE: $48/yr. institutions, $25/yr. personal. PUBLISHER: Carnegie Mellon University Press, Schenley Park, Pittsburgh, PA 15213. EDITOR: Peter N. Stearns. ILLUSTRATIONS. INDEX. ADVERTISEMENTS. CIRCULATION: 1,900. MANUSCRIPT SELECTION: Editor, Refereed. MICROFORMS: MIM, UMI. REPRINTS: UMI. BOOK REVIEWS. INDEXED/ABSTRACTED: AHCI, AmBibSlav, AmerH, BoRvI, CrimJusAb, CurrCont, HistAb, LLBA, RecPubArt, SageFamStudAb, SocAb,

SOCI, SocSc, SocWAb, SPDA, WomAb. TARGET AUDIENCE: AC, SP.

The *Journal of Social History* is the American counterpart to the British publication, *Social History*. Topics recently covered are: education, industrialization, status attainment, race politics, pluralist theory, ethics and medicine, family studies and morality. Recent titles of interest are: "Managers and Engineers in French Big Business of the 19th Century," and "Prosperity and Industrial Emigration from Britain During the Early 1850's." This is an international journal covering the wide range of social history subjects as a discipline.

Each issue publishes an average of seven substantial research articles of usually twenty pages. There are fifteen to twenty signed book reviews per issue. They are two to three pages long.

197 *Journal of Social Issues*. DATE FOUNDED: 1945. FREQUENCY: q. PRICE: $120/yr. institutions, $29.50/yr. personal. PUBLISHER: Plenum Publishing Corporation, 233 Spring Street, New York, NY 10013. EDITOR: Stuart Oskamp. ILLUSTRATIONS. INDEX. ADVERTISEMENTS. CIRCULATION: 7,500. MANUSCRIPT SELECTION: Editors, Editorial Advisory Board. MICROFORMS: UMI. REPRINTS: UMI. INDEXED/ABSTRACTED: AbAnthro, ABCPolSci, AbCrimPen, AbSocWor, AdolMentHlthAb, AmerH, ASSIA, BI, BibAg, CIJE, CommAb, CrimJusAb, CurrCont, CurrLit-FamPlan, EdAdAb, GeoAb, HistAb, HRA, LLBA, PAIS, PeaceResAb, PsyAb, Psycscan, SageFamStudAb, SagePAA, SageUrbStudAb, SocAb, SocEdAb, SOCI, SocSc, SPDA, StudWomAb, WomAb. TARGET AUDIENCE: AC, SP.

The *Journal of Social Issues* is sponsored by the Society for the Psychological Study of Social Issues, "a group of over three thousand psychologists and allied social scientists who share a concern with research on the psychological aspects of important social issues." The Society seeks to bring theory and practice into focus on human problems of groups, communities, the nation and international bodies. It seeks to communicate "scientific findings and interpretations in a nontechnical manner." Previous issues have included such topics as "Productivity and Satisfaction in the Public Sector," "Beyond Nine to Five: Sexual Harassment on the Job," and "Black Employment Opportunities: Macro and Micro Perspectives."

Each issue focuses on a special topic. There are usually ten to fifteen articles of under twenty pages in length per issue. Mostly written by American academics the articles are both empirical and conceptual in nature.

198   *Journal of Social Policy.* DATE FOUNDED: 1972. FREQUENCY: q. PRICE: $108/yr. PUBLISHER: Cambridge University Press, The Pitt Building, Trumpington Street, Cambridge CB2 1RP, England. EDITOR: Alan Deacon. ILLUSTRATIONS. INDEX. ADVERTISEMENTS. MANUSCRIPT SELECTION: Editor, Editorial Board. MICROFORMS: UMI. REPRINTS: UMI. BOOK REVIEWS. INDEXED/ABSTRACTED: ABCPolSci, AbHyg, ASSIA, CurrCont, HospLitI, IntLabDoc, LLBA, MedCareRev, PAIS, PovHumResAb, PsyAb, RecPubArt, SocAb, SOCI, SocSc, SPDA, TropDisBull. TARGET AUDIENCE: AC, SP.

This is the journal of the British Social Policy Association. It publishes empirical, methodological and conceptual research on such topics as sick pay, social class, gender, social security, labor, poverty, and comparable worth, among others. Recent articles have included: "Early Retirement in a Period of High Unemployment," "A Case Study in Public Sector Labour Relations" and "Back to the Future: Statutory Sick Pay, Citizenship and Social Class."

Each issue has four or five substantial articles. Other features include "Research Notes," "Comment," and "Discussion." There is a regular book review section which usually averages ten signed reviews per issue.

199   *Journal of Social Psychology.* DATE FOUNDED: 1930. FREQUENCY: 6/yr. PRICE: $68/yr. PUBLISHER: HELDREF Publications, 4000 Albemarle Street, N.W., Washington, D.C. 20016. EDITOR: Penny S. Atkins. ILLUSTRATIONS. INDEX. CIRCULATION: 2,350. MANUSCRIPT SELECTION: Editor, Editorial Board. MICROFORMS: UMI. REPRINTS: Publisher. INDEXED/ ABSTRACTED: AbSocWor, AdolMentHlthAb, ASSIA, BioAb, BrAbMedSc, ChildDevAb, CIJE, CommAb, CrimJusAb, CurrCont, ECER, ExMed, IMed, IndPsyAb, IntPolSc, LLBA, MgtRes, PersLit, PovHumResAb, PsyAb, ResHiEdAb, RevRelRes, SageUrbStudAb, SchPsyDig, SocEdAb, SocSc, SOCI. TARGET AUDIENCE: AC, SP.

The *Journal of Social Psychology* was founded by John Dewey and Carl Murchison. It is devoted to experimental, empirical and especially field studies of groups, cultural effects, cross-national problems, language and ethnicity. This journal is particularly strong in field studies on cross-national problems while the *British Journal of Social Psychology* publishes original research dealing with theory and methodology as well as empirical studies. Important to industrial relations scholarship, recent articles have included: "The Impact of Occupation, Performance and Sex on Sex Role Stereotyping," and "Economic Factors and Suicide."

Each issue includes ten to fifteen mainly empirically based articles. It includes regular sections on "Current Problems," "Cross-cultural Notes" and summaries of recent studies titled "Replications and Refinements."

200   *Journal of the American Statistical Association.* DATE FOUNDED: 1888. TITLE CHANGES: *Publications of the American Statistical Association* (1888-1918); *Quarterly Publication of the American Statistical Association* (1919-1921). PRICE: $73/yr. PUBLISHER: American Statistical Association, 1429 Duke Street, Alexandria, VA 22314. EDITOR: J. Sedransk. ILLUSTRATIONS. INDEX. ADVERTISEMENTS. CIRCULATION: 17,172. MANUSCRIPT SELECTION: Editors, Associate Editor. MICROFORMS: MIM, UMI. REPRINTS: UMI. BOOK REVIEWS. INDEXED/ABSTRACTED: AbHyg, ABIn, BI, BioAb, BusI, ChildDevAb, CompConAb, CompRev, Compumath, CurrCont, CurrIStat, ElecComA, ElecElecAb, EnerInfoAb, EnvAb, ExMed, IEconArt, IntAeroAb, ISMEC, JContQuanMeth, JEL, MathR, PollAb, PopInd, PhysAb, PsyAb, RiskAb, SafSciA, SOCI, StatThMethAb, TraIndI, TropDisBull, WorBankAb. TARGET AUDIENCE: AC, SP.

Journal of the American Statistical Association divides each issue into three major sections. "Applications" publishes original practical articles on data sets, statistical methods, new data, and evaluations of data sources. "Theory and Methods" publishes articles that make original contributions to the foundations, theoretical development, and methodology of statistics and probability. "Invited Essays in Review" appears occasionally and is usually a review of an area of applied statistics or a review of statistical methods or theory. Typical articles of all three types have been: "Estimating a Common Relative Risk: Application in Equal Employment," "Minimax Estimation of the Mixing Proportion of Two Known Distributions" and "Introductory Textbooks: A Framework for Evaluation."

Each issue publishes eight to ten applications articles, as many as twenty theory and methods articles, and usually one review essay. All articles are variable in length but average around eight pages. There are usually twenty signed book reviews per issue.

201   *Journal of Vocational Behavior.* DATE FOUNDED: 1971. FREQUENCY: 6/yr. PRICE: $170/yr. PUBLISHER: Academic Press, Inc., 1 East First St., Duluth, MN 55802. EDITOR: Nancy E. Betz. ILLUSTRATIONS. INDEX. MANUSCRIPT SELECTION: Editor. INDEXED/ABSTRACTED: ASSIA, CIJE, CINAHL,

CurrCont, LLBA, PersLit, PsyAb, Psycscan, SocAb, SOCI, SPDA, WomAb. TARGET AUDIENCE: AC, SP.

The *Journal of Vocational Behavior* publishes "...empirical, methodological, and theoretical articles related to such issues as the validation of theoretical constructs, developments in instrumentation, program comparisons and research methodology as related to vocational development, preference, choice and selection, implementation, satisfaction, and effectiveness throughout the life-span and across cultural, national, sex and other demographic boundaries." Recent articles have included: "Periodicity in Seniority-job Satisfaction Relationship" and "The Relationship Between Congruent Specialty Choice Within Occupations and Satisfaction."

Articles vary in length. The number of articles per issue also varies widely. One recent issue had four articles of between seventy to less than twenty pages in length while another issue had as many as eight articles of fifteen to twenty pages in length. There are no book reviews, although there are some review articles.

202   *Labor.* DATE FOUNDED: 1951. TITLE CHANGES: *Christlabor* (1951-1955). FREQUENCY: m. PRICE: $15/yr. institutions, $12/yr. personal. PUBLISHER: Labor, rue de Treves, 33, B-1040, Brussels, Belgium. EDITOR: Jan Kulakowski. ILLUSTRATIONS. MANUSCRIPT SELECTION: Editorial Board. SPECIAL ISSUES: m. TARGET AUDIENCE: GP, HS, SP.

Labor is written by trade unionists from around the world and published by the World Confederation of Labor. This publication is aimed at promotion of the world trade union movement. It is a highly sophisticated publication trying to develop a consciousness out of which will grow a universal overall trade union strategy.

Ten to twelve substantive articles are included in each monthly issue. "Gatt and Protectionism" and "Towards a European Coal Policy" are sample entries. It includes a monthly "Review on Trade Union Information and Training." It is published in several languages.

203   *Labor Arbitration in Government.* DATE FOUNDED: 1970. FREQUENCY: m. PRICE: $90/yr. PUBLISHER: American Arbitration Association, 140 W. 51st Street, New York, NY 10020. EDITOR: Colleen J. McCann. INDEX. CIRCULATION: 300. MANUSCRIPT SELECTION: Editor. MICROFORMS: Publisher. REPRINTS: Publisher. INDEXED/ABSTRACTED: PersLit. TARGET AUDIENCE: AC, SP.

Each month, labor arbitration awards (submitted by America Arbitration Association regional offices) involving employees of federal, state, city and local agencies are summarized here for publication. There are twenty-six regional offices of the AAA across the U.S. and they deal with such subjects as "the effects of statutes on the collective bargaining agreement; arbitrability; absenteeism; and just cause for discharge." Decisions on grievances arising in health care facilities are also included.

204   *Labor Herald.*   DATE FOUNDED: 1936. TITLE CHANGES: *Baltimore Labor Herald* (1936-1939). FREQUENCY: bw. PRICE: $5/ yr. PUBLISHER: Labor Herald, 4005 Seven Mile Lane, Baltimore, MD 21208-6114. EDITOR: Daniel Bernstein. ILLUSTRATIONS. ADVERTISEMENTS. CIRCULATION: 33,902. MANUSCRIPT SELECTION: Editor. REPRINTS: Publisher. BOOK REVIEWS. SPECIAL ISSUES: 4-8/yr. TARGET AUDIENCE: GP, SP. SAMPLE COPIES: Libraries, individuals.

This newspaper is published in Maryland for Marylanders described as "workers of hand and brain." There are many short articles but it does include some substantial articles of interest to labor. One recent issue had an article written by Maryland Congressman Benjamin L. Cardin, "We Must Act Now to Reduce Federal Deficit."

It includes signed book reviews varying in number with each issue. The publication also includes four to eight special issues each year, usually around Labor Day and election dates.

205   *Labor History.*   DATE FOUNDED: 1953. TITLE CHANGES: *Labor Historians' Bulletin* (1953-1959). FREQUENCY: q. PRICE: $25/ yr. institutions, $19.50/yr. personal. PUBLISHER: Tamiment Institute, New York University, 70 Washington Square South, New York, NY 10012. EDITOR: Daniel J. Leab. INDEX. ADVERTISEMENTS. CIRCULATION: 1,800. MANUSCRIPT SELECTION: Editorial Board. MICROFORMS: UMI. BOOK REVIEWS. INDEXED/ABSTRACTED: AHCI, AmerH, API, HistAb, HumI, IEconArt, RecPubArt, SOCI, WomAb, WorAb, WritAmHis. TARGET AUDIENCE: AC.

This journal focuses on original research in labor history, studies of specific unions, the impact of labor problems upon ethnic and minority groups, theories of the labor movement and comparative studies and analysis of foreign labor movements as they influence American labor developments. Writers are American academics. This title focuses on American labor in contrast with *International Labor and Working Class History* which takes a more international approach.

A typical issue has four to six lengthy articles plus two essays. There is an annual bibliography on American labor compiled by a librarian. It is divided by subject but without annotations. An average of six to eight signed book reviews are included in each issue. These have been reviewed by academics and are at least one page in length. A "Newsnotes" section provides short notices regarding awards and grants, conferences, exhibits, publications and societies' activities.

206   *Labor Law Journal.* DATE FOUNDED: 1949. FREQUENCY: m. PRICE: $80/yr. PUBLISHER: Commerce Clearing House, Inc., 4025 W. Peterson Ave., Chicago, IL 60646. EDITOR: Allen E. Schecter. ILLUSTRATIONS. INDEX. ADVERTISEMENTS. CIRCULATION: 3,100. MANUSCRIPT SELECTION: Editor. MICROFORMS: UMI. INDEXED/ABSTRACTED: BusI, CLI, CurrCont, HospLitI, ILegPer, IntLabDoc, LRI, ManI, PAIS, PersLit, SOCI, TraIndI, WomAb, WorAb. TARGET AUDIENCE: AC, SP.

Labor Law Journal is published by Commerce Clearing House "to promote sound thinking on labor law problems." Its articles survey important legislative, administrative, and judicial developments pertaining to legal problems in the labor field. Recent articles have included "Job Safety and Health," "Right-to-Work Referendum Voting: Observations on the Aggregate Historical Statistics" and "A Brief History of the Fair Labor Standards Act."

Each issue contains six to eight articles of varying length but usually ten pages or so. An annual index is also published.

207   *Labor Notes.* DATE FOUNDED: 1979. FREQUENCY: m. PRICE: $20/yr. institutions, $10/yr. personal. PUBLISHER: Labor Education & Research Project, 7435 Michigan Ave., Detroit, MI 48210. EDITOR: Jim Woodward. CIRCULATION: 6,500. MANUSCRIPT SELECTION: Editor, Staff. MICROFORMS: State Historical Society of Wisconsin. BOOK REVIEWS. INDEXED/ABSTRACTED: API. TARGET AUDIENCE: AC, GP. SAMPLE COPIES: Libraries, individuals.

From the viewpoint of the grassroots labor activist, this publication attempts to spread the news on issues affecting labor. It maintains a definite political bent left of center. Substantial articles in each issue are on current labor issues. An example would be "Dissent Grows at California GM-Toyota Plant," and "Flight Attendants at American Airlines Fight Two-Tier Wage System."

It includes occasional book reviews which are signed. The masthead motto "Let's Put the Movement Back in Labor Movement" should speak volumes.

208 **Labor Relations Reporter.** DATE FOUNDED: 1937. TITLE CHANGES: *Labor Relations Report* (1937-1939); *War Labor Reports* (1942-1945). MERGER: *Labor Arbitration Reports* (1946-). Published in conjunction with *Labor Relations Reporter*. FREQUENCY: Looseleaf. PRICE: $1,718/yr. PUBLISHER: Bureau of National Affairs, 1231 25th St., N.W. Washington, D.C. 20037. ILLUSTRATIONS. INDEX. INDEXED/ABSTRACTED: IntLabDoc. TARGET AUDIENCE: AC, SP.

Labor Relations Reporter is another looseleaf service from BNA. It is divided into five sections. *The Expediter* is an encyclopedic desk reference providing explanations of labor statutes, cases and issues plus summaries of cases concerning labor on the Supreme Court docket. *Labor-Management Relations* publishes full text federal and state labor-related court decisions, digests of NLRB Rulings, and selected state laws dealing with labor, and the *Fair Employment Practice Service* which is a guide to EEO laws, policies, programs, and rules. *Labor Arbitration* gives rulings of arbitrators, boards and fact finding bodies. *Wages and Hours* gives full text of federal court decisions in wage-hour cases plus regulations, interpretations, enforcement procedures, and administrative decisions.

This service comes in fourteen reference binders and is updated in all sections on a weekly basis. The fifth section is a *Master Index* for the entire service by topic, case names or BNA classification number.

209 **Labor Studies Journal.** DATE FOUNDED: 1976. FREQUENCY: 3/yr. PRICE: $25/yr. institutions, $15/yr. personal. PUBLISHER: Transaction, Rutgers - The State University, New Brunswick, NJ 08903. EDITOR: Richard Humphreys. INDEX. ADVERTISEMENTS. CIRCULATION: 800. MANUSCRIPT SELECTION: Editor, Refereed. REPRINTS: Publisher. BOOK REVIEWS. SPECIAL ISSUES. INDEXED/ABSTRACTED: AmerH, HistAb, MgtC, PerManAb, WorAb. TARGET AUDIENCE: AC, SP. SAMPLE COPIES: Libraries.

A scholarly journal, *Labor Studies Journal* focuses on the publication of materials, teaching methods, philosophy and substance of labor studies and industrial relations. It tends to concentrate on trade unionism, the status of collective bargaining, union administration, and contract administration. Authors are usually American academics. Special issues are published once every three years. They focus on a theme for the issue such as occupational safety and health.

Each issue usually contains four articles. Regular features include an Audio-Visual Reference Shelf which reviews recent appropriate A-V materials, and a book review section with an average of twelve signed, critical reviews containing 500 words.

210   *Labor-Management Relations Service Newsletter*.   DATE FOUNDED: 1970. TITLE CHANGES: *LMRS Newsletter* (1970-1979). FREQUENCY: 6/yr. PUBLISHER: U.S. Conference of Mayors, 1620 Eye Street, N.W., 4th Floor, Washington, D.C. 20006. INDEX. MANUSCRIPT SELECTION: Editorial Staff. TARGET AUDIENCE: AC, SP.

This newsletter is published by the U.S. Conference of Mayors as an information source for current news on labor-management relations. Typical lead articles have included: "Benefit Plans Must Meet Section 89 Tests," "Candidates State Positions on Workplace Issues" and "IRS Rescinds Ruling on Section 457."

Each issue includes one lead article usually a page and a half in length. Other features include "Negotiated Settlements Across the Nation," "National News Briefs", "Legislative Watch" and "Upcoming Conferences."

211   *Labour and Society*. DATE FOUNDED: 1966. TITLE CHANGES: *IILS Bulletin* (1966-1974). FREQUENCY: q. PRICE: SwF. 45./yr. institutions, SwF. 17./yr. personal. PUBLISHER: International Institute for Labour Studies, CH-1211 Geneva 22, Switzerland. EDITOR: Rose Marie Greve. ILLUSTRATIONS. INDEX. ADVERTISEMENTS. CIRCULATION: 1,200. MANUSCRIPT SELECTION: Editor, Refereed. MICROFORMS: Publisher. BOOK REVIEWS. SPECIAL ISSUES. INDEXED/ABSTRACTED: BMTA, HRA, IntLabDoc, LLBA, MgtC, PAIS, RuralRecrTourAb, SocAb, SPDA. TARGET AUDIENCE: AC, SP.

The journal reflects one of the basic aims of IILS which is to serve as a forum for "deeper understanding...of the processes of social change and its implications for labour relations and labour policy." Hence, the journal covers "social and labour issues and particular prominence is given to the three programme areas of the IILS: new industrial organisation, labour markets and workers participation."

There are eight to ten articles per issue and four to five signed book reviews of one to one and one-half pages in length.

212   ***Labour Education.*** DATE FOUNDED: 1964. FREQUENCY: q. PRICE: $22.80/yr. PUBLISHER: Worker's Education Branch, International Labour Office, CH-1211 Geneva 22, Switzerland. EDITOR: Clara Foucault-Mohammed. ILLUSTRATIONS. ADVERTISEMENTS. CIRCULATION: 3,500. MICROFORMS: UMI. BOOK REVIEWS. INDEXED/ABSTRACTED: CIJE, ContPgMgt, IntLabDoc. TARGET AUDIENCE: AC, GP, SP.

Published in English, French and Spanish by the Worker's Education Branch of the ILO, this publication targets trade union organizations, worker's education institutions, as well as public authorities and individuals concerned with labor education. Most articles are written by the staff and designed to help "trade union organisations to provide training and knowledge to their members, enabling them to fulfill their trade union, social and economic responsibilities."

Several articles are included under the headings "Labour Education in the World," "Activities of the ILO," "Methods and Techniques" and "Workers in History." There are several, short unsigned book reviews per issue.

213   ***Labour, Capital and Society.*** DATE FOUNDED: 1968. TITLE CHANGES: *Manpower and Unemployment Research in Africa* (1968-1975); *Manpower and Unemployment Research* (1976-1978). FREQUENCY: 2/yr. PRICE: Can. $18/yr. institutions, Can. $12/yr. personal. PUBLISHER: Centre for Developing Area Studies, McGill University, 3715 Peel Street, Montreal, Quebec H3A 1X1. EDITOR: Rosalind E. Boyd. ILLUSTRATIONS. INDEX. ADVERTISEMENTS. CIRCULATION: 800. MANUSCRIPT SELECTION: Editor, Editorial Committee, Refereed. BOOK REVIEWS. INDEXED/ABSTRACTED: API, ASSIA, GeoAb, HRA, IntLabDoc, PAIS, RecPubArt, RuralRecrTourAb, SOCI, SocSc, WorldAgEcon-RuralSocAb. TARGET AUDIENCE: AC, SP.

Labour, Capital and Society is published by McGill University's Centre for Developing Area Studies. It is billed as a journal of the Third World and "invites contributions in English or French on diverse aspects of labour research." Recent titles have included: "Structural Change and Organizational Development of Petty Manufacturers in Ecuador" and "Manual Workers in Uganda." This journal is a good source for comparative, international labor/industrial relations information.

One issue averages several substantial articles of usually twenty-five to thirty-five pages. Some articles are only in French. There is usually a shorter "Research Report." Usually eight to ten signed book reviews per issue are published. They average several pages in length. A recent issue included an extensive "Bibliography on Unemployment," which is a continuing series for the publication. It is a list of hundreds of monographs on the subject.

214   *Labour/Le Travail.* DATE FOUNDED: 1971. TITLE CHANGES: *Bulletin - Committee on Canadian Labour History* (1971-1971); *Canadian Labour History* (1973-1975); *Bulletin of the Committee on Canadian Labour History* (1976-1979). FREQUENCY: 2/yr. PRICE: $25/yr. institutions, $20/yr. personal. PUBLISHER: Committee on Canadian Labour History, Department of History, Memorial University, St. John's, Newfoundland A1C 5S7. EDITOR: Gregory S. Kealey. ILLUSTRATIONS. INDEX. ADVERTISEMENTS. CIRCULATION: 1,300. MANUSCRIPT SELECTION: Editorial Board, Refereed. MICROFORMS: Publisher. REPRINTS: Publisher. BOOK REVIEWS. SPECIAL ISSUES: Occasional. INDEXED/ABSTRACTED: AHCI, AmerH, API, CanPerI, CurrCont, HistAb, HRA, PAIS, SagePAA. TARGET AUDIENCE: AC, GP, SP. SAMPLE COPIES: Libraries, individuals.

This title is a bilingual, biannual review devoted to the study of Canadian labour history. Articles dealing with teaching and research in labour studies are included in this scholarly academic journal.

There are ninety signed book reviews of approximately 1000 words and eight to ten substantial articles in each issue.

215   *Law and Contemporary Problems.* DATE FOUNDED: 1933. FREQUENCY: q. PRICE: $32.50/yr. PUBLISHER: School of Law, Duke University, Durham, NC 27706. EDITOR: Joyce S. Rutledge. INDEX. ADVERTISEMENTS. CIRCULATION: 2,700. MANUSCRIPT SELECTION: Editor. MICROFORMS: FBR, UMI. REPRINTS: RRI. INDEXED/ABSTRACTED: ABCPolSci, AccI, ASSIA, CLI, CoalA, CommAb, CrimJusAb, CurrCont, EnerI, EnerInfoAb, HospLitI, IEconArt, ILegPer, LegCont, LLBA, LRI, MarAffBib, PAIS, SocAb, SOCI, SocSc, SPDA, WritAmHis. TARGET AUDIENCE: AC, SP.

Law and Contemporary Problems is published by the Duke University School of Law. Each issue focuses on a special area and the articles published under the rubric include legal, economical, administrative, and sociological aspects of the subject. Topics of volumes have included: "Federal Regulation of Work from Recruitment to Retirement," "Extraterritoriality of Economic Legislation" and "Reweaving the Corporate Veil."

Each issue has a unifying topic under which ten to fifteen articles are published. Articles vary in length but average twenty pages. A recent issue included an extensive bibliography titled "Economists as Judges."

216 *Law and Society Review.* DATE FOUNDED: 1966. TITLE CHANGES: *Law and Society Association. Newsletter* (nd). FREQUENCY: 5/yr. PRICE: $65/yr. PUBLISHER: Law and Society Association, Hampshire House, University of Massachusetts, Amherst, MA 01003. EDITOR: Robert L. Kidder. ILLUSTRATIONS. INDEX. ADVERTISEMENTS. CIRCULATION: 2,400. MANUSCRIPT SELECTION: Editor, Editorial Advisory Board, Refereed. MICROFORMS: UMI, RRI, WSH. REPRINTS: ISI. SPECIAL ISSUES: Occasional. INDEXED/ABSTRACTED: ABCPolSci, AbCrimPen, AdolMentHlthAb, AmerH, ASSIA, CLI, CrimJusAb, CurrCont, HistAb, HRIS, ILegPer, IntBibSoc, LegCont, LLBA, LRI, PAIS, PeaceResAb, PsyAb, RecPubArt, SageUrbStudAb, SocAb, SOCI, SocSc, SPDA, WritAmHis. TARGET AUDIENCE: AC, SP.

Law and Society Review is published by the Law and Society Association which in turn is supported by its offices at UMass (Amherst). The Association is an international group whose purpose is to stimulate and support research and teaching on the cultural, economic, political, psychological and social aspects of law and the legal system. Recent articles in this academically focused journal include: "Class Structure and Legal Practice" and "Pain, Suffering and Jury Awards." Written by American law school professors, this journal is a useful source for some labor law interpretation.

Each issue publishes five to eight articles of thirty pages in length. There is usually a research note of shorter length. Contributors read like a legal profession "Who's Who."

217 *The Leader/Le Leader.* DATE FOUNDED: 1986. FREQUENCY: m. PRICE: Free. PUBLISHER: Canadian Union of Public Employees, 21 Florence St., Ottawa, Ontario K2P OW6. EDITOR: Ron Verzuh. ILLUSTRATIONS. CIRCULATION: 140,000. MANUSCRIPT SELECTION: Editors. SPECIAL ISSUES. TARGET AUDIENCE: GP, SP. SAMPLE COPIES: Libraries, individuals.

A newspaper format providing short articles supporting its union's position on any issue or event affecting the public sector of the economy. *The Leader* is published by Canada's largest trade union and represents a large cross-section of trade union activity across the country. It is a news supplement to the *Facts* and the *Public Employee* and is compiled by the editor and an in-house staff.

A typical issue has thirty-five short articles covering such topics as workers in nursing homes, pay equity for women, the jailing of labor leaders, and deregulation of Canadian airlines.

218   *Leadership Action Line*. DATE FOUNDED: 1981. FREQUENCY: m. PUBLISHER: Brotherhood of Railway, Airline & Steamship Clerks, Freight Handlers, Express & Station Employees (BRAC), 3 Research Place, Rockville, MD 20850. EDITOR: R.I. Kilroy. ILLUS-TRATIONS. CIRCULATION: 3,200. MANUSCRIPT SELEC-TION: Editor. SPECIAL ISSUES. TARGET AUDIENCE: SP. SAMPLE COPIES: Libraries, individuals.

One of many newsletters written for the members of a trade/labor union, *Leadership Action Line* explores collective bargaining, legislative goals, industry trends, and issues affecting transportation industry workers, both as taxpayers and consumers. The issues are presented from a labor union point of view. The writers who are journalists or researchers are drawn from the U.S. labor movement. For more in-depth coverage, the union also publishes the *International President's Bulletin*.

A typical newsletter consists of several short news items dealing with drug testing, extension of health coverage, union elections, and con-tract settlements. Special issues are published as needed.

219   *Leadership and Organization Development Journal*.   DATE FOUNDED: 1980. FREQUENCY: 5/yr. PRICE: $359.95/yr. PUB-LISHER: MCB University Press Ltd., 62 Toller Lane, Bradford BD8 9BY, England. EDITOR: Dr. David Butcher. ILLUSTRATIONS. INDEX. ADVERTISEMENTS. MANUSCRIPT SELECTION: Editor, Editorial Advisory Board. BOOK REVIEWS. INDEXED/ABSTRACTED: ABIn, AccDataProcAb, ASEANMgtAb, BI, CurrCont, MgtC, MgtMarA, PsyAb. TARGET AUDIENCE: AC, SP.

Written for practicing organizational development specialists as well as academics teaching applied leadership, *Leadership and Organization Development Journal* focuses on leadership style, team building, conflict management, politics in organizations, technology, communication, business policy and managing planned change. Recent titles have included "A Survey of Difference in Communication between Manag-ers and Subordinates" and "Stress and the Employee."

Each issue contains four to six major articles of varying length. Regular features include "News and Views," "Letters to the Editor" and "Bookshelf" which averages five signed book reviews.

220   *Legislative Information*. DATE FOUNDED: 1984. FREQUENCY: 11/yr. PUBLISHER: Publications, International Labour Office, CH-1211 Geneva 22, Switzerland. EDITOR: Legislative Information Branch. CIRCULATION: 500. MANUSCRIPT SELECTION: Staff. MICROFORMS: Publisher (1984-1986 only). REPRINTS: Publisher. TARGET AUDIENCE: AC, SP. SAMPLE COPIES: Libraries, individuals.

This is a supplement of *Legislative Series* which is annotated elsewhere in this bibliography as providing "a selection of labor and social security legislation." *Legislative Information* is that same selection which is available from the ILO on microfiche.

Each issue is an annotated listing of labor and social security legislation from virtually all countries of the world. Most issues run twenty-five to thirty typewritten pages.

221   *Legislative Series*. DATE FOUNDED: 1906. TITLE CHANGES: *International Labour Office. Bulletin* (1906-1919). FREQUENCY: 3/yr. PRICE: 60 SwF./yr. PUBLISHER: Publications, International Labour Office, CH-1211 Geneva 22, Switzerland. EDITOR: Legislative Information Branch. INDEX. CIRCULATION: 2,000. MANUSCRIPT SELECTION: Staff. REPRINTS: Editor. SPECIAL ISSUES: Annual. TARGET AUDIENCE: AC, SP. SAMPLE COPIES: Libraries, individuals.

Legislative Series is a selection of world labor and social security legislation. Published simultaneously in French, English and Spanish, this publication consists of translations and edited reprints of a selection of the most important laws and regulations affecting labor and social security adopted by various countries.

Each issue contains five to seven reprints of laws and/or regulations. Recent issues have covered employment equity in Canada, workers' liability in Spain and social insurance in Ecuador. Each issue has a "List of Recent Legislation" passed in all countries of the world. It also includes a chronological list of legislation.

222   *LMI Review: A Quarterly Review of Washington State Labor Market Information*. DATE FOUNDED: 1985. FREQUENCY: q. PUBLISHER: Employment Security Department, Labor Market & Economic Analysis Branch, KG-11, Olympia, WA 98504-5311. EDITOR:

Carol Welch. ILLUSTRATIONS. INDEX. CIRCULATION: 2,000. MANUSCRIPT SELECTION: Director, Editor. RE-PRINTS: Publisher. TARGET AUDIENCE: AC, GP, SP. SAMPLE COPIES: Libraries, individuals.

"The ultimate purpose of *LMI* is to expand employment opportunities and to reduce unemployment by providing...labor market information." This is a substantial publication for a state agency.

LMI Review includes many statistical analyses. It always includes a detailed and lengthy "Quarterly Analysis" of Washington State economy along with feature articles. One recent article was titled "The Labor Market Experience of the Unemployed."

223   *Management.*   DATE FOUNDED: 1981. FREQUENCY: q. PRICE: $15/yr. PUBLISHER: John E. Anderson Graduate School of Management at UCLA, 405 Hilgard Ave., Rm. 4250, Los Angeles, CA 90024. EDITOR: Cathleen Watkins. ILLUSTRATIONS. ADVER-TISEMENTS. CIRCULATION: 23,000. MANUSCRIPT SELEC-TION: Editor, Editorial Advisory Board. REPRINTS: Publisher. INDEXED/ABSTRACTED: PAIS. TARGET AUDIENCE: AC, SP. SAMPLE COPIES: Libraries, individuals.

This journal discusses issues pertinent to mid- and upper-level managers, entrepreneurs and business leaders. The articles are written by the journal staff or business journalists. More than one-half of the audience are MBA alumni of the Anderson Graduate Management School at UCLA.

Each issue contains one main article and several shorter ones. Frequently articles appear focusing on distinguished faculty and their research; other focus on alumni. There is a regular calendar of events and a column devoted to alumni.

224   *Management and Labour Studies.* DATE FOUNDED: 1975. FRE-QUENCY: q. PRICE: $20/yr. PUBLISHER: Xavier Labour Relations Institute, P.O. Box 222, Jamshedpur, India 831001. EDITOR: Rev. T.A. Mathias. INDEX. ADVERTISEMENTS. CIRCULA-TION: 1,000. MANUSCRIPT SELECTION: Editor, Refereed. RE-PRINTS: Editor. BOOK REVIEWS. INDEXED/ABSTRACTED: HRA, PerManAb, PsyAb, SagePAA, SageUrbStudAb. TARGET AUDIENCE: AC, SP. SAMPLE COPIES: Libraries, individuals.

This journal is addressed to professional managers and academicians and focuses on the latest thinking and research in the areas of management, labor, and related subjects. Although the authors are drawn from international scholars, researchers and managers, a large number of the articles are particularly appropriate to India. A human approach to business and industrial relations is the viewpoint which is espoused. The journal is well indexed but may not be readily available in the United States.

A representative issue contains an average of six articles and a book review section with six reviews. Recent articles covered women in the corporate world in the 21st century, alternative organizations in the 21st century, Zen and its impact on Japanese management. The signed book reviews are critical and lengthy consisting of about 1500 words.

225 *Management Decision.*   DATE FOUNDED: 1963. TITLE CHANGES: *Scientific Business: A Quarterly Review of the Application of Scientific Method in Business* (1963-1967). FREQUENCY: 6/yr. PRICE: $479.95/yr. PUBLISHER: MCB University Press Ltd., 62 Toller Lane, Bradford BD8 9BY, England. EDITOR: Gordon Wills. INDEX. MANUSCRIPT SELECTION: Editor, Editorial Advisory Board, Refereed. REPRINTS: Publisher. SPECIAL ISSUES: Occasional. INDEXED/ABSTRACTED: ABIn, BrHumI, BusI, IntLab-Doc, MgtC, MgtMarA, PAIS, WorAb. TARGET AUDIENCE: AC, GP, SP.

This journal provides in-depth articles in all areas of management such as corporate planning, management training and development, marketing and multinational management. It provides practical help to managers for problems in the industrial field. It combines the best articles from more specialized journals from this publisher which have been reworked by professional writers before presentation to a more general audience. New articles are also written specifically for this publication as well. The journal is objective and international in scope and maintains a balance between theory and practice. The authors are international academics or managers.

A typical issue contains about six articles. From time to time special issues are published which devote the complete issue to an in-depth look at a particular topic. Some topics have focused on practical financial management and effective communications.

226 *Management International Review.*   DATE FOUNDED: 1961. TITLE CHANGES: *Management International* (1961-1966). FREQUENCY: q. PRICE: DM 158/yr. institutions, DM 44,50/yr. personal. PUBLISHER: Betriebswirthschaftlicher, Verlag Dr. Th. Galbler Gmb H, Taunusstr. 54, Postfach 1546, 6200 Wiesbaden 1, West Germany. EDITOR: K. Macharzina. ILLUSTRATIONS. IN-

DEX. ADVERTISEMENTS. CIRCULATION: 3,000. MANU-SCRIPT SELECTION: Editor, Editorial Board, Refereed. MICRO-FORMS: UMI. SPECIAL ISSUES. INDEXED/ABSTRACTED: ABIn, AccDataProcAb, BI, BusI, CurrCont, ExMed, KeyEconSci, MgtC, MgtMarA, PAIS, RefSo, SOCI, WorAb. TARGET AUDI-ENCE: AC, SP.

Management International Review aims at the advancement and dissemi-nation of international applied research in the fields of management and business. The scope of the publication comprises management and business policy, international business and transnational corporations. *MIR* stresses the interaction between theory and practice of manage-ment by publishing articles, research notes and reports which concen-trate on the application of existing and potential research for business and other organizations. Recent titles have included: "The Measuring of Organizational Effectiveness" and "Cultural Differences in the Learning Style of Managers."

Each issue has an editorial, and eight or so articles of under twenty pages. Occasionally there is a "Research Note" or two per issue which is usually a shorter article. Some issues have a special focus and the articles revolve around that theme.

227   *Management Review.* DATE FOUNDED: 1914. TITLE CHAN-GES: *Bulletin* (National Association of Corporation Schools) (1914-1920); *Bulletin* (National Association of Corporation Training) (1920-1921); *Corporation Training* (1922-1922); *Personnel Administration* (1922-1923); *American Management Review* (1923-1925). MERGER: *Management in Practice* (1970-1977). FREQUENCY: m. PRICE: $40/yr. PUBLISHER: American Management Association, 135 W. 50th Street, New York, NY 10020. EDITOR: Rod Willis. ILLUSTRA-TIONS. INDEX. ADVERTISEMENTS. CIRCULATION: 90,000. MANUSCRIPT SELECTION: Editors. MICROFORMS: UMI. REPRINTS: Publisher. BOOK REVIEWS. INDEXED/AB-STRACTED: ABIn, BusI, CompLitI, HospLitI, IntAeroAb, MgtC, PAIS, PerManAb, PersLit, PsyAb, RefSo, WorAb. TARGET AUDI-ENCE: AC, GP, SP.

This journal is aimed at the busy manager who needs to be aware of current trends in the business world. It is written in much the same vein as *Business Week* although its articles tend to examine issues in somewhat more depth.

There are regular features or departments in each issue including "Memo for Management," "Management in Practice," "Washington Perspective," and "Global Perspective." Book reviews are included with an average of seven to ten per issue. The majority of them are written anonymously in 100-200 words. Occasionally there is a longer signed review. A recent issue focused on young people and business. It included several articles dealing with childcare and family leave policies in corporations as well as young people starting businesses and an investigation of family businesses.

228   *Management Services.*   DATE FOUNDED: 1942. TITLE CHANGES: *Work Study and Management Services* (1942-1975). FREQUENCY: m. PRICE: £2.50/yr. PUBLISHER: Institute of Management Services, 1 Cecil Court, London Road, Enfield, Middlesex EN2 6DD, England. EDITOR: David Charlton. ILLUSTRATIONS. INDEX. ADVERTISEMENTS. CIRCULATION: 14,000. MANUSCRIPT SELECTION: Editorial Panel. MICROFORMS: UMI. REPRINTS: Publisher. BOOK REVIEWS. SPECIAL ISSUES. INDEXED/ABSTRACTED: ABIn, CompConAb, ElecElecAb, MgtMarA, PhysAb, ShipA. TARGET AUDIENCE: AC, SP.

This is the official journal of the Institute of Management Services. The majority of writers are British academic and management executives who support and encourage productivity and efficiency among its members.

A typical issue has three to six articles of two to three pages each. There are regular features such as short reports for branches of the Institute in the United Kingdom, a fairly lengthy column on new technology and short news items pertaining to management. About one-third to one-half of the publication consists of classified advertisements for management positions. There are an average of two book reviews per issue of one-third page each. There are also items outlining activities taking place in the Institute including various conferences, seminars and educational courses.

229   *Management Solutions.*   DATE FOUNDED: 1955. TITLE CHANGES: *Supervisory Management* (1955-1986). FREQUENCY: m. PRICE: $25/yr., $22.50/yr. American Management Association members. PUBLISHER: American Management Association, 135 W. 50th St., New York, NY 10020-1201. EDITOR: Florence Stone. ILLUSTRATIONS. INDEX. ADVERTISEMENTS. CIRCULATION: 30,000. MANUSCRIPT SELECTION: Editor. MICROFORMS: UMI. REPRINTS: Publisher. INDEXED/ABSTRACTED: ABIn, BibAg, BusI, CINAHL, MgtC, WorAb. TARGET AUDIENCE: SP. SAMPLE COPIES: Libraries, individuals.

This publication is aimed at managers, chief executive officers and division heads providing them with short articles exemplifying supervisory and management issues which are regularly encountered, and some suggested ways in which to handle them. The authors are academics, researchers and managerial staff drawn mostly from the United States, Canada and the United Kingdom. *Management Solutions* and *Supervisory Scene*, other AMA publications, cover very similar topics. The former covers more articles per issue in less depth while the latter presents a more rounded, intensive approach to one topic.

There are an average of seven articles per issue. There are also regular features such as an arbitration issue, a case study and responses to previously published case studies.

230   *Management Today*. DATE FOUNDED: 1966. FREQUENCY: m. PRICE: £34/yr. PUBLISHER: Management Publications Limited, 30 Lancaster Gate, London WZ 3LP, England. EDITOR: Lance Knobel. ILLUSTRATIONS. INDEX. ADVERTISEMENTS. CIRCULATION: 100,000. MANUSCRIPT SELECTION: Editor. REPRINTS: Editor. BOOK REVIEWS. INDEXED/ABSTRACTED: ABIn, BusI, ExMed, IntLabDoc, MgtC, MgtMarA, ShipA, TraIndI, WorAb, WorTexA. TARGET AUDIENCE: AC, GP, SP. SAMPLE COPIES: Libraries.

A British publication which is geared toward upper management. It provides practical articles which are written by British and American journalists and business people. The major focus is definitely British; for a comparable American focus, one should consult *Sloan Management Review*.

A typical issue contains ten to twelve articles including regular columns such as "Inside Europe" and "Inside America" expressing points of view on appropriate and current topics. Some issues may revolve around a theme such as finances. There are usually three signed book reviews of 800 words each.

231   *Management World*.   DATE FOUNDED: 1960. TITLE CHANGES: *AMS Management Bulletin* (1960-1971). FREQUENCY: 6/yr. PRICE: $22/yr. PUBLISHER: Administrative Management Society, 2360 Maryland Rd., Willow Grove, PA 19090. EDITOR: Joseph E. McKendrick. ILLUSTRATIONS. INDEX. ADVERTISEMENTS. CIRCULATION: 13,000. MANUSCRIPT SELECTION: Editor. MICROFORMS: UMI. REPRINTS: Publisher. BOOK REVIEWS. INDEXED/ABSTRACTED: ABIn, AccDataProAb, BI, BusI, HospLitI, MgtC, PersLit. TARGET AUDIENCE: AC, GP, SP. SAMPLE COPIES: Libraries, individuals.

This magazine is focused to provide practical approaches to problems and situations which arise in the management and development of one's career in today's business world. The writers of articles are usually U.S. or Canadian academics or people who are themselves business managers.

A typical issue has eight to ten articles dealing with topics such as stress, the automated office, marketing oneself for career advancement and conducting successful but short meetings. There are eight to ten regular features dealing with the workplace environment, resources (reviews of one appropriate book or video tape), and a forum column.

232   *Managerial Law*. DATE FOUNDED: 1975. TITLE CHANGES: *Knights Industrial Law Reports* (1975). FREQUENCY: 6/yr. PRICE: £119.95/yr. PUBLISHER: Barmarick Publications, Enholmes Hall, Partrington, Hull HU12 OPR, England. EDITOR: J.R. Carby-Hall. CIRCULATION: 250. MANUSCRIPT SELECTION: Editor. INDEXED/ABSTRACTED: CurrCont. TARGET AUDIENCE: SP. SAMPLE COPIES: Libraries, individuals.

The major purpose of this journal is to provide a forum for British managers to keep abreast of current trends and developments in the field of business legislation. It covers in-depth the areas of labor relations, employment conditions, training, marketing, accounting and taxation. Its authors are British academics.

A typical issue is a monograph covering a single topic such as discrimination and collective agreements, the transfer of employees, and balloting for closed shops.

233   *Managers Digest: An International Journal of Management and Organisation Behaviour*. DATE FOUNDED: 1971. FREQUENCY: 2/yr. PRICE: $40/yr. institutions, $20/yr. personal. PUBLISHER: M.A. Mabud, Management Development Centre, 1 Shakespeare Sarani, Calcutta 700 071, India. EDITOR: M.A. Mabud. INDEX. ADVERTISEMENTS. CIRCULATION: 500. MANUSCRIPT SELECTION: Editor, Refereed. REPRINTS: Editor. BOOK REVIEWS. INDEXED/ABSTRACTED: WorAb. TARGET AUDIENCE: AC, SP. SAMPLE COPIES: Libraries.

Managers Digest is written for academics and specialists. Recent articles have focused on empirical research, critical surveys, theoretical contributions, prescriptive guidelines in the areas of management, training, organizational behavior and allied sciences. Recent titles have been

"Management—Indian Style," "Work Alienation in a Psycho-Social Perspective" and "Organisational Climate."

Each issue contains six articles (ten to fifteen pages in length). On average, there are usually three signed book reviews per issue.

234   *Massachusetts Labor Leader.* DATE FOUNDED: 1960. FRE-QUENCY: q. PRICE: Free. PUBLISHER: Massachusetts AFL/CIO, 8 Beacon St., 3rd Floor, Boston, MA 02108. EDITOR: John S. Laughlin. ILLUSTRATIONS. CIRCULATION: 8,000. MANU-SCRIPT SELECTION: Staff. TARGET AUDIENCE: AC, SP. SAMPLE COPIES: Libraries, individuals.

This is a union newsletter which is directed at its 8,000 members. It includes a few short, topical articles written by staff. It provides legislative updates on the state and federal levels. Other regular features include "Labor Names and Faces" and a calendar of events, "Labor Dates."

235   *Metropolitan Washington, D.C. Area Labor Summary.* DATE FOUNDED: 1969. TITLE CHANGES: *Greater Washington Labor Summary* (nd). FREQUENCY: m. PRICE: Free. PUBLISHER: Department of Employment Services, 500 C Street, N.W., Suite 201, Washington, D.C. 20001. EDITORS: Richard Groner and Eileen Dent. ILLUSTRATIONS. CIRCULATION: 1,100. MANU-SCRIPT SELECTION: Editors. INDEXED/ABSTRACTED: SRI. TARGET AUDIENCE: AC, SP. SAMPLE COPIES: Libraries.

This is a Washington, D.C. labor market information publication focusing on labor force/labor market statistics and analysis. Statistically focused articles include: "Job Growth in the District of Columbia," "Labor Force Profile: City-wide Unemployment 1983 to 1985," and "Employment of District Residents Increases-Unemployment Drops to 7.9%."

Each issue usually contains seven or eight articles. Articles written by the department staff who also compile and analyze the area labor statistics.

236   *Monthly Benefit Statistics.* DATE FOUNDED: 1968. FREQUEN-CY: m. PRICE: Free. PUBLISHER: U.S. Railroad Retirement Board, Office of Public Affairs, 844 Rush Street, Chicago, IL 60611. EDI-TOR: W. Poulos. CIRCULATION: 2,000. INDEXED/ABSTRAC-TED: ASI, IndUSGovPer. TARGET AUDIENCE: AC, SP. SAM-PLE COPIES: Libraries, individuals.

This journal consists primarily of statistics on railroad retirement and unemployment insurance for railroad workers. The focus is on retirement and survivor programs, financial statistics, and unemployment and sickness programs available to the membership.

237   ***Monthly Labor Review***.   DATE FOUNDED: 1915. TITLE CHANGES: *Monthly Review* (1915-1918). FREQUENCY: m. PRICE: $16/yr. PUBLISHER: U.S. Department of Labor, Bureau of Labor Statistics, 441 G St., N.W., Washington, D.C. 20212. EDITOR: Henry Lowenstein. ILLUSTRATIONS. INDEX. CIRCULATION: 15,000. MANUSCRIPT SELECTION: Editor. MICROFORMS: UMI. REPRINTS: Publisher. BOOK REVIEWS. SPECIAL IS-SUES: Occasional. INDEXED/ABSTRACTED: AbHlthCareMgtS, ABIn, AccI, ASI, BoRvI, BusI, CIJE, CISAb, CLI, CLOA, HistAb, HospLitI, IndUSGovPer, IntLabDoc, LRI, MagArtSum, MagInd, PAIS, PopInd, Pred, RG, SOCI, SocSc, TraIndI, WorAb. TARGET AUDIENCE: AC, GP, HS, SP. SAMPLE COPIES: Libraries, individuals.

This is the flagship publication of the many issued by the Bureau of Labor Statistics. It is also a major research journal essential to the study of industrial and labor relations. Recently published, statistically based, empirical articles have included "Major Labor Contracts in 1986 Provided Record Low Wage Adjustments," "Productivity in the Furniture and Home Furnishing Stores Industry," and "International Trends in Productivity, Labor Costs in Manufacturing."

Each issue contains four or five articles analyzing recently compiled labor statistics. Regular departments include: "Labor Month in Review," "Research Summaries," "Major Agreements Expiring Next Month," "Developments in Industrial Relations," "Book Reviews" (three to ten, signed), and the famous "Current Labor Statistics." Occasional special issues.

238   ***National Business Woman***.   DATE FOUNDED: 1919. FREQUEN-CY: 6/yr. PRICE: $8.50/yr. PUBLISHER: National Federation of Business & Professional Women, 2012 Massachusetts Ave., N.W., Washington, D.C. 20036. EDITOR: Karen Suchenski. ILLUSTRA-TIONS. INDEX. ADVERTISEMENTS. CIRCULATION: 130,000. MANUSCRIPT SELECTION: Editor. INDEXED/AB-STRACTED: PersLit, WorAb. TARGET AUDIENCE: AC, GP, SP.

The publication like the parent organization "promotes full participa-tion, equity and economic self-sufficiency for working women." It is printed in a newspaper format. It focuses on such issues as: the changing family, pay equity, comparable worth, discrimination against working women, women in the political process and family economics.

Each issue contains three to five substantive articles written by such people as Ellen Goodman. There are occasional book reviews and announcements of conferences on women's issues.

239 *National Center for the Study of Collective Bargaining in Higher Education and the Professions. Newsletter.* DATE FOUNDED: 1973. FREQUENCY: 5/yr. PRICE: $20/yr. PUBLISHER: National Center for the Study of Collective Bargaining in Higher Education and the Professions, Baruch College, City University of New York, 17 Lexington Ave., Box 332, New York, NY 10010. EDITOR: Joel M. Douglas. ILLUSTRATIONS. INDEX. CIRCULATION: 350. MANUSCRIPT SELECTION: Editor. MICROFORMS: ERIC. BOOK REVIEWS. INDEXED/ABSTRACTED: ERIC. TARGET AUDIENCE: AC, SP. SAMPLE COPIES: Libraries, individuals.

The newsletter analyzes current trends, new developments and major decisions of courts and regulatory bodies in the field of faculty collective bargaining in higher education. Most of the writers are academics of the United States. It also provides an annual update on the state of collective bargaining in higher education and an annual update on the effects of the Yeshiva Supreme Court decision regarding the managerial status of faculty at Yeshiva University. There are usually one or two articles per issue.

240 *National News Update.* DATE FOUNDED: 1985. TITLE CHANGES: *Personnel Update* (nd-1985); *Personnel Manager's Policy and Practice Update* (198?-198?). FREQUENCY: m. PRICE: $175/yr. PUBLISHER: Business and Legal Reports, 64 Wall Street, Madison, CT 06443-1513. EDITOR: Robert L. Brady. ILLUSTRATIONS. CIRCULATION: 5,000. MANUSCRIPT SELECTION: Editor in Chief. REPRINTS: Publisher. BOOK REVIEWS. SPECIAL ISSUES: 8 to 10/yr. TARGET AUDIENCE: SP. SAMPLE COPIES: Libraries, individuals.

This newsletter is a supplement to the basic volume, *What to Do About Personnel Problems*, which is updated periodically. The newsletter is customized for twenty-nine of the states. The newsletter covers federal and appropriate state laws and regulations affecting all areas of personnel practice and procedure. Periodically, surveys of wages, turnovers, and benefits are also tailored to specific states. The authors are lawyers and personnel experts.

The monthly newsletter has a section covering the updating of national news relating to personnel matters. It is written in a short, concise format. There is a separate section dealing with personnel issues affecting a specific state. Frequently a brief description of an appropriate new book or film is included.

241   *New York's Finest.* DATE FOUNDED: 1980. TITLE CHANGES: *PBA Front and Center* (nd-1979). FREQUENCY: 6/yr. PRICE: membership dues. PUBLISHER: Patrolmen's Benevolent Association, 250 Broadway, New York, NY 10007. EDITOR: Beth Castronovo. ILLUSTRATIONS. CIRCULATION: 32,000. MANUSCRIPT SELECTION: Editor, Union President. BOOK REVIEWS. TARGET AUDIENCE: SP. SAMPLE COPIES: Libraries, individuals.

A publication dedicated to providing news within the New York City Police Department for its active members and retired police officers. It focuses on local New York City criminal justice matters, local police, labor negotiations and other related news. The articles are usually prepared by professional freelancers although contributions are accepted from police officers. The articles advocate the position of police officers.

A typical issue contains ten to twelve short articles plus regular features such as a president's message, services provided by the Association, and notices of personal interest. There is usually one article highlighting the life and/or career of one of its officers.

242   *Northeast Journal of Business and Economics.* DATE FOUNDED: 1965. TITLE CHANGES: *Rhode Island Business Quarterly* (1965-1974); *New England Journal of Business and Economics* (1975-1983). FREQUENCY: 2/yr. PRICE: Free. PUBLISHER: College of Business Administration, Research Center in Business and Economics, 210 Ballentine Hall, University of Rhode Island, Kingston, RI 02881. EDITORS: Peter E. Koveos and Blair M. Lord. ILLUSTRATIONS. INDEX. CIRCULATION: 2,000. MANUSCRIPT SELECTION: Editors, Refereed. INDEXED/ABSTRACTED: ABIn, MgtC. TARGET AUDIENCE: AC, SP. SAMPLE COPIES: Libraries, individuals

The *Northeast Journal of Business and Economics* is the former *Rhode Island Business Quarterly.* The purpose of the journal is to provide an outlet for business and economic research and particularly that research concerning the Northeast. Most articles are written by academics from the University of Rhode Island or other New England business schools. Recent titles have included "Employment Growth and the Turn

Around in the New England Economy," and "Relative Price Variability and the Labor Supply of Married Persons."

Each issue has five or six empirically based research articles. The articles usually run under twenty-five pages in length. There is good coverage from a regional perspective not much unlike the *Akron Business and Economic Review*.

243   ***Occupational Health Review***.   DATE FOUNDED: 1986. FRE-QUENCY: 6/yr. PRICE: £78/yr. PUBLISHER: Industrial Relations Services, 18-20 Highbury Place, London N5 1QP, England. EDI-TORS: John Green and John Manos. INDEX. MANUSCRIPT SELECTION: Editors. REPRINTS: Publisher. BOOK REVIEWS. SPECIAL ISSUES: Occasional. TARGET AUDIENCE: AC, SP.

This is the definitive British journal of occupational health. Although it is basically published for English managers dealing with health concerns as well as occupational health specialists and physicians, many of the articles have relevancy to the United States. Articles are written by physicians and occupational health specialists and tend to be of general interest as well as specific.

In a typical issue there are six to eight articles on such topics as shiftwork and its effect on health, the labelling of substances hazardous to health and occupational skin diseases. There is a review section of four to six 400-500 word signed critical evaluations. A sample issue included the reviews of two videos on AIDS. A unique section contains twenty to twenty-five lengthy abstracts of pertinent articles from journal literature. These are identified by subject.

244   ***Occupational Outlook Quarterly***.   DATE FOUNDED: 1957. TITLE CHANGES: *Occupational Outlook* (1957-1958). FREQUENCY: q. PRICE: $5/yr. PUBLISHER: U.S. Department of Labor, Bureau of Labor Statistics, Washington, D.C. 20212. EDITOR: Melvin Fountain. ILLUSTRATIONS. INDEX. CIRCULATION: 15,000. MANUSCRIPT SELECTION: Editor, Staff. MICROFORMS: Bell and Howell, UMI. REPRINTS: Government Printing Office. IN-DEXED/ABSTRACTED: ABIn, ASI, BI, CIJE, HospLitI, In-dUSGovPer, MagInd, PAIS, PersLit, SocSc, TraIndI, WorAb. TAR-GET AUDIENCE: AC, GP, HS, SP.

This major journal publishes relevant information about careers, jobs, training, earning and working conditions on the national level. One of its strong points is the summary of projected changes in employment which are prepared every two years. Occupations that are to be added to future editions of the *Occupational Outlook Handbook* are also identified in this quarterly. The journal is basically written by government employees and academics.

An average issue contains six to eight articles. There are certain features which appear on a regular basis. "The Job Outlook in Brief" is published in the spring of even numbered years. It summarizes new projections from the Bureau of Labor Statistics. "The Job Outlook for College Graduates" is published in the summer of even numbered years and focuses on occupations requiring a college degree. "Matching Yourself to the World of Work" is published every two to three years and provides the major characteristics of more than 200 occupations. The occupations are both at the professional level as well as vocational level.

Most of the articles provide statistical information and/or sources of additional information.

245   *Occupational Pensions.* FREQUENCY: m. PUBLISHER: Industrial Relations Services, 18-20 Highbury Place, London N5 1QP, England. EDITOR: Colin Sherwood. INDEX. MANUSCRIPT SELECTION: Editor. REPRINTS: Publisher. SPECIAL ISSUES: Occasional. TARGET AUDIENCE: AC, SP.

An objectively written British publication whose focus provides information to managers and executives about pensions. It presents guidelines for new legislation and changes to current legislation, major surveys on pensions in specific organizations, detailed studies on specific problems, and information on basic aspects of pension administration.

Each issue has a section on the most current news written as short items. There are four to six longer articles. A recent issue covered such topics as equalizing retirement ages, additional voluntary contributions, and a guide to the Social Security Act.

246   *OECD Employment Outlook.* DATE FOUNDED: 1967. FREQUENCY: sa. PUBLISHER: Organisation for Economic Co-operation & Development, 2, rue Andre-Pascal, 75775 Paris Cedex 16, France. MANUSCRIPT SELECTION: Staff. MICROFORMS: OECD. TARGET AUDIENCE: AC, SP.

The *OECD Employment Outlook* provides an annual assessment of labor market developments and prospects in member countries (Australia, Western Europe and the U.S.). Each issue contains an overall analysis of the latest labor market trends and short-term forecasts, and examines key labor market developments. Reference statistics are also included.

A recent annual had a lead article, "Policies for Employment in a Changing Economy." The major portion of the annual is divided into two parts: "Labour Market Developments in the OECD Area," and "Detailed Analysis of Key Labour Market Issues." Other features include an extensive bibliography and a "Statistical Annex" and a "Technical Annex."

247   *Official Bulletin. Series A.*   DATE FOUNDED: 1919. TITLE CHANGES: *Official Bulletin-International Labour Office* (1919-1974). FREQUENCY: 3/yr. PRICE: $66.50/yr. PUBLISHER: International Labour Office, CH-1211 Geneva 22, Switzerland. ILLUSTRA-TIONS. INDEX. MICROFORMS: UMI. TARGET AUDIENCE: AC, SP.

This is an official publication of the *International Labour Office*. It is a news bulletin of information on the activities of the ILO and includes texts adopted by the International Labour Conference and other official documents. It is published three times per year.

248   *Official Bulletin. Series B.*   DATE FOUNDED: 1919. TITLE CHANGES: *Official Bulletin-International Labour Office* (1919-1974). FREQUENCY: 3/yr. PRICE: $66.50/yr. PUBLISHER: International Labour Office, CH-1211 Geneva 22, Switzerland. ILLUSTRA-TIONS. INDEX. MICROFORMS: UMI. TARGET AUDIENCE: AC, SP.

This is an official publication of the International Labour Office. It publishes the reports of the Committee on Freedom of Association of the Governing Body of the ILO and other related issues. It is published three times a year.

249   *Oklahoma Employment Security Review.* DATE FOUNDED: 1941. TITLE CHANGES: *Monthly Report of Commission Activities* (1941-1946); *Review of Activities* (1947-1948). FREQUENCY: m. PUB-LISHER: Oklahoma Employment Security Commission, 310 W. Will Rogers Bldg., Oklahoma City, OK 73105. EDITOR: Mary Slyman. CIRCULATION: 150. MANUSCRIPT SELECTION: Editor. TARGET AUDIENCE: GP, SP. SAMPLE COPIES: Libraries, indi-viduals.

This state publication is published and written by employees of the Oklahoma Employment Security Commission to disseminate informa-tion, statistics and studies relating to the Oklahoma labor market. It is almost completely statistical information compiled by the Commission.

250   *Omega*. DATE FOUNDED: 1973. FREQUENCY: 6/yr. PRICE: $240/yr. PUBLISHER: Pergamon Press, Maxwell House, Elmsford, NY 10523. EDITOR: Samuel Eilon. ILLUSTRATIONS. INDEX. ADVERTISEMENTS. CIRCULATION: 1,400. MANUSCRIPT SELECTION: Editor, Editorial Advisory Board. MICROFORMS: UMI, MIM. INDEXED/ABSTRACTED: AccDataProcAb, AppMechRev, BI, CIJE, CompConAb, DataProcD, ElecElecAb, ExMed, GeoAb, HiEdCurrAwareBull, LegCont, MgtC, PhysAb. TARGET AUDIENCE: AC, SP.

Omega is an international journal of management science. It publishes empirical and conceptual research articles. There are articles on theory and applications which have included: "Labour Productivity: Is There Such a Measure? (The Case of Greek Industry)," "Matching Problem Diagnostic Tools to Managers' Decision Styles: A Contingency Approach," and "Change-Related Behaviour and Information Systems."

Each issue has an average of ten articles of from ten to twenty pages. Other features include "Memoranda" which are short contributions and "Feedback" which is reader correspondence. Regularly appearing is a "Software Survey Section" which gives a signed review of a piece of software.

251   *Ontario Labour*. DATE FOUNDED: 1957. TITLE CHANGES: *Ontario Labour Review* (1957-1961); *Labour Review* (1962-1977). FREQUENCY: q. PRICE: Free. PUBLISHER: Ontario Federation of Labour, 15 Gervais Drive, Suite 202, Don Mills, Ontario M3C IY8. EDITOR: Sheila Keenan. ILLUSTRATIONS. CIRCULATION: 8,000. MANUSCRIPT SELECTION: Editor. MICROFORMS: Micromedia. REPRINTS: Publisher. BOOK REVIEWS. INDEXED/ABSTRACTED: CanBusI. TARGET AUDIENCE: AC, HS, SP. SAMPLE COPIES: Libraries, individuals.

This magazine is regional in appeal and its focus is mainly union organizing. Typical articles include "Polling and New Campaign Techniques Give Unions a Key to Public Support," and "The Cultural, Economic and Political Assault on Canadians." Major topics covered are union education, collective bargaining, labor law, economics and technological change.

Each issue contains five or six substantive articles, and occasional unsigned book reviews. Ten to fifteen small news articles are also included.

252   *Opsearch: Journal of the Operational Research Society of India.*
DATE FOUNDED: 1964. FREQUENCY: q. PRICE: $30/yr. PUB-
LISHER: Operational Research Society of India, c/o Institute for
Systems Studies & Analyses, T-44 Metcalfe House, Delhi 110054,
India. EDITOR: Dr. N.K. Jaiswal and Dr. S. Subba Rao. ILLUSTRA-
TIONS. INDEX. ADVERTISEMENTS. CIRCULATION: 2,000.
MANUSCRIPT SELECTION: Editor, Refereed. BOOK RE-
VIEWS. INDEXED/ABSTRACTED: CompConAb, ElecElecAb,
IntAbOpRes, JContQuanMeth, MathR, PhysAb. TARGET AUDI-
ENCE: AC, SP. SAMPLE COPIES: Libraries, individuals.

This is an empirically based journal for the publication of research by
academics from a variety of countries. The focus of the publication is
operational research/management science. Recent articles have included "Optimum Repair Limit Replacement Policy When the Lifetime Depends on the Number of Repairs," and "Expediting Work-in-
Process."

There are four to five substantial theoretical papers per issue. Three to
four one-half page signed book reviews are occasionally included.

253   *Organizational Behavior and Human Decision Processes.* DATE
FOUNDED: 1966. TITLE CHANGES: *Organizational Behavior and
Human Performance* (1966-1984). FREQUENCY: 6/yr. PRICE: $210/
yr. PUBLISHER: Academic Press, Inc., 1 East First Street, Duluth,
MN 55806. EDITOR: James C. Naylor. ILLUSTRATIONS. IN-
DEX. ADVERTISEMENTS. MANUSCRIPT SELECTION: Edi-
tor, Editorial Board. INDEXED/ABSTRACTED: ASSIA, BI, BusI,
CINAHL, CommAb, CurrCont, HospLitI, IntLabDoc, PsyAb,
Psycscan, RiskAb, SOCI. TARGET AUDIENCE: AC, SP.

Organizational Behavior and Human Decision Processes publishes research
articles "describing original empirical research and theoretical developments in all areas of human performance theory and organizational
psychology." Typical articles include: "Time Pressure and Strategic
Choice in Mediation," and "Measuring Attitudes Across Job Levels."
This journal is one of fundamental research and theory in applied
psychology.

Each issue publishes six or seven empirically based articles per issue.
They are usually twenty-five pages or less in length. They are written
by U.S. academics.

254   *Organizational Dynamics.* DATE FOUNDED: 1972. FREQUEN-
CY: q. PRICE: $50/yr. PUBLISHER: American Management Associa-

tion, 135 W. 50th St., New York, NY 10020. EDITOR: Peter B. Vaill. INDEX. CIRCULATION: 8,000. MANUSCRIPT SELECTION: Editor. REPRINTS: Publisher. INDEXED/ABSTRACTED: ABIn, BusI, HospLitI, IntLabDoc, MgtC, PsyAb, WorAb. TARGET AUDIENCE: AC, SP. SAMPLE COPIES: Libraries, individuals.

The articles which appear in this journal deal with organizational development and the dynamics of organizations. The majority of the authors are academics. The reading audience is most likely to be scholars or specialists in this area. Articles are selected by the editor.

An average issue contains four to five articles. Topics of articles in a recent issue present various viewpoints on "the role basic values and beliefs play in the ability of organization members to come together in concerted and sustained action." One article attempts to clarify values and priorities in helping organizations change. Another article reports the results of an experiment with telephone operators, and the discussion of basic values in the approach to job design it engendered.

255   *Our Times Magazine.* DATE FOUNDED: 1982. FREQUENCY: 10/yr. PRICE: $25/yr. institutions, $15/yr. personal. PUBLISHER: Our Times Co-operative, 390 Dufferin St., Toronto, Ontario M6K 2A3. EDITOR: Stuart Crombie. ILLUSTRATIONS. ADVERTISE-MENTS. CIRCULATION: 4,000. MANUSCRIPT SELECTION: Editorial Board. MICROFORMS: Micromedia. BOOK REVIEWS. SPECIAL ISSUES: Occasional. INDEXED/ABSTRACTED: CanPerI, CMI. TARGET AUDIENCE: GP, SP. SAMPLE COPIES: Libraries, individuals.

This is in magazine format and is committed to "social change through democratic pluralism." It presents a Canadian focus on issues current to the labor union movement. It is published by a cooperative to showcase positive achievements of the Canadian labor movement.

There are fifteen substantive articles per issue, including three to four book reviews which are about 1,000 words in length and signed.

256   *Pacific Tribune.* DATE FOUNDED: 1946. FREQUENCY: w. PRICE: $25/yr. PUBLISHER: Tribune Publishing Co., Ltd., c/o 2681 E. Hastings St., Vancouver, British Columbia V5K 1Z5. EDITOR: Sean Griffin. ILLUSTRATIONS. ADVERTISEMENTS. CIRCU-LATION: 5,000. MANUSCRIPT SELECTION: Editor, Staff. MICROFORMS: University of Washington, State Historical Society of Washington. BOOK REVIEWS. SPECIAL ISSUES. TARGET AUDIENCE: AC, GP, SP. SAMPLE COPIES: Libraries, individuals.

This is Canada's only independent weekly labor newspaper. It covers local, national, and international issues reported from the working class perspective and not usually presented through traditional print media. Writers are Canadian journalists.

An average issue contains approximately four pages of local labor issues and eight pages devoted to international labor issues. These issues include those which customarily appear in a labor periodical but also include articles devoted to antinuclear issues and environmental concerns such as acid rain. One or two book reviews of one-half page are also included. Weekly issues may have enclosed supplements on special topics including free trade, acid rain, and Soviet policies. Special issues are published at Christmas and May Day.

257   *Paperworker.* DATE FOUNDED: 1972. FREQUENCY: m. PUBLISHER: United Paperworkers International Union, P.O. Box 1475, Nashville, TN 37202. EDITOR: Monte L. Byers. ILLUSTRATIONS. CIRCULATION: 285,000. MANUSCRIPT SELECTION: Editor. MICROFORMS: Founders Memorial Library. SPECIAL ISSUES: 1 to 2/yr. INDEXED/ABSTRACTED: WorAb. TARGET AUDIENCE: SP. SAMPLE COPIES: Libraries, individuals.

Tabloid in format, this publication centers mainly on work-related and political/legislative issues. It is usually published only in relation to an organizing drive or national political elections.

Articles are lengthy and in depth analyses on labor issues. Usually there are endorsements of political candidates ("UPIU Members Have Voice in Endorsement") or analysis ("America's Trade Crisis."). It is well done for a union membership publication.

258   *Pay and Benefits Bulletin.* DATE FOUNDED: 1979. FREQUENCY: bw. PRICE: £90/yr. PUBLISHER: Industrial Relations Services, 18-20 Highbury Place, London N5 1QP, England. EDITOR: James Hillage. INDEX. CIRCULATION: 1,000. MANUSCRIPT SELECTION: Editor. REPRINTS: Publisher, UMI. SPECIAL ISSUES: Occasional. TARGET AUDIENCE: AC, SP.

This journal is devoted to providing regular analysis of settlement levels and trends in collective bargaining in the United Kingdom. It is an integral part of *Industrial Relations Review and Report.*

A typical issue presents the full details of all major pay settlements and arbitration awards on an industry by industry approach. It also provides a short section of concise articles dealing with issues that are relevant to future negotiations. The third major section is a review of salary surveys and earning statistics.

259   *Pension World.* DATE FOUNDED: 1964. TITLE CHANGES: *Pension and Welfare News* (1964-1975). FREQUENCY: m. PRICE: $44/yr. PUBLISHER: Communication Channels, Inc., 6255 Barfield Rd., Atlanta, GA 30328. EDITOR: Kathleen N. Crighton. ILLUSTRATIONS. INDEX. ADVERTISEMENTS. CIRCULATION: 28,000. MANUSCRIPT SELECTION: Editor, Advisory Board. MICROFORMS: UMI. REPRINTS: UMI. SPECIAL ISSUES. INDEXED/ABSTRACTED: ABIn, AccI, BankLitI, BI, BusI, MgtC, MgtMarA, PAIS, PersLit, SRI, WorAb. TARGET AUDIENCE: AC, SP.

This monthly is produced for investment managers, pension plan sponsors, and employee benefits coordinators. Focus is on investments ("Japan's Increasing Yen for Global Investing Draws Attention") and employee benefits ("Lessons Learned In the Battle to Control Health-Care Costs").

Each issue contains columns such as "Perspective of Investments" written by notables such as Thomas H. Clark of Shearson, Lehman, Hutton. There are eight to ten substantial articles per issue and seven 'columns' and seven other regular departments such as the calendar. Twelve to fifteen unsigned book reviews are included per issue. Special issues include directories of "State Retirement Systems Survey" (August), "Real Estate Portfolio Managers" (September), "Trust Services".

260   *People's Daily World.* DATE FOUNDED: 1936. TITLE CHANGES: *Worker* (1936-1968); *Daily World* (1968-1986). FREQUENCY: d. PRICE: $15/yr. PUBLISHER: Long View Publishing Co., Inc., 239 W. 23rd Street, New York, NY 10011. EDITOR: Barry Cohen. ILLUSTRATIONS. ADVERTISEMENTS. CIRCULATION: 60,000. MANUSCRIPT SELECTION: Editor, Staff. MICROFORMS: 3R Microfilm, UMI. TARGET AUDIENCE: AC, GP, SP.

The *People's Daily World* is a daily newspaper published by a wing of the communist movement in the United States. It is a longtime member of the Marxist press. Typical articles include: "Soviets Challenge West to Match Their Arms Cuts," and "Akron Teachers Settle Strike." This newspaper is useful for its different perspective on labor relations.

Each issue of this tabloid includes thirty to forty news stories of varying length. The paper itself usually runs ten to twelve pages. As with all newspapers, it also includes editorials, letters and other typical features including a sports page.

261   *Personnel.* DATE FOUNDED: 1919. FREQUENCY: m. PRICE: $45/yr., $40.50/yr. American Management Association members. PUBLISHER: American Management Association, 135 West 50th St., New York, NY 10020. EDITOR: Thomasine Rendero. ILLUSTRATIONS. INDEX. ADVERTISEMENTS. CIRCULATION: 20,000. MANUSCRIPT SELECTION: Editor. MICROFORMS: UMI. REPRINTS: UMI, ISI. INDEXED/ ABSTRACTED: ABIn, AccI, ASEANMgtAb, BusI, CompLitI, CurrCont, EdAdAb, ExMed, HospLitI, KeyEconSci, MgtMarA, OperRes, PerManAb, PersLit, PsyAb, RefSo, SOCI, TraIndI, WorAb. TARGET AUDIENCE: AC, GP, SP.

This is a practical publication for practitioners in the human resource field. Magazine in format, this publication is similar to *Personnel Administrator*. Recent topics of articles have included: drug testing, strikes, leadership styles, training, resumes, cost reduction, labor compensation and women in the workplace.

Each issue of this monthly contains six to eight substantive articles. Regular departments include "Technology Tie-In," "Career Development Calendar," and among several others, "Product Showcase." A signed column "New on the Shelf" includes reviews of books (usually ten or so), media, and other new products. "Special Sections" have included "Outplacement" and "Training-Disney Style."

262   *Personnel Administrator: The Magazine of Human Resource Management.* DATE FOUNDED: 1954. TITLE CHANGES: *Journal for Personnel Administration* (1954-1955). FREQUENCY: m. PRICE: $44/yr. PUBLISHER: American Society for Personnel Administration, 606 N. Washington St., Alexandria, VA 22314. EDITOR: John T. Adams III. ILLUSTRATIONS. INDEX. ADVERTISEMENTS. CIRCULATION: 36,279. MANUSCRIPT SELECTION: Editor. MICROFORMS: Bell & Howell, UMI. REPRINTS: Publisher, UMI. BOOK REVIEWS. INDEXED/ABSTRACTED: ABIn, AccDataProAb, ASEANMgtAb, BI, BusI, CIJE, EdAdAb, HospLitI, MgtC, MgtMarA, PAIS, PerManAb, PersLit, Pred, PROMT, PsyAb, TraIndI, WorAb. TARGET AUDIENCE: SP.

A practical, no-nonsense publication (much like *Personnel*) with the subtitle, "The magazine of human resource management," which reflects the scope of the journal. Designed for the practicing professional, recent articles have dealt with such subjects as work patterns, contingent time off, telecommuting, employee attitudes, career development, termination of employees, and AIDS and the law.

There are five to six major articles of varying length in each issue. "Focus" is a regular column as is "Also in this Issue." "Departments" include "Books in Brief" (ten or so signed reviews), "Further Reading," "What's New," "HRM Update" and in a recent issue, "1988 Editorial Index."

263   *Personnel Journal: Magazine for Industrial Relations and Personnel Management.* DATE FOUNDED: 1922. TITLE CHANGES: *Journal of Personnel Research* (1922-1927). FREQUENCY: m. PRICE: $38/ yr. PUBLISHER: Betty Hartzell, 245 Fischer Avenue, B-2, Costa Mesa, CA 92626. EDITOR: Margaret Magnus. ILLUSTRATIONS. INDEX. ADVERTISEMENTS. CIRCULATION: 25,000. MANUSCRIPT SELECTION: Panel of Editors. MICROFORMS: UMI, BLH. REPRINTS: Publisher. SPECIAL ISSUES: 6/yr. INDEXED/ ABSTRACTED: ABIn, AccDataProAb, ASEANMgtAb, BankLitI, BI, BibAg, BoRvI, BusI, CIJE, CINAHL, CurrCont, DataProcD, EdAdAb, ExMed, KeyEconSci, MgtC, MgtMarA, OperRes, PAIS, PerManAb, PersLit, PROMT, PsyAb, Psycscan, SOCI, WomAb, WorAb. TARGET AUDIENCE: AC, SP. SAMPLE COPIES: Libraries.

This is the "management magazine for personnel professionals." Focus is on the importance and responsibilities of the human resources manager, human resource management and development and their evolving role in an organization and society. The journal provides articles with information on the how-to's of hiring, firing, training, supervising, compensating and managing of employees. It does include theoretical as well as practical articles.

There are an average of fifteen articles per issue. Special issues/ supplements are issued on a regular basis such as a recent "Subject Index 1977-1986." The journal also focuses on such professional issues as current trends, activities and other pertinent information.

264   *Personnel Manager's Legal Reporter.* DATE FOUNDED: 1978. FREQUENCY: m. PRICE: $78/yr. PUBLISHER: Business and Legal Reports, 64 Wall Street, Madison, CT 06443-1513. EDITOR: Robert L. Brady. INDEX. CIRCULATION: 4,500. MANUSCRIPT SELECTION: Editor in Chief. REPRINTS: Publisher. BOOK REVIEWS. SPECIAL ISSUES: Occasional. TARGET AUDIENCE: AC, SP. SAMPLE COPIES: Libraries, individual.

This monthly publication focuses on the employment law area. Its major aim is to communicate to personnel management the current laws, regulations, guidelines, court decisions and administrative developments. It is written by lawyers and personnel experts but appropriate for laypersons. It pertains to the United States. There appears to be considerable overlap with a similar publication, *What To Do About Personnel Problems*.

An average issue has twelve articles written in a concise fashion which allows for the highlighting of the major points. There are occasional book reviews consisting of two to three paragraphs.

265   *Personnel Psychology*. DATE FOUNDED: 1948. FREQUENCY: q. PRICE: $45/yr. PUBLISHER: Personnel Psychology, 9660 Hillcroft, Suite 337, Houston, TX 77096. EDITOR: Paul R. Sackett. ILLUSTRATIONS. INDEX. ADVERTISEMENTS. CIRCULATION: 3,200. MANUSCRIPT SELECTION: Editor, Editorial Board, Refereed. MICROFORMS: UMI. REPRINTS: UMI. BOOK REVIEWS. INDEXED/ABSTRACTED: ABIn, BI, BoRvI, BusI, CIJE, CommAb, CurrCont, EdAdAb, MgtC, PerManAb, PersLit, PsyAb, Psycscan, RefSo, SOCI, WomAb, WorAb. TARGET AUDIENCE: AC, SP.

Personnel Psychology publishes empirical applied research dealing with a wide range of personnel problems facing public and private sector organizations. Articles deal with all aspects of personnel psychology including employee selection, training and development, job analysis, productivity improvement programs, work attitudes, labor-management relations, and compensation and reward systems. Typical articles include: "Some New Frontiers in Personnel Selection Research" and "Does Pre-employment Drug Use Predict On-The-Job Suitability."

Each issue includes eight substantial research articles of under twenty pages. They are written in the main by U.S. academics. There is a book review section. Usually twenty-five, three to four page, signed book reviews are published with each issue. There is also a list of books received but not reviewed.

266   *Philippine Journal of Industrial Relations*. DATE FOUNDED: 1978. TITLE CHANGES: *Labor Review* (1964-1965). FREQUENCY: 2/yr. PRICE: $8/yr. PUBLISHER: Institute of Industrial Relations, University of the Philippines, DiLiman, Quezon City 3004, Philippines. EDITOR: Rene E. Ofrenco. ILLUSTRATIONS. INDEX. ADVERTISEMENTS. CIRCULATION: 1,000. MANUSCRIPT SELECTION: Editorial Board. BOOK REVIEWS. SPE-

CIAL ISSUES. INDEXED/ABSTRACTED: IntLabDoc. TARGET
AUDIENCE: AC, SP.

An academic journal published under the sponsorship of the Institute of
Industrial Relations at the University of the Philippines. The focus of
recent articles include: labor relations in the Philippines, employee
participation, agrarian workers and their relationship to industrial
relations and a methodology for understanding industrial relations.

There are five to seven substantial empirical and expository articles per
issue. Special theme issues are published occasionally such as "Towards
a More Participatory Philippine Industrial Society." Two to three
signed book reviews appear in each issue.

267   *Planning Review*. DATE FOUNDED: 1972. FREQUENCY: 6/yr.
PRICE: $55/yr. PUBLISHER: Planning Forum, 5500 College Corner
Pike, P.O. Box 70, Oxford, OH 45056. EDITOR: Liam Fahey. ILLUS-
TRATIONS. INDEX. ADVERTISEMENTS. CIRCULATION:
7,700. MANUSCRIPT SELECTION: Editor. MICROFORMS:
UMI. REPRINTS: UMI. BOOK REVIEWS. SPECIAL ISSUES.
INDEXED/ABSTRACTED: ABIn, AccDataProcAb, AccI, ASE-
ANMgtAb, BI, BusI, CompLitI, FutAb, MgtC, MgtMarA, PAIS, Pred,
PROMT. TARGET AUDIENCE: AC, SP.

Planning Review is a publication of the Planning Forum, The International Society for Planning and Strategic Management. The Forum
monitors new developments in planning and strategic management,
conducts research, evaluates complementary and conflicting information, and disseminates information and viewpoints on issues and tools
related to corporate performance. Many of the articles use a case study
approach. The writers are international academics, practitioners or
consultants. Recent articles from the *Review* include: "Managing for the
Share Holders" and "The Westinghouse Shareholder Value Culture."

A typical issue contains six articles which are complete with charts,
tables and figures if appropriate. There are usually two signed book
reviews of one page in length. Recent special issues have focused on
"Shareholder Value."

268   *Policies for Manpower and Social Affairs Newsletter*. DATE
FOUNDED: 1976. FREQUENCY: 2/yr. PRICE: Free. PUBLI-
SHER: Directorate for Manpower, Social Affairs and Education,
Organisation for Economic Co-operation and Development, 2, rue
Andre Pascal, 75775 Paris Cedex 16, France. MANUSCRIPT SELEC-

TION: Staff. REPRINTS: Publisher. BOOK REVIEWS. TARGET
AUDIENCE: AC, SP. SAMPLE COPIES: Libraries, individuals.

Policies for Manpower and Social Affairs is published twice a year by the
OECD. It is a "commentary on work being pursued at the interface of
economic, employment and social policies by the Organisation for
Economic Co-operation and Development." Recent issues have fo-
cused on "Public Pension Reform," "Outlook for Employment,"
"Current Work on Social Policy" and "Manpower and Employment."

Each issue runs four pages with double columns. There are usually two
topics per issue. It includes a "Recent Publications" feature of unsigned
reviews and/or recent pertinent OECD publications.

269   *Political Affairs.* DATE FOUNDED: 1918. TITLE CHANGES:
Workers Monthly (1924-1927); *Communist* (1927-1944). MERGER:
Liberator (1918-1924); *Labor Herald* (1922-1924); *Soviet Russia Pictorial*
(1923-1924). FREQUENCY: 11/yr. PRICE: $15/yr. institutions, $10/
yr. personal. PUBLISHER: Political Affairs Publishers, Inc., 235 West
23rd Street, New York, NY 10011. EDITOR: Michael Zagarell.
ILLUSTRATIONS. INDEX. ADVERTISEMENTS. CIRCULA-
TION: 5,000. MANUSCRIPT SELECTION: Editor, Editorial
Board. MICROFORMS: UMI. REPRINTS: UMI. BOOK RE-
VIEWS. INDEXED/ABSTRACTED: AmBibSlav, API, PAIS. TAR-
GET AUDIENCE: AC, GP, SP.

Political Affairs is the theoretical journal of the Communist Party, USA.
A regular contributor is the well known Gus Hall, a long time moving
force behind the Communist Party, USA. Recent articles have included:
"Who Profits from the Homeless' Plague," "Labor's Shift to the Left,"
"The Bechtel Story," "World Working Class Unity Can Defeat the
TNC's" and "Confronting the Nation's Crisis in Education."

Each issue contains an average of six articles of under fifteen pages.
There is usually a signed book review, an editorial and letters to the
editor. An index of issues is also published.

270   *Politics and Society.* DATE FOUNDED: 1970. FREQUENCY: q.
PRICE: $48/yr. institutions, $25/yr. personal. PUBLISHER: Butter-
worth, 80 Montvale Avenue, Stoneham, MA 02180. EDITOR: Mary
Nolan. ILLUSTRATIONS. INDEX. ADVERTISEMENTS. CIR-
CULATION: 1,000. MANUSCRIPT SELECTION: Editorial
Board. INDEXED/ABSTRACTED: ABCPolSci, AmBibSlav,
AmerH, API, ASSIA, CurrCont, HistAb, LeftI, SOCI, SocSc. TAR-
GET AUDIENCE: AC, SP.

Politics and Society is "committed to developing Marxist, post-Marxist, and other radical perspectives and to examine what Robert Lynd once called 'some outrageous hypotheses'." Interdisciplinary in nature, it publishes theoretical essays, as well as empirical research which encompasses politics in the broadest sense whether "conflicts over the shape of social life...on the shop floor, within the family, or in the realms of the state and the world economy." Recent titles have included "Historical and Ideological Orientations in the Italian Workers' Movement" and "Beyond Mass Production: Production and the Labor Process in Japan."

Each issue has four to seven articles. The articles are substantial and average thirty to forty pages in length.

271   *Post.* DATE FOUNDED: 1920. FREQUENCY: m. PRICE: £1/yr. PUBLISHER: Union of Communication Workers, Crescent Lane, London SW4 9RN, England. EDITOR: Allen Slater. ILLUSTRA-TIONS. ADVERTISEMENTS. CIRCULATION: 68,000. MANU-SCRIPT SELECTION: Editor. TARGET AUDIENCE: SP.

A newspaper tabloid, this publication keeps its membership aware of the activities of the postal workers' union in England. The approximate twenty-five articles are short and deal with issues which affect union workers. These include the activities of members of Parliament, union negotiations for increased wages, and activities in the various parts of the country. There is a page for "After Hours" including items on gardening, woodworking, cooking, and crossword puzzles.

272   *Postal and Telecommunications Workers Journal.* DATE FOUNDED: 1923. TITLE CHANGES: *Postal Worker* (1923-1985). FREQUENCY: m. PUBLISHER: Postal and Telecommunications Workers Union, 53 Parnell Square, Dublin 1, Ireland. EDITOR: D.T. Begg. ILLUSTRATIONS. CIRCULATION: 9,000. MANU-SCRIPT SELECTION: Editor. TARGET AUDIENCE: SP. SAMPLE COPIES: Libraries, individuals.

This is a newsletter published in Ireland for the membership of the Postal and Telecommunications Union. It does support that union's point of view. It provides information regarding issues of pay, benefits, and other issues affecting the socioeconomics of the membership. Items of news about various members are also featured.

273   *Proceedings of the National Center for the Study of Collective Bargaining in Higher Education and the Professions Annual Conference.*

DATE FOUNDED: 1973. FREQUENCY: a. PRICE: $20/yr. PUB-LISHER: National Center for the Study of Collective Bargaining in Higher Education and the Professions, Baruch College, City University of New York, 17 Lexington Ave., Box 322, New York, NY 10010. EDITOR: Joel M. Douglas. CIRCULATION: 500. MANUSCRIPT SELECTION: Editor. MICROFORMS: ERIC. INDEXED/ABSTRACTED: ERIC. TARGET AUDIENCE: AC, SP.

The Proceedings of the Annual Conference are the speeches which have been presented. The conference devotes its concerns to topics of interest in higher education, labor relations and collective bargaining. The presenters are usually United States academics and practitioners in academic collective bargaining.

274   *Productivity*. DATE FOUNDED: 1980. FREQUENCY: m. PRICE: $167/yr. PUBLISHER: Norman Bodek, 750 Summer St., Stamford, CT 06901. EDITOR: Norman Bodek. ILLUSTRATIONS. INDEX. CIRCULATION: 3,000. MANUSCRIPT SELECTION: Editor. REPRINTS: Publisher. BOOK REVIEWS. SPECIAL ISSUES. INDEXED/ABSTRACTED: PersLit, TexTechD. TARGET AUDIENCE: AC, SP. SAMPLE COPIES: Libraries, individuals.

The mission of *Productivity* is to discover and disseminate "The best methods of productivity and quality improvement for American companies in the industrial and service sectors." Recently it has had particularly strong coverage of the most successful Japanese industrial production methods such as "Just-in-Time" which is revolutionizing the production of goods. The publication also translates Japanese management books into English.

This is a newsletter with three to four brief articles per issue. Other features include "Productivity Calendar" of events, an editorial, and news briefs.

275   *Public Choice*. DATE FOUNDED: 1966. TITLE CHANGES: *Papers on Non-Market Decision Making* (1966-67). FREQUENCY: q. PRICE: $176/yr. institutions, $36/yr. personal. PUBLISHER: Kluwer Academic Publishers (Martinus Nijhoff), P.O. Box 989, 3300 AZ Dordrecht, The Netherlands. EDITOR: Peter H. Aranson. ILLUSTRATIONS. INDEX. ADVERTISEMENTS. CIRCULATION: 3,000. MANUSCRIPT SELECTION: Editor, Refereed. MICROFORMS: UMI. REPRINTS: Publisher, UMI. BOOK REVIEWS. SPECIAL ISSUES. INDEXED/ABSTRACTED: ABCPolSci, CurrCont, GeoAb, IEconArt, JEL, LLBA, PAIS, SagePAA, SageUrbStudAb,

SocAb, SOCI, SPDA, USPSD. TARGET AUDIENCE: AC, SP. SAMPLE COPIES: Libraries, individuals.

Public Choice "deals with the intersection between economics and political science. It started when economists and political scientists became interested in the application of essentially economic methods to problems normally dealt with by political scientists." The empirical research articles are written with the focus of application "to heal world problems." The journal is associated with the Center for Public Choice at George Mason University.

Each issue includes eight major articles. Recent typical titles include: "The Distribution of Income, Incomplete Information and the Rank and Pareto Criteria," and "The Public Choice Theory of the Great Contraction."

276   *Public Employee.* DATE FOUNDED: 1937. TITLE CHANGES: *Journal of State and Local Government Employees* (1937-1947). FREQUENCY: 8/yr. PRICE: Membership. PUBLISHER: AFSCME, 1625 L Street, N.W., Washington, D.C. 20036. EDITOR: Marshall O. Donley, Jr. ILLUSTRATIONS. CIRCULATION: 1,200,000. MANUSCRIPT SELECTION: Editor, Staff. MICROFORM: UMI. REPRINTS: Editor. BOOK REVIEWS. SPECIAL ISSUES: Occasional. INDEXED/ABSTRACTED: PersLit, WorAb. TARGET AUDIENCE: AC, SP. SAMPLE COPIES: Libraries, individuals.

This is the official publication of AFSCME. It is pro-union and in magazine format. Recent subjects have included voting records of congressmen, South Africa, working place drug testing, employee assistance programs, child care, working women and pay equity.

Each issue has an average twenty-five to fifty articles. The articles run a page or two in length. There have been special issues such as a recent one on the history of the union. Six two-paragraph, unsigned book reviews per issue are included.

277   *Public Personnel Management. The Journal of the International Personnel Management Association.* DATE FOUNDED: 1973. MERGER: *Public Personnel Review* (1940-1972); *Personnel Administration* (1938-1972). FREQUENCY: q. PRICE: $40/yr. PUBLISHER: International Personnel Management Association, 1617 Duke Street, Alexandria, VA 22314. EDITOR: Lourie W. Shaker. ILLUSTRATIONS. INDEX. ADVERTISEMENTS. CIRCULATION: 9,700. MANUSCRIPT SELECTION: Editor, Publications Advisory Board. MICROFORMS: Kraus, MIM, UMI. REPRINTS: Kraus, UMI.

INDEXED/ABSTRACTED: ABCPolSci, ABIn, AccDataProAb, AccI, BI, BoRvI, BusI, CurrCont, DataProcD, EdAdAb, IntLabDoc, PerManAb, PersLit, PsyAb, Psyscan, SagePAA, SOCI, WorAb. TARGET AUDIENCE: AC, SP.

Considered a membership service for the International Personnel Management Association, *Public Personnel Management* is directed not only at academics but professionals in the field as well. Several typical articles have included: "Working Women," "A Typology for Union Discrimination: A Public Sector Perspective," "Roleplay Simulation for Employee Selection" and "Alcohol Problems in the Workplace."

Each issue contains four to five articles of varying length. There is an occasional special issue, the last of which was "Employee Assistance Programs."

278   *Quality Assurance New Zealand.* DATE FOUNDED: 1981. FREQUENCY: 2/yr. PRICE: NZ $14/yr. PUBLISHER: International Quality Consultants Ltd., P.O. Box 33-664, Takapuna, New Zealand. EDITOR: A.R. Stephenson. ILLUSTRATIONS. ADVERTISEMENTS. CIRCULATION: 1,200. MANUSCRIPT SELECTION: Editor. REPRINTS: NZOQA, P.O. Box 622, Palmerston North, New Zealand. BOOK REVIEWS. TARGET AUDIENCE: SP.

This highly specialized journal is the major publication of the New Zealand Organisation for Quality Assurance. Its purpose is to "spread the adoption of good quality control/management practices." Recent articles have included "Quality Assurance in Different Job Functions" and "Quality in the Service Industries."

There are eight to twelve substantial articles per issue of an empirical rather than expository nature. It includes three to four signed book reviews of 300 words per issue.

279   *Quarterly Journal of Economics.* DATE FOUNDED: 1886. FREQUENCY: q. PRICE: $65/yr. institutions, $20/yr. personal. PUBLISHER: MIT Press, 55 Hayward Street, Cambridge, MA 02142. EDITORS: Olivier J. Blanchard, Eric S. Maskin, Lawrence H. Summers. ILLUSTRATIONS. INDEX. ADVERTISEMENTS. CIRCULATION: 4,600. MANUSCRIPT SELECTION: Editors, Associate Editors, Refereed. MICROFORMS: MIM, UMI. REPRINTS: UMI. INDEXED/ABSTRACTED: ABIn, AmerH, BI, BusI, CoalA, CREJ, CurrCont, EnerResAb, ExMed, GeoAb, HistAb, HRA, IEconArt, IntLabDoc, JEL, KeyEconSci, MathR, MgtC, RG, RuralRecrTourAb, SagePAA, SageUrbStudAb, SOCI, SocSc, SocWAb,

WorAb, WorBankAb, WorldAgEconRuralSocAb. TARGET AUDI-
ENCE: AC, SP.

The *Quarterly Journal of Economics* is an objective scholarly publication published under the auspices of the Department of Economics of Harvard University. The majority of the authors are American acade-micians. The publication does not espouse a particular point of view. The scope is to report theoretical and empirical studies.

A typical issue has eight to ten lengthy articles complete with a 100 word abstract on such topics as unemployment, industrial diversity, and management. There are two or three "Notes" included which are shorter empirical presentations.

280   ***Quarterly Report of the General Counsel.*** DATE FOUNDED: 1960. FREQUENCY: q. PUBLISHER: National Labor Relations Board, 1717 Pennsylvania Ave., N.W., Washington, D.C. 20570. GENERAL COUNSEL: Rosemary M. Collyer. MANUSCRIPT SELECTION: General Counsel. TARGET AUDIENCE: AC, SP.

The *Quarterly Report* is published by the General Counsel of the NLRB, who selects those cases that will be of most interest to the labor relations community and bar. It discusses and summarizes cases "which were decided upon a request for advice from a Regional Director (NLRB) or an appeal from a Regional Director's dismissal of unfair labor practice charges."

Each issue summarizes eight to ten cases. Each summary is usually two single-spaced, typewritten pages.

281   ***Quarterly Review of Economics and Business.*** DATE FOUNDED: 1938. TITLE CHANGES: *Opinion and Comment* (1938-1948); *Current Economic Comment* (1949-1960). FREQUENCY: q. PRICE: $29.70/yr. institutions, $18/yr. personal. PUBLISHER: Bureau of Economic and Business Research, University of Illinois at Urbana-Champaign, 428 Commerce Building West, 1206 South Sixth Street, Champaign, IL 61820. EDITORS: Richard J. Arnould and C.F. Lee. ILLUSTRA-TIONS. INDEX. ADVERTISEMENTS. CIRCULATION: 2,000. MANUSCRIPT SELECTION: Editors, Editorial Board. MICRO-FORMS: MIM, UMI. REPRINTS: UMI. BOOK REVIEWS. IN-DEXED/ABSTRACTED: ABIn, AccI, AmerH, BI, BusI, CREJ, CurrCont, EnerResAb, HistAb, HospLitI, IEconArt, JEL, MgtC, OperRes, PAIS, PerManAb, RiskAb, RuralRecrTourAb, SOCI, SocSc, WorAb, WorldAgEconRuralSocAb.

The *Quarterly Review of Economic and Business* is the official journal of the

Midwest Economics Association. It publishes factual information and interpretive comment on business and economic issues. The authors are drawn from the academic world which also comprises the bulk of the readership. The scholarly studies and analyses are abstracted in the front of the issue.

A typical issue has eight to ten articles. A recent copy reported a study completed on wage growth and the black-white wage differential; a second piece examined prices, labor costs and wages in the United States over a thirty-five year period. A simple listing of approximately eighty-five scholarly or professional books is included.

282   *Radical History Review*. DATE FOUNDED: 1974. TITLE CHANGES: *MARHO Newsletter* (1974-1974). FREQUENCY: 3/yr. PRICE: $40/yr. institutions, $20/yr. personal. PUBLISHER: Radical History Review, 445 W. 59th Street, Room 4312, New York, NY 10019. EDITOR: Amy Ward. ILLUSTRATIONS. INDEX. ADVERTISEMENTS. CIRCULATION: 1,800. MANUSCRIPT SELECTION: Editor. MICROFORMS: Em-Cee Microfilm, UMI. REPRINTS: ISI. BOOK REVIEWS. SPECIAL ISSUES. INDEXED/ABSTRACTED: AHCI, AmerH, API, BoRvI, CurrCont, HistAb, LeftI, RecPubArt, SocAb, SOCI, WritAmHis. TARGET AUDIENCE: AC, SP.

If the *American Historical Review* is the publication of the staid, historical establishment, *Radical History Review* is the organ through which the historical left presents its research. Recent titles have included: "Moving Beyond Beard, A Symposium," and "Women's Labors."

Each issue has an average of ten articles of varying length from under ten pages to over fifty. Usually each issue has a special theme around which the feature articles are brought together. The publication is supported by City University of New York.

283   *RBER, Review of Business and Economic Research*. DATE FOUNDED: 1965. TITLE CHANGES: *Mississippi Valley Journal of Business and Economics* (1965-1975). FREQUENCY: 2/yr. PRICE: $10/yr. PUBLISHER: Division of Business and Economic Research, College of Business Administration, University of New Orleans, New Orleans, LA 70148. EDITOR: Jerry P. Simpson. ILLUSTRATIONS. INDEX. CIRCULATION: 1,000. MANUSCRIPT SELECTION: Editor, Editorial Board. MICROFORMS: UMI. REPRINTS: UMI. INDEXED/ABSTRACTED: ABIn, AccI, BI, BusI, CREJ, IEconArt, JEL, MgtC, PAIS, SOCI, WorBankAb. TARGET AUDIENCE: AC, SP.

RBER publishes the empirical and conceptual research of predominantly American academics whose credentials usually include membership on a business school faculty. Recent subjects have included: research in business, foreign trade, mortgage rates, input and output models, pricing and salaries, and labor relations.

Each issue has six to eight research articles of fifteen to twenty pages in length. Recent articles have included "Research Productivity of American Business Schools, 1975-85," and "A Comparison of Large and Small Firm Productivity, Labor Compensation and Investment Rates."

284   *Relations Industrielles/Industrial Relations.* DATE FOUNDED: 1945. TITLE CHANGES: *Industrial Relations Bulletin* (1945-1950). FREQUENCY: q. PRICE: $48/yr. institutions, $26/yr. personal. PUBLISHER: Department des relations industrielles, Université Laval, Quebec, Canada G1K 7P4. EDITOR: Gerard Dion. INDEX. ADVERTISEMENTS. CIRCULATION: 2,400. MANUSCRIPT SELECTION: Editorial Board, Refereed. MICROFORMS: UMI, MIM. REPRINTS: UMI. BOOK REVIEWS. INDEXED/ABSTRACTED: AmerH, CanBusI, CanPerI, CurrCont, EmpRelAb, ForLangI, HistAb, HRA, ICanLegPerLit, LRI, MarAffBib, MgtC, PAIS, RecPubArt, SageFamStudAb, SagePAA, SageUrbStudAb, SOCI, TraIndI, WorAb. TARGET AUDIENCE: AC.

This scholarly journal which covers all aspects of industrial relations is written in both English and French. It is considered the "dean of all university periodicals in industrial relations." Articles are both empirical and theoretical in the areas of labor history, unionism, collective bargaining, human resources, and occupational health. Authors are predominately Canadian and American academicians.

A typical issue contains eight to ten articles preceded by an author abstract. There is a discussion section which consists of papers presented at meetings or contains summaries of research. Part of this section is also legislative changes and decisions relating to employment in Canada. There are ten to twelve signed book reviews of one to one and one-half pages in length. In addition there is a separate listing of books which have been received including bibliographic information. The third regular feature is a bibliography of recent journal publications. These are grouped by a broad subject approach.

285   *Review of Black Political Economy.* DATE FOUNDED: 1970. FREQUENCY: q. PRICE: $30/yr. institutions, $20/yr. personal. PUBLISHER: National Economic Association and the Southern Center for Studies in Public Policy of Clark College, Transaction Periodicals

Consortium, Rutgers-The State University, New Brunswick, NJ 08903. EDITOR: Margaret C. Simms. ILLUSTRATIONS. INDEX. ADVERTISEMENTS. CIRCULATION: 1,500. MANUSCRIPT SELECTION: Editor. MICROFORMS: UMI, MIM. REPRINTS: UMI. BOOK REVIEWS. INDEXED/ABSTRACTED: AmerH, BI, CurrCont, HistAb, IEconArt, PAIS, SagePAA, SageUrbStudAb, SOCI, SocSc, TraIndI, WorAb, WritAmHis. TARGET AUDIENCE: AC, SP.

Black Political Economy examines the issues "related to the economic status of black and third world peoples." Its primary focus is in identifying and analyzing policy prescriptions designed to reduce racial economic inequality. Recent articles of interest in the area of labor relations include subjects such as the right to work legislation, the economic position of black workers and the post-1964 earnings gains by black women.

This journal focuses on the appraisal of policy and each issue has an average of six substantive articles. There is an occasional book review section with an average of one to three signed, lengthy reviews. Other features include "Responses," "Announcements" and "About the Authors."

286   *Review of Economics and Statistics.* DATE FOUNDED: 1919. TITLE CHANGES: *Review of Economic Statistics* (1919-1947). FREQUENCY: q. PRICE: $133/yr. institutions, $52.50/yr. personal. PUBLISHER: Elsevier Science Publishers B.V., P.O. Box 1991, 1000 BZ Amsterdam, The Netherlands. EDITOR: Hendrik S. Houthakker. ILLUSTRATIONS. INDEX. ADVERTISEMENTS. CIRCULATION: 5,400. MANUSCRIPT SELECTION: Editor, Associate Editors, Refereed. MICROFORMS: Publisher, RPI. INDEXED/ABSTRACTED: ABIn, AmerH, BI, BibAg, BusI, CREJ, CurrCont, EnerI, EnerInfoAb, EnerResAb, ExMed, GeoAb, HistAb, IEconArt, IntAeroAb, IntLabDoc, JContQuanMeth, KeyEconSci, MagInd, MarAffBib, MathR, MedCareRev, MgtC, PAIS, PopInd, RiskAb, RuralRecrTourAb, SageUrbStudAb, SOCI, SocSc, TraIndI, WomAb, WorBankAb, WorldAgEconRuralSocAb. TARGET AUDIENCE: AC, SP.

This scholarly publication is published by the Department of Economics at Harvard University. The articles which are empirically based or theoretical are written by academicians or upper level management which comprise its audience. Its focus is on the entire business world including articles dealing with multinational phenomena as well as labor and management perspectives.

Each issue has twelve to fifteen articles of ten to twelve pages. There are about one-half the number and length of "Notes" covering the same topics. Each article and note has a one paragraph abstract.

287   ***Review of Public Personnel Administration.*** DATE FOUNDED: 1980. FREQUENCY: 3/yr. PRICE: $30/yr. institutions, $15/yr. personal. PUBLISHER: Bureau of Governmental Research and Service, University of South Carolina, Columbia, SC 29208. EDITOR: Charlie B. Tyer. ILLUSTRATIONS. CIRCULATION: 1,500. MANUSCRIPT SELECTION: Editor, Refereed. BOOK REVIEWS. SPECIAL ISSUES. INDEXED/ABSTRACTED: ABCPolSci, PAIS, PerManAb, PersLit, SagePAA, SageUrbStudAb, UrbAffAb. TARGET AUDIENCE: AC, SP.

ROPPA is a scholarly journal of public personnel administration. It is the only academic journal which focuses primarily on public personnel issues. It is designed to promote the advancement of personnel theory and the study and practice of public personnel management. The focus of several recent articles have been on the personnel manager's role in public organizations, labor-management relations, employee recruitment selection and promotion, and other specific personnel programs and articles.

About five to seven articles appear per issue. Three to five signed book reviews per issue are included. There is usually one special issue per year with such topics as "Merit Pay."

288   ***Review of Radical Political Economics.*** DATE FOUNDED: 1969. FREQUENCY: q. PRICE: $60/yr. institutions, $40/yr. Union for Radical Political Economics members. PUBLISHER: Union for Radical Political Economics, 122 West 27th Street, 10th Floor, New York, NY 10001. EDITOR: Bill James. ILLUSTRATIONS. INDEX. ADVERTISEMENTS. CIRCULATION: 3,000. MANUSCRIPT SELECTION: Editor, Editorial Board. MICROFORMS: UMI. REPRINTS: UMI. BOOK REVIEWS. INDEXED/ABSTRACTED: AmBibSlav, AmerH, API, BibAg, CurrCont, GeoAb, HistAb, IEconArt, LeftI, PAIS, SOCI. TARGET AUDIENCE: AC, SP.

The *Review* is published by the Union for Radical Political Economics and welcomes research from a perspective which continues the "critique of the capitalist system and of all forms of oppression and (builds on) the construction of progressive social policy." Its perspective was formed by its founders of the Socialist left in the United States. Some articles with an international focus are published. Recent titles of articles include: "A

Reconsideration of Racial Earning Inequality," "Class and Socialist Politics in France," and "Economic Theory of Marriage."

Each issue has four substantive research articles, empirical rather than conceptual. They run an average of twenty pages in length. There is a notes and comments section, a call for papers, and book reviews. There are usually five, signed book reviews per issue, one to two pages in length.

289   *RWDSU Record.* DATE FOUNDED: 1941. TITLE CHANGES: *Retail, Wholesale & Department Store Employee* (1941-1954). FREQUENCY: 6/yr. PRICE: $3/yr. PUBLISHER: Retail, Wholesale & Department Store Union, 30 E. 29th St., New York, NY 10016. EDITOR: J. Spellane. ILLUSTRATIONS. CIRCULATION: 275,000. MANUSCRIPT SELECTION: Editor, Assistant Editor, Union President. MICROFORMS: UMI. REPRINTS: Publisher. INDEXED/ABSTRACTED: WorAb. TARGET AUDIENCE: AC, GP, HS, SP. SAMPLE COPIES: Libraries, individuals.

Tabloid format, this is a trade union publication directed at its membership. The content is mostly limited to activities and issues related to department stores and department store employees.

Although mostly newsy and certainly not scholarly, this publication does contain some interesting information with such articles as "The New Immigration Law" or "How the Union Came to Bloomingdales."

290   *Sacramento Valley Union Labor Bulletin.* DATE FOUNDED: 1929. FREQUENCY: bw. PRICE: $10/yr. PUBLISHER: Sacramento Central Labor Council, 2640 Cordova Lane, Suite 104, Rancho Cordova, CA 95670. EDITOR: Rita A. Carroll. ILLUSTRATIONS. ADVERTISEMENTS. CIRCULATION: 14,000. MANUSCRIPT SELECTION: Editor. MICROFORMS: State of California Library; State Historical Society of Wisconsin. SPECIAL ISSUES: 3/yr. TARGET AUDIENCE: GP, SP. SAMPLE COPIES: Libraries, individuals.

The *Labor Bulletin* is owned by three AFL-CIO affiliated councils and reports on labor news in the Sacramento Valley area. Subscribers are union members of AFL-CIO affiliated locals.

It contains area labor-related information and hard news. Generally it serves as an educational vehicle to stimulate union activity and strength. Some longer features project a broader scope such as a recent example, "Stress: an Occupational Hazard."

291   *Screen Actor Hollywood.* DATE FOUNDED: 1959. TITLE
       CHANGES: *Screen Actor* (1959-1979). FREQUENCY: q. PRICE:
       $10/yr. PUBLISHER: Screen Actors Guild, 7065 Hollywood Boule-
       vard, Hollywood, CA 90028. EDITOR: Mark Locher. ILLUSTRA-
       TIONS. CIRCULATION: 75,000. MANUSCRIPT SELECTION:
       Editor. REPRINTS: Publisher. BOOK REVIEWS. INDEXED/
       ABSTRACTED: FLI. TARGET AUDIENCE: GP, SP. SAMPLE
       COPIES: Libraries.

       This is the official publication of the Screen Actors Guild and reflects
       the views of its 70,000 member union of the performing arts. It focuses
       on the craft and business of professional screen acting. Articles are
       written by American journalists and freelance writers.

       Quarterly issues cover such topics as biographies of or interviews with
       actors and actresses, historical and future glimpses at the motion picture
       business, and union news as well as general information on acting.
       There are an average of twelve articles per issue and one to two unsigned
       book reviews consisting of 300 words.

292   *Seafarers Log.* DATE FOUNDED: 1937. FREQUENCY: m. PRICE:
       Free. PUBLISHER: Seafarers International Union, 5201 Auth Way,
       Camp Springs, MD 20746. EDITOR: Charles Svenson. ILLUSTRA-
       TIONS. CIRCULATION: 32,000. MANUSCRIPT SELECTION:
       Editor. MICROFORMS: Paul Hall Library. SPECIAL ISSUES:
       Occasional. INDEXED/ABSTRACTED: WorAb. TARGET AUDI-
       ENCE: SP. SAMPLE COPIES: Libraries, individuals.

       A publication generated specifically for those in the Maritime unions.
       As such it provides relevant, up-to-date information on legislative and
       political issues, health and pension information for its members, and
       general union news. The viewpoint from which the material is pre-
       sented by the in-house editorial staff is pro-labor.

       Typical issues contain an average of thirty articles. There are occasion-
       ally special reports of several pages. Recent articles have been written on
       the decline of U.S. sealift and meeting the changing vocational and edu-
       cational needs of members. There are articles and regular features
       highlighting union members who have been outstanding, have retired
       or died, and a digest of ships' meetings and dispatchers' reports.

293   *Selections.* DATE FOUNDED: 1984. FREQUENCY: 3 to 4/yr.
       PRICE: Free. PUBLISHER: Graduate Management Admission
       Council, 11601 Wilshire Blvd. #1060, Los Angeles, CA 90025. EDI-
       TOR: Deborah Perrin. ILLUSTRATIONS. CIRCULATION:

7,000. MANUSCRIPT SELECTION: Editorial Board. SPECIAL ISSUES: Occasional. TARGET AUDIENCE: SP. SAMPLE COPIES: Libraries, individuals.

The major focus of this publication is to present debate about the substance and quality of graduate management education both in the United States as well as internationally. It is the only publication of its kind in this field. The writers are usually American academics or researchers. The major readers of this publication are educators in graduate management programs.

There are usually five articles per issue. Special issues are occasionally published focusing on a specific topic. One such recent issue deals with "Curriculum and Pedagogy." It consists of a group of essays debating the positive and negative aspects of management education; the past, present and future of management education and the international aspect of this education. There are two lengthy interviews with noted professors in the field.

294   *Service Employees Union.* DATE FOUNDED: 1942. TITLE CHANGES: *Building Service Employee* (1942-1956); *Service Employee* (1957-1987). FREQUENCY: 8/yr. PUBLISHER: Service Employees International Union, 1313 L St., Washington, D.C. 20005. EDITOR: David Ransom. ILLUSTRATIONS. CIRCULATION: 20,000. MANUSCRIPT SELECTION: Editor/Publisher. INDEXED/ABSTRACTED: WorAb. TARGET AUDIENCE: SP. SAMPLE COPIES: Libraries, individuals limited.

This professional tabloid news magazine is aimed at the SEIU membership and the trade-union leaders in the health care, building services, the public sector and office industries.

It is filled with short news stories aimed at organizing American labor. There are one to three major stories published per issue. The editorial viewpoint, as expected, is left of center.

295   *Skill: the UAW's International Magazine for Skilled Trades Members.* DATE FOUNDED: 1981. FREQUENCY: q. PRICE: $5/yr. PUBLISHER: International Union, UAW, 8000 E. Jefferson Ave., Detroit, MI 48214. EDITOR: Peter Laarman. ILLUSTRATIONS. CIRCULATION: 165,000. MANUSCRIPT SELECTION: Editors. TARGET AUDIENCE: GP, SP. SAMPLE COPIES: Libraries, individuals.

Unlike the other UAW publication, *Solidarity*, which is aimed at the general membership, *Skill* directs itself to those UAW members in the skilled trades such as technicians and engineers.

Written by journalists and researchers, each issue contains about eight to ten articles with such focus as "Hi-Tech Hits the Skilled Trades Dept." A definite working class/union bias.

296   ***Sloan Management Review.*** DATE FOUNDED: 1960. TITLE CHANGES: *Industrial Management Review* (1960-1970). FRE-QUENCY: q. PRICE: $32/yr. PUBLISHER: Alfred P. Sloan School of Management, Massachusetts Institute of Technology, 50 Memorial Drive, Cambridge, MA 02139. EDITOR: Rosemary Brutico. ILLUS-TRATIONS. INDEX. ADVERTISEMENTS. CIRCULATION: 19,500. MANUSCRIPT SELECTION: Editor, Refereed. MICRO-FORMS: UMI. REPRINTS: Publisher. BOOK REVIEWS. IN-DEXED/ABSTRACTED: BusI, PAIS, WorAb. TARGET AUDI-ENCE: AC, SP. SAMPLE COPIES: Libraries, individuals.

The principal goal of this publication which is affiliated with a prestig-ious academic institution provides the practicing manager with in-depth analysis of the latest tools and information needed for effective problem solving and decision making. Articles are selected that discuss new techniques, case studies, models, and research trends of practical significance to the professional manager. The articles are written by mostly academics and researchers but also some top managers usually from the United States. The *Sloan Management Review* provides more in-depth analysis than other comparable journals.

A sample journal has four to five articles plus three forum pieces. There are two to three book reviews per issue which are signed by the reviewer and are two to three pages long. In addition, there is a listing of recent management publications complete with lengthy annotations.

297   ***Social and Economic Studies.*** DATE FOUNDED: 1953. FRE-QUENCY: q. PRICE: $40/yr. institutions, $25/yr. personal. PUB-LISHER: Institute of Social and Economic Research, University of the West Indies, Mona, Kingston 7, Jamaica, West Indies. PUBLISHER: J. Edward Greene. ILLUSTRATIONS. INDEX. ADVERTISE-MENTS. CIRCULATION: 2,000. MANUSCRIPT SELECTION: Editor, Refereed. MICROFORMS: UMI. REPRINTS: ISI, UMI. BOOK REVIEWS. SPECIAL ISSUES. INDEXED/AB-STRACTED: AbAnthro, AmerH, AnthroI, ASSIA, CREJ, CurrCont, GeoAb, HistAb, IEconArt, IntLabDoc, LLBA, PAIS, PopInd, PsyAb, RuralRecrTourAb, SocAb, SOCI, SocSc, SPDA, WorldAgEconRural-SocAb. TARGET AUDIENCE: AC, SP.

Social and Economic Studies is the official publication of the Institute of Social and Economic Research of the University of the West Indies. In addition to reports of the Institute, it publishes research on the social, economic and political problems and policy issues of the Caribbean, Latin America, and the Third World. Recent topics have included: West Indian trade, colonial policy and industrialization and balance of payments. Recent titles include "The U.S. and Canada: The Struggle for British West Indian Trade," and "The Circuit of Capital and the Labour Problem in Capitalist Development."

An average of ten articles of varying length are published in each issue. An occasional review essay is published as is "Notes on Contributors."

298   *Social and Labour Bulletin.* DATE FOUNDED: 1974. FRE-QUENCY: q. PRICE: $28.50/yr. PUBLISHER: International Labour Office, Publication Sales Service, CH-1211 Geneva 22, Switzerland. EDITOR: Margaret Cove. INDEX. ADVERTISEMENTS. MANU-SCRIPT SELECTION: Editorial Team. MICROFORMS: UMI. REPRINTS: Publisher. SPECIAL ISSUES: Annual. INDEXED/ ABSTRACTED: AbHyg, ErgAb, ExMed, MedCareRev, TropDis-Bull, WorAb. TARGET AUDIENCE: AC, SP.

This journal provides comprehensive news coverage on industrial relations developments in the 150 member states of the International Labour Office. The International Labour Organization is the only international agency within the United Nations system with a tripartite constituency, i.e. representing governments, workers' and employees' organizations. Its articles are written by multilingual academicians, government representatives and industrial relations experts and high-light events and new approaches to labor legislation, collective bargaining, employment policies, working conditions, social security and equal opportunity. These articles aim at giving a balanced view of the response by governments and both sides of industry to on-going social and labor questions.

A typical issue has an average of 130 short articles of 200-300 words each which have been printed in other sources in the member states. The original source is cited. A table of content is divided by a broad subject approach under topics such as working conditions, wages, employment, etc. Topics are further subdivided by geographical area.

299   *Social Forces.* DATE FOUNDED: 1922. TITLE CHANGES: *Journal of Social Forces* (1922-1925). FREQUENCY: q. PRICE: $30/yr. institutions, $19/yr. personal, $16/yr. American Sociological Association members. PUBLISHER: University of North Carolina Press, P.O.

Box 2288, Chapel Hill, NC 27515-2288. EDITOR: Richard L. Simpson. ILLUSTRATIONS. INDEX. ADVERTISEMENTS. CIRCULATION: 4,800. MANUSCRIPT SELECTION: Editor, Editorial Board. MICROFORMS: UMI, MIM. REPRINTS: UMI. BOOK REVIEWS. INDEXED/ABSTRACTED: AbAnthro, ABCPolSci, AbSocWor, AdolMentHlthAb, AmBibSlav, AmerH, ASSIA, BoRvI, CIJE, CommAb, CrimJusAb, CurrCont, CurrLitFam-Plan, EdAdAb, GeoAb, HistAb, LLBA, PAIS, PopInd, PsyAb, RefSo, RuralRecrTourAb, SageFamStudAb, SageUrbStudAb, SocAb, SOCI, SocSc, SocWAb, SPDA, WomAb, WorldAgEconRuralSocAb, Writ-AmHis.

Social Forces is, as the subtitle states, "an international journal of social research." Empirical and conceptual articles published have included: "Time with Children: The Impact of Couples' Work-Time Commitments," "Labor Market Structure, Human Capital, and Earnings Inequality in Metropolitan Areas," and "The Family Wage System in Pennsylvania's Anthracite Region: 1850-1900."

Each issue has ten to fifteen articles of ten to twenty pages in length. Book reviews are signed and on average twenty are published. Biographies of contributors are published under a feature titled "Take Note."

300   *Social History* (London). DATE FOUNDED: 1976. FREQUENCY: 3/yr. PRICE: $70/yr. institutions, $50/yr. personal. PUBLISHER: Routledge, 11 New Fetter Lane, London EC4P 4EE, England. EDITORS: Janet Blackman and Keith Nield. ILLUSTRATIONS. INDEX. ADVERTISEMENTS. CIRCULATION: 1,000. MANUSCRIPT SELECTION: Editors, Editorial Board. BOOK REVIEWS. INDEXED/ABSTRACTED: AHCI, AmerH, HistAb, SocSc, WritAmHis. TARGET AUDIENCE: AC, SP.

Published under the sponsorship of the Department of Economic and Social History at the University of Hull, this highly respected academic journal is important to the field of industrial and labor relations. Recent theoretical and empirical articles have included: "Issues of Gender and Employment," "Trade Unionism, Sex Segregation and the State" and "Employers' Organizations, Unemployment and Social Politics in Britain During the Inter-War Period."

Each issue contains five to eight articles of ten to twenty pages in length. Each issue contains a varying number of signed book reviews and a list of books received for review.

301   *Social Indicators Research*. DATE FOUNDED: 1974. FREQUEN-
CY: 6/yr. PRICE: $152/yr. institutions, $49/yr. personal. PUB-
LISHER: Kluwer Academic Publishers, P.O. Box 17, 3300 AA Dordre-
cht, The Netherlands. EDITOR: Alex C. Michalos. ILLUSTRA-
TIONS. INDEX. ADVERTISEMENTS. MANUSCRIPT SELEC-
TION: Editor, Editorial Board. MICROFORMS: UMI. BOOK
REVIEWS. INDEXED/ABSTRACTED: AdolMentHlthAb, ASSIA,
BibAg, CommAb, CurrCont, FutSurv, HRA, LLBA, MidEast,
MgtMarA, PAIS, PhilI, PsyAb, PubAdAb, RuralDevAb, RuralExtE-
dTrAb, RuralRecrTourAb, SageFamStudAb, SagePAA, SageUrb-
StudAb, SocAb, SOCI, SPDA, WorldAgEconRuralSocAb, Writ-
AmHis. TARGET AUDIENCE: AC, SP.

Social Indicators Research is a leading journal dealing with "problems
relating to the measurement of all aspects of the quality of life."
Research published is empirical, philosophical and methodological.
Topics covered are: labor, populations, social customs, morality, poli-
tics, education, economics, technology, and poverty, among others.
Recent articles have included: "Migration and Job Satisfaction—a
Logistic Regression Analysis of Satisfaction of Filipina Domestic
Workers in Hong Kong."

Each issue has seven to nine articles, fifteen to thirty pages in length.
Each issue usually contains a review article of some length.

302   *Social Psychology Quarterly*. DATE FOUNDED: 1937. TITLE
CHANGES: *Sociometry* (1937-1977); *Social Psychology* (1978-1978).
FREQUENCY: q. PRICE: $53/yr. institutions, $27/yr. personal, $13/
yr. American Sociological Association members. PUBLISHER:
American Sociological Association, 1722 N Street, N.W., Washington,
D.C. 20036. EDITOR: Karen S. Cook. ILLUSTRATIONS. INDEX.
ADVERTISEMENTS. CIRCULATION: 5,000. MANUSCRIPT
SELECTION: Editor, Editorial Board. MICROFORMS: UMI,
MIM. REPRINTS: UMI. SPECIAL ISSUES: Occasional. IN-
DEXED/ABSTRACTED: AdolMentHlthAb, ASSIA, CrimJusAb,
CurrCont, EdAdAb, IntPolSc, LLBA, PsyAb, SocAb, SOCI, SocSc,
SPDA. TARGET AUDIENCE: AC, SP.

A journal of the American Sociological Society, it publishes empirically
based, scholarly articles. It includes articles of importance to industrial
relations which focus on such topics as the psychology of work, interpersonal and intergroup behavior, and group dynamics. Recent articles
have included "Models of Participation in Status Differentiated
Groups."

Each issue contains six to ten empirical, methodologically, rigidly defined articles. Each issue also includes editorials and "Research Notes." Special issues focus on a subject in greater depth.

303 *Social Science History*. DATE FOUNDED: 1976. FREQUENCY: q. PRICE: $50/yr. institutions, $20/yr. personal. PUBLISHER: Duke University Press, 6697 College Station, Durham, NC 27708. EDITORS: James Q. Graham, Jr. and Robert P. Swierenga. ILLUSTRATIONS. INDEX. ADVERTISEMENTS. CIRCULATION: 1,200. MANUSCRIPT SELECTION: Editors, Board of Editors. MICROFORMS: MIM. BOOK REVIEWS. INDEXED/ABSTRACTED: AmBibSlav, AmerH, ASSIA, CurrCont, HistAb, LLBA, RecPubArt, SagePAA, SageUrbStudAb, SocAb, SOCI, SocWAb, SPDA, USPSD, WritAmerHis. TARGET AUDIENCE: AC, SP.

This publication is the official journal of the Social Science History Association. *Social Science History* is published to improve "the quality of historical explanation in teaching and research of relevant theories and methods from the social science disciplines." Recent articles have included: "The Transplanted: Workers, Class and Labor," and "American Labor Law: Its Impact on Working-Class Militancy, 1901-1980."

Each issue publishes from three to six research articles. The articles average about thirty pages in length. There is a research note. Occasionally one lengthy, signed book review is published.

304 *Social Science Quarterly*. DATE FOUNDED: 1920. TITLE CHANGES: *Southwestern Political Science Quarterly* (1920-1923); *Southwestern Political and Social Science Quarterly* (1923-1931); *Southwestern Social Science Quarterly* (1931-1968). FREQUENCY: q. PRICE: $36/yr. institutions, $20/yr. personal. PUBLISHER: Southwestern Social Science Association, University of Texas Press, P.O. Box 7819, Austin, TX 78713. EDITOR: Charles M. Bonjean. ILLUSTRATIONS. INDEX. ADVERTISEMENTS. CIRCULATION: 2,300. MANUSCRIPT SELECTION: Editor, Editorial Board. MICROFORMS: UMI, JAI, Kraus, MIM. REPRINTS: UMI. BOOK REVIEWS. INDEXED/ABSTRACTED: ABCPolSci, AmBibSlav, AmerH, ASSIA, BoRvI, CIJE, CommAb, CrimJusAb, CurrCont, CurrIStat, EdAdAb, EnerInfoAb, EnvAb, ERIC, HistAb, IEconArt, ILegPer, IntBibPolSc, IntBibSoc, IntPolSc, JEL, LLBA, PAIS, PolScAb, PopInd, RecPubArt, ResHiEdAb, RuralRecrTourAb, SageFamStudAb, SagePAA, SageUrbStudAb, SocAb, SocEdAb, SOCI, SocSc, SPDA, USPSD, WomAb, WorAb, WorldAgEconRuralSocAb. TARGET AUDIENCE: AC, SP.

"SSQ is dedicated to developing communication across traditional disciplinary boundaries. Authors with diverse perspectives consider the same subjects in special issues and symposia." Recent symposia have included "Employment and Earnings." Recent articles of importance to labor/industrial relations include: "Labor Union Ideology in the Screen Actors Guild" and "Explaining Participation in Coproduction."

Each issue has eight to fifteen articles of substantial length (ten to twenty pages). "Current Research" is another regular feature of two to three articles as is "Research Notes." Fifteen to twenty signed, substantial book reviews per issue are included.

305   *Socialist Review*. DATE FOUNDED: 1959. TITLE CHANGES: *Studies on the Left* (1959-1967); *Socialist Revolution* (1970-1977). MERGER: *Marxist Perspectives* (1978-1980). FREQUENCY: q. PRICE: $42/yr. institutions, $21/yr. personal. PUBLISHER: Center for Social Research and Education, 3202 Adeline Street, Berkeley, CA 94703. EDITOR: Ron Silliman. ILLUSTRATIONS. INDEX. ADVERTISEMENTS. CIRCULATION: 5,500. MANUSCRIPT SELECTION: Editor, Collectives. MICROFORMS: UMI. RE- PRINTS: UMI. BOOK REVIEWS. INDEXED/ABSTRACTED: API, IntBibSoc, IntPolSc, LeftI, LLBA, SocAb, SOCI. TARGET AUDIENCE: AC, SP.

The *Socialist Review* is an intellectual, unorthodox, wide-ranging, inde- pendent journal that boasts it is the only U.S. socialist review for political analysis. They are right. The wide range of subjects it considers for publication are contemporary society, politics, economics and culture. Recently published articles are: "The Politics of New-Style Workforce," "Debt Crisis Update: 1988," "The Promise of Compa- rable Worth" and "Feminization of the Workplace."

Each issue publishes five to six expository articles of under thirty pages. There is also a comments section. Book reviews are included. They are usually five pages in length, signed, and four per issue.

306   *Society*. DATE FOUNDED: 1963. TITLE CHANGES: *Transaction* (1963-1972). FREQUENCY: 6/yr. PRICE: $50/yr. institutions, $30/ yr. personal. PUBLISHER: Transactions, Inc., Rutgers-The State University, New Brunswick, NJ 08903. EDITOR: Irving Louis Hor- owitz. ILLUSTRATIONS. INDEX. ADVERTISEMENTS. CIR- CULATION: 15,000. MANUSCRIPT SELECTION: Editor. MICROFORMS: Bell & Howell, Johnson Associates, UMI, MIM. REPRINTS: UMI. BOOK REVIEWS. INDEXED/ABSTRAC- TED: ABCPolSci, AmerH, BoRvI, CIJE, CommAb, CurrCont, EdA-

dAb, EnerInfoAb, EnvAb, ExMed, FLI, FutSurv, HistAb, LLBA, MagInd, MedCareRev, PAIS, PeaceResAb, PolScAb, RG, SagePAA, SageUrbStudAb, SocAb, SOCI, SocWAb, SPDA, USPSD, WomAb. TARGET AUDIENCE: AC, GP, SP.

Society is "the periodical of record in the social science and public policy for the past 25 years." It gives a readable and useful presentation of research not only for the academic but also for the educated layperson. Recent articles have included "Planning, Power and Politics" and "Human Service Corporations and the Welfare State." Special features have included "Comparable Worth."

Each issue includes articles under the headings "Commentaries," "Special Feature," "Articles," "Social Science and Public Policy," "Culture and Society," "Social Science and the Citizen" and "Social Science Books of the Month." Each issue also has a photo essay. Five to eight substantial, signed book reviews are included in each issue.

307 *Socio-Economic Planning Sciences.* DATE FOUNDED: 1967. FRE-QUENCY: 6/yr. PRICE: $180/yr. PUBLISHER: Pergamon Press Inc., Maxwell House, Elmsford, NY 10523. EDITOR: Barnett R. Parker. ILLUSTRATIONS. INDEX. ADVERTISEMENTS. CIR-CULATION: 1,700. MANUSCRIPT SELECTION: Editor, Editorial Board. MICROFORMS: UMI, MIM. SPECIAL ISSUES. IN-DEXED/ABSTRACTED: ABCPolSci, AbHlthCareMgtS, ASSIA, BI, CIJE, CREJ, CurrCont, CurrLitFamPlan, EdAdAb, ElecComA, ExMed, GeoAb, HospLitI, ISMEC, JContQuanMeth, LegCont, LLBA, MedCareRev, MgtC, PAIS, PollAb, RiskAb, RuralRe-crTourAb, SafSciA, SagePAA, SageUrbStudAb, SocAb, SOCI, SPDA, WorldAgEconRuralSocAb. TARGET AUDIENCE: AC, SP.

Socio-Economic Planning Sciences is devoted to research dealing with applications of quantitative models and techniques to important decision problems in the service and public sectors. Recent articles have included: "Problem Statements in Managerial Problem Solving," "Optimization of Task Allocation for Community Health Workers in Haiti" and "Reducing Attrition Among Village Health Workers in Rural Nigeria through Supervision."

Each issue contains an average of six to eight articles usually under twenty pages in length. Special issues are occasional, the most recent being "Field Application of Operations Research in Primary Health Care."

308 *Sociological Perspectives.* DATE FOUNDED: 1958. TITLE CHANGES: *Pacific Sociological Review* (1958-1982). FREQUENCY: q.

PRICE: $65/yr. institutions, $30/yr. personal. PUBLISHER: Sage Publications, Inc., 2111 West Hillcrest Drive, Newbury Park, CA 91320. EDITOR: Bernard Farber. ILLUSTRATIONS. INDEX. ADVERTISEMENTS. MANUSCRIPT SELECTION: Editor. MICROFORMS: UMI. REPRINTS: UMI. INDEXED/ABSTRACTED: ABCPolSci, AbCrimPen, AbSocWor, AmerH, CurrCont, HistAb, HRA, IntBibSoc, LLBA, PsyAb, SageFamStudAb, SageUrbStudAb, SocAb, SocEdAb, SOCI, USPSD. TARGET AUDIENCE: AC, SP.

This is the official publication of the Pacific Sociological Association. Empirical and conceptual research topics have recently included: leisure, marriage, social theory, immigration, and consumption. Typically important articles for labor and industrial relations might be "Overeducation and the Earnings of Black, Hispanic, and White Male Workers," and "Economic Segmentation and Worker Earnings in a U.S.-Mexico Border Enclave."

Each issue has five or six articles twenty to thirty pages in length. They are written by U.S. academics publishing original research.

309   *Sociological Quarterly.*   DATE FOUNDED: 1938. TITLE CHANGES: *Midwest Sociologist* (1938-1959). FREQUENCY: q. PRICE: $75/yr. institutions, $35/yr. personal. PUBLISHER: JAI Press, Inc., 55 Old Post Road-No. 2, P.O. Box 1678, Greenwich, CT 06836-1678. EDITOR: Gary L. Albrecht. ILLUSTRATIONS. INDEX. ADVERTISEMENTS. CIRCULATION: 2,550. MANUSCRIPT SELECTION: Editor, Editorial Review Board. MICROFORMS: JAI, UMI, AMS, WSH. REPRINTS: UMI. INDEXED/ABSTRACTED: ABCPolSci, AbPopCult, AbSocWor, AdolMenthHlthAb, AmBibSlav, AmerH, ASSIA, CommAb, CrimJusAb, CurrCont, HistAb, IntPolSc, LLBA, PsyAb, SocAb, SOCI, SocSc, SocWAb, SPDA, WomAb.

Theoretical and empirical in nature, the *Sociological Quarterly* welcomes articles from a variety of perspectives—a truly interdisciplinary journal. Of interest to all labor specialists, recent topics covered have been: mediation and negotiation, employees' credentials, homicide refugees, organizational behavior, labor market and migrants. Specific titles have included: "A Multivariate Model of Job Stress and Alcohol Consumption" and "Punishment and Social Structure Revisited: Unemployment and Imprisonment in the United States."

Each issue contains an average of ten articles. The articles usually run twenty to thirty pages each and are empirically as well as conceptually based.

310   ***Soundview Executive Book Summaries***. DATE FOUNDED: 1978.
TITLE CHANGES: *Soundview Summaries* (1978-1984). FRE-
QUENCY: m. PRICE: $82/yr. PUBLISHER: Cynthia Folino, Sound-
view, 5 Main St., Bristol, VT 05443. EDITOR: Roger Griffith. ILLUS-
TRATIONS. CIRCULATION: 24,000. MANUSCRIPT SELEC-
TION: Editor. REPRINTS: Publisher. BOOK REVIEWS. TAR-
GET AUDIENCE: AC, GP, SP.

This is a looseleaf binder service which provides summaries of business
books which are of particular importance to business people. This
format allows executives to examine new ideas, methods, and techniques in a minimum of reading time. As an additional service, a book
sales service is available for those wishing to purchase the reviewed
materials.

Each issue has two to three lengthy summaries of books written by the
author. These provide a brief overview. There is a lengthier essay of
seven to ten pages about the book content. There is also a separate
section called "Speed Reviews" consisting of three unsigned reviews of
400 to 500 words. Each book has an editorial opinion section.

311   ***South African Labour Bulletin***. DATE FOUNDED: 1974. FRE-
QUENCY: 8/yr. PRICE: $75-$150/yr. institutions and companies,
$36/yr. personal. PUBLISHER: SALB, P.O. Box 31073, Braamfontein
2017, South Africa. EDITOR: Jon Lewis. ILLUSTRATIONS.
ADVERTISEMENTS. CIRCULATION: 2,000. MANUSCRIPT
SELECTION: Editor, Refereed. BOOK REVIEWS. SPECIAL IS-
SUES. INDEXED/ABSTRACTED: HRRep, IndSAPer, PAIS,
RecPubArt. TARGET AUDIENCE: AC, GP, SP.

SALB is a journal "which supports the democratic labour movement in
South Africa. It is a forum for analyzing, debating and recording the
aims and activities of this movement....Constructive criticism of unions
or federations in the democratic labour movement is welcome. However, articles with unwarranted attacks or of a sectarian nature which
have a devisive effect on the labour movement will not be published."

Seven to eight analytical articles such as "Transition To A Socialist
Agriculture" per issue. It occasionally publishes a special issue.

312   ***South Dakota Labor Bulletin***. DATE FOUNDED: 1949. TITLE
CHANGES: *Manpower Bulletin* (1949-1975). FREQUENCY: m.
PUBLISHER: South Dakota Department of Labor, Labor Market
Information Center, 420 S. Roosevelt, P.O. Box 4730, Aberdeen, SD
57402. ILLUSTRATIONS. CIRCULATION: 1,450. REPRINTS:

Publisher. SPECIAL ISSUES: a. TARGET AUDIENCE: AC, GP, HS. SAMPLE COPIES: Libraries, individuals.

Many states publish information similar to material in this publication. South Dakota does a comprehensively good job including statistics on workers (hours, earnings, etc.), consumer price index, county-to-county statistics on South Dakota unemployment, and employment compared with previous years. It draws heavily from U.S. Labor Department sources.

There are two to three substantive articles per issue. In January of each year, an article is published offering a narrative analysis of the labor economics in the state over the previous year.

313.   *Studies for Trade Unionists*. DATE FOUNDED: 1974. TITLE CHANGES: *Background Notes on Industrial Relations* (1974-1975). FREQUENCY: q. PRICE: £4.50/yr. PUBLISHER: Workers' Educational Association, 9 Upper Berkeley Street, London W1H 8BY, England. EDITOR: Mel Doyle. ILLUSTRATIONS. CIRCULATION: 4,000. MANUSCRIPT SELECTION: Editorial Committee. REPRINTS: Publisher. TARGET AUDIENCE: AC, SP. SAMPLE COPIES: Libraries.

This publication is largely aimed at members of the trade unions in the United Kingdom. Its major purpose is to offer a comprehensive overview of questions which affect union members. Each issue consists of a single article written usually by a trade union officer, researcher or academician from the United Kingdom.

A recent issue was devoted to the subject of death at work. The 12,000 word piece contained an introduction reviewing who gets sick from work, proposed reforms and organizing for change.

314   *Suara Buruh*. DATE FOUNDED: 1956. TITLE CHANGES: *Suara Buroh* (1956-1978). FREQUENCY: m. PRICE: $7.20/yr. PUBLISHER: Malaysian Trades Union Congress, Bangunan Buruh, P.O. Box 38, 46700 Pitaling Jaya, Selangor, Malaysia. EDITOR: V. David. ILLUSTRATIONS. ADVERTISEMENTS. CIRCULATION: 10,000. MANUSCRIPT SELECTION: Editor. SPECIAL ISSUES. TARGET AUDIENCE: AC, GP, SP. SAMPLE COPIES: Libraries, individuals.

This tabloid newspaper is written for Communist labor and trade union members. It concentrates on providing its membership with the type of information included in most union newsletters dealing with national and local union activities. It focuses on issues that affect the welfare of its members. A special issue appears in May to commemorate Workers' Day on May 1st.

A typical issue may have up to twenty-five articles, some of one to two pages in length. A copy recently reviewed had articles dealing with the occupational and wage discrimination against women, provisions to provide more and better health and safety, methods and strategy of collective bargaining, and a lengthy historical sketch of the labor movement.

315   *Supervision.*   DATE FOUNDED: 1925. TITLE CHANGES: *Foreman's Magazine* (1925-1929); *Foreman* (1930-1930); *Industrial Executive Foreman and The Industrial Executive* (1931-1933). FRE-QUENCY: m. PRICE: $30.50/yr. PUBLISHER: National Research Bureau, 424 N. Third Street, Burlington, IA 52601-5224. EDITOR: Barbara Boeding. ILLUSTRATIONS. INDEX. ADVERTISE-MENTS. CIRCULATION: 7,816. MANUSCRIPT SELECTION: Editor. MICROFORMS: UMI. REPRINTS: UMI. INDEXED/ABSTRACTED: ABIn, BI, BusI, ExMed, PersLit, TraIndI, WorAb. TARGET AUDIENCE: AC, SP.

Supervision is aimed at the supervisor on the job and as such provides professional insight to help identify and accomplish goals and objectives, strengthen management skills, and provide guidance and resources to meet supervisory needs. Authors are free lance writers in the area of business, upper level managers, or academics.

There are an average of ten to twelve articles of three to four pages in length. Two regular features appear each month dealing with labor law for supervisors and "Treasure Chest" which is a column with ideas and problem solving solutions.

316   *Supervisory Management.*   DATE FOUNDED: 1955. TITLE CHANGES: *Supervisory Management* (1955-1986); *Management Solutions* (1986-1988). FREQUENCY: m. PRICE: $27/yr., $24.30 American Management Association members. PUBLISHER: American Management Association, 135 W. 50th Street, New York, NY 10020. EDITOR: Florence Stone. ILLUSTRATIONS. INDEX. ADVER-TISEMENTS. CIRCULATION: 33,000. MANUSCRIPT SELEC-TION: Editor, Editorial Advisory Board. MICROFORMS: UMI. REPRINTS: Publisher, ISI, UMI. INDEXED/ABSTRACTED: ABIn, BankLitI, BibAg, BusI, CINAHL, MgtC, PerManAb, PersLit, WorAb. TARGET AUDIENCE: AC, SP.

Supervisory Management is a pragmatic journal expressing authoritative views on the problems arising in the area of management. Authors are drawn from the academic world, executives, and other professionals working in the field.

A typical issue covers topics on the relationship of the supervisor to workers, communication skills, and the problems involved in managing a culturally diverse workforce. Regular features include "Cost Cutting/ Profit Making Ideas," "If You Were the Arbitrator," and "Let's Get Down to Cases," a report on a legal case.

317   *Supervisory Sense*. DATE FOUNDED: 1980. FREQUENCY: m. PRICE: $22.20/yr., $19.92/yr. American Management Association members. PUBLISHER: American Management Association, 135 W. 50th St., New York, NY 10020-1201. EDITOR: Florence Stone. ILLUSTRATIONS. CIRCULATION: 21,000. MANUSCRIPT SELECTION: Editor. TARGET AUDIENCE: SP. SAMPLE COPIES: Libraries; individuals.

Each issue of *Supervisory Sense* is devoted to a single topic written by an author versed in supervisory and management issues. One of its major purposes is to be as a tool in group instruction. Each issue usually contains a self test. Recent topics covered are communicating unpopular decisions, using performance appraisal, practical decision making, and drug addiction in the workplace.

318   *Talkin' Union*. DATE FOUNDED: 1981. FREQUENCY: 2/yr. PRICE: $12/yr. institutions, $7.50/yr. personal. PUBLISHER: Talkin' Union, Box 5349, Takoma Park, MD 20912. EDITOR: Paul Schniderman. ILLUSTRATIONS. CIRCULATION: 1,000. MICROFORMS: Bell and Howell. TARGET AUDIENCE: GP.

This is a very interesting publication designed to present the music, folklore and history of today's labor movement. Pithy articles include the likes of "The 1913 Massacre: The Italian Hall and the Copper Strike."

The magazine features songs, stories, poems, photos and cartoons collected by the editors from working people.

319   *Texas A & M Business Forum*. DATE FOUNDED: 1975. TITLE CHANGES: *Texas Business Executive* (1975-1984). FREQUENCY: a. PRICE: Free. PUBLISHER: College of Business Administration, Texas A & M University, College Station, TX 77840-4113. EDITOR: Estelle P. Buffa. ILLUSTRATIONS. CIRCULATION: 3,000. MANUSCRIPT SELECTION: Editor. REPRINTS: Editor. SPE-

CIAL ISSUES: Occasional. TARGET AUDIENCE: AC, SP. SAMPLE COPIES: Libraries, individuals.

The annual edition has a timely issue as a focus thus allowing an in-depth view of the topic. The writers are invited to prepare papers on the current topic. These writers are chosen from business managers, executives, civic leaders, administrators and academicians. The presentation of articles presents a balanced approach to the topic under discussion.

A typical issue contains about eight articles of a scholarly or managerial nature presented in a visually pleasing format. There is subtle promotion for Texas A & M in such areas as notices of Professional Development Programs and the Center for International Business Studies; however, this does not carry over to the articles.

320   *Texas Labor Market Review*. DATE FOUNDED: 1945. TITLE CHANGES: *Texas Labor Market* (1945-1967); *Texas Manpower Trends* (1967-1977). FREQUENCY: m. PRICE: Free. PUBLISHER: Texas Employment Commission, 15th & Congress Avenue, Austin, TX 78778. EDITOR: Dianne Dobie. ILLUSTRATIONS. CIRCULATION: 12,000. MANUSCRIPT SELECTION: Editor. INDEXED/ABSTRACTED: SRI. TARGET AUDIENCE: AC, GP, SP. SAMPLE COPIES: Libraries, individuals.

Just as the title implies, this monthly focuses on economic changes in Texas and its twenty-eight metropolitan statistical areas. It includes statistics and analysis of labor force totals, unemployment, and employment by industry sectors.

Each issue runs ten to fifteen pages and includes analyses written by Commission employees. It contains mainly tables, charts and graphs.

321   *Theory & Society*. DATE FOUNDED: 1974. FREQUENCY: 6/yr. PRICE: $113.50/yr. institutions, $40/yr. personal. PUBLISHER: Kluwer Academic Publishers, P.O. Box 17, 3300 AA Dordrecht, The Netherlands. EDITOR: Janet Gouldner. INDEX. ADVERTISEMENTS. CIRCULATION: 1,500. MANUSCRIPT SELECTION: Editors. MICROFORMS: Elsevier Sequoia S.A. BOOK REVIEWS. INDEXED/ABSTRACTED: ASSIA, CommAb, CurrCont, LeftI, LLBA, PAIS, SocAb, SOCI, SPDA. TARGET AUDIENCE: AC.

Theory & Society is an international academic journal whose scope is "renewal and critique in social theory." Empirically based articles on social theory research report on such subjects as state and urban resolutions, socialist fiscal crises, intellectual and social organizations, and reconsidering Stalinism. Recent titles have included labor history as well: "Inside Contracting at the Sargent Hardware Company: A Case Study of a Factory in Transition at the Turn of the Century."

Usually four articles are included in each issue with each about forty to fifty pages in length. Three to five signed book reviews of substantial length running three to five pages each are a regular feature.

322   *Trade Union Studies Journal.* DATE FOUNDED: 1980. FRE-QUENCY: 2/yr. PRICE: £5/yr. PUBLISHER: Workers' Educational Association, 9 Upper Berkeley Street, London W1H 8BY, England. EDITOR: Mel Doyle. ILLUSTRATIONS. CIRCULATION: 1,000. MANUSCRIPT SELECTION: Editorial Committee. REPRINTS: Publisher. BOOK REVIEWS. TARGET AUDIENCE: AC, SP. SAMPLE COPIES: Libraries.

This journal is the only journal devoted to trade union education and adult education in the United Kingdom. It publishes articles on theory and practice for tutors and students involved in this type of education. It includes the relationship between industrial relations and trade unions, issues of race and gender, educational methods and practices and historical perspectives. The material which is authored by academics, researchers and trade union officers presents a trade union perspective.

A typical issue has five to eight articles plus columns on local and international concerns. An average of four books are reviewed by signed reviewers in about 500 words.

323   *Training and Development Journal.* DATE FOUNDED: 1947. TITLE CHANGES: *Journal of Industrial Training* (1947-1953); *Journal of the American Society of Training Directors* (1954-1962); *Training Directors Journal* (1963-1966). MERGER: *Training Research Abstracts* (1961-1965). FREQUENCY: m. PRICE: $60/yr., $20/yr. American Society for Training and Development members. PUBLISHER: American Society for Training and Development, 1630 Duke Street, Box 1443, Alexandria, VA 22313. EDITOR: Patricia A. Galagan. ILLUSTRATIONS. INDEX. ADVERTISEMENTS. CIRCULA-TION: 30,000. MANUSCRIPT SELECTION: Editor. MICRO-FORMS: UMI. REPRINTS: UMI. BOOK REVIEWS. INDEXED/ ABSTRACTED: ABIn, AccDataProAb, BI, BibAg, BusI, CIJE, ContPgEd, CurrCont, KeyEconSci, LLBA, MgtC, OperRes, Per-ManAb, PersLit, PsyAb, Psycscan, RiskAb, SciAb, SocAb, SOCI, TraIndI, WorAb. TARGET AUDIENCE: AC, SP.

This journal is aimed at professionals in the field. As such, it is pragmatic in approach. The authors are from academe, top level managers, or executives from the private sector. The focus is to provide innovative ideas to vexing social problems encountered in the work force. Articles on the issues of illiteracy in the workplace, parental-leave policy, and training for quality improvement are some of the topics addressed.

There are regular features in each issue: letters to the editor; new training tools consisting of video cassettes, magazines, and seminars; and a classified section on positions open. Books are reviewed, unsigned, lengthy, and critically. There are three to four books reviewed in each issue with an additional number listed but not reviewed.

324   *Training Digest.* DATE FOUNDED: 1978. FREQUENCY: m. PRICE: $140/yr. PUBLISHER: John Chittock, Training Digest, 37 Gower Street, London WC1E 6HH, England. EDITOR: Christie Quinn. INDEX. MANUSCRIPT SELECTION: Editor. BOOK REVIEWS. SPECIAL ISSUES: 4/yr. TARGET AUDIENCE: AC, SP. SAMPLE COPIES: Libraries.

This British journal has a unique format which allows for very concise, pertinent information, quick to read and refer to, and comprehensive in its range of coverage. Its major focus of coverage is in the field of training especially in business, commerce, and industry. The writers are usually British specialists in the training field or journalists.

Each issue presents about 110 items in categories such as general, administrative and service training, manual and technical training, new products and services, methodology, techniques and research. Brief descriptions of approximately 100 words are included in each of the items. There is a listing of events and courses. One section lists new publications, books, industry reports, and films and videos with an annotation.

325   *Training: The Magazine of Human Resources Development.* DATE FOUNDED: 1964. TITLE CHANGES: *Training in Business and Industry* (1964-1976). FREQUENCY: m. PRICE: $42/yr. PUBLISHER: Jerry Noack, Lakewood Publications, 50 South Ninth St., Minneapolis, MN 55402. EDITOR: Jack Gordon. ILLUSTRATIONS. INDEX. ADVERTISEMENTS. CIRCULATION: 50,000. MANUSCRIPT SELECTION: Editor. MICROFORMS: UMI, Bell and Howell. REPRINTS: Reprint Services. BOOK REVIEWS. SPECIAL ISSUES: 2/yr. INDEXED/ABSTRACTED: BusI, CIJE, MgtC, PersLit, SageFamStudAb, WorAb. TARGET AUDIENCE: SP. SAMPLE COPIES: Libraries.

The major focus of this journal is to provide information on training, development and performance improvement in organizations. It claims to be the "world's leading publication on corporate training and development." Authors are drawn from the corporate training field. Special issues are published twice yearly. The October issue is an "Industry Report" consisting of a research report on corporate training activity; the August issue is the *Annual Marketplace Directory*.

The monthly issue consists of five to six feature length articles and upward to thirty shorter articles. Usually two books are reviewed in about 500 word signed reviews.

326   *Transport Salaried Staff Journal.* DATE FOUNDED: 1904. TITLE CHANGES: *Railway Clerk* (1904-1919); *Railway Service Journal* (1919-1951). FREQUENCY: m. PRICE: Free. PUBLISHER: Transport Salaried Staff Association, Walkden House, 10 Melton Street, London NW1 2EJ, England. EDITOR: Jim Cobley. ILLUSTRATIONS. INDEX. ADVERTISEMENTS. CIRCULATION: 50,000. MANUSCRIPT SELECTION: Editor. BOOK REVIEWS. TARGET AUDIENCE: SP. SAMPLE COPIES: Libraries, individuals.

This British journal is a tabloid newspaper which provides union news to people working in the public transport sphere. As such, it supports the Labour party. The writers are from Great Britain and the Irish Republic. The articles provide information on union activities such as conferences, elections, special events, and negotiations.

A typical issue has twenty articles of one page or less complete with pictures. There is a book review section containing two signed reviews of 250 words. A "Leisure Time" page is included with an article or reviews on music, a consumer column, crossword puzzle, and recipe.

327   *Transport Workers of the World.* DATE FOUNDED: 1949. FREQUENCY: q. PRICE: $6/yr. PUBLISHER: Trade Unions International of Transport Workers, H-1139 Budapest, Vaci ut 73, Hungary. EDITOR: K.C. MATHEW. ILLUSTRATIONS. ADVERTISEMENTS. CIRCULATION: 5,000. MANUSCRIPT SELECTION: Editorial Board. TARGET AUDIENCE: SP. SAMPLE COPIES: Libraries, individuals.

The viewpoint of this journal is to promote the interests of transport workers throughout the world. Other union publications claim to be international; however, this one truly lives up to that claim presenting items from such diverse countries as Angola, Bangladesh, Trinidad and Australia. The articles are informative regarding current issues in the transport workers' trade unions and the political, social, and economic problems facing them. The articles are written by union and non-union individuals from around the world.

Recent issues have an average of twenty-five articles; some are of one-half page length, others are one to two pages. They cover such specific topics as containerization, South Africa and the boycott, British ferries, women in the French transport union. There are articles written on an international scope which are of vital concern to the U.S., such as air safety, transport of dangerous materials and air pollution. The journal is published in English, French and Spanish.

328   *UAW Solidarity.* DATE FOUNDED: 1936. TITLE CHANGES: *United Automobile Worker* (1936-1957). FREQUENCY: m. PRICE: $5/yr. PUBLISHER: International Union, UAW, 8000 E. Jefferson Ave., Detroit, MI 48214. EDITOR: David Elsila. ILLUSTRATIONS. CIRCULATION: 1,400,000. MANUSCRIPT SELECTION: Editors. BOOK REVIEWS. INDEXED/ABSTRACTED: WorAb. TARGET AUDIENCE: GP, SP. SAMPLE COPIES: Libraries, individuals.

Solidarity is the official publication of the United Automobile, Aerospace and Agriculture Implement Workers of America. As such, its scope and purpose is to provide information and commentary on labor and social issues. These issues are viewed from the labor perspective. The short articles are written by researchers and journalists in the United States.

Each issue contains an average of twenty-eight articles. One or two signed book reviews are included that consist of approximately 500 words. There are also equal length reviews of films and records which have a relationship to the labor movement. A Reader's Forum is included in each issue.

329   *UE News.* DATE FOUNDED: 1941. TITLE CHANGES: *UE News* (1941-1943); *Canadian UE News* (1943-1967). FREQUENCY: sm. PUBLISHER: United Electrical, Radio and Machine Workers of Canada (UE), 137 Boultbee Ave., Toronto, Ontario M4J 1B2. EDITOR: Elias Stavrides. CIRCULATION: 10,000. MANUSCRIPT SELECTION: Editor, Union Officers. MICROFORM: State Historical Society of Wisconsin. TARGET AUDIENCE: SP. SAMPLE COPIES: Libraries, individuals.

UE News is written for workers and political activists. Left of center in political perspective, this publication is designed to help with the "...mobilization of workers for social/international causes..."

Around for fifty years, this publication is mainly short news articles dealing with labor oriented current events. Some longer articles have titles such as "New Study Reveals Jobs at Great Risk Under Free Trade."

330   *UI Quarterly Review*. DATE FOUNDED: 1985. FREQUENCY: q. PRICE: Free. PUBLISHER: New Mexico Employment Security Department, P.O. Box 1928, Albuquerque, NM 87103. EDITOR: Martin L. Reiter. ILLUSTRATIONS. CIRCULATION: 120. MANUSCRIPT SELECTION: Editor. TARGET AUDIENCE: AC, GP, HS, SP. SAMPLE COPIES: Libraries, individuals.

This New Mexico state publication is a quarterly compilation of unemployment insurance data including claims, insured unemployment, benefit payments, claimant characteristics and trust fund solvency. Data is by county and statewide.

Each issue contains mainly statistical tables, graphs and charts with little analysis. It also contains a detailed glossary. The publication runs thirty to fifty pages in length.

331   *UITBB Information*. DATE FOUNDED: 1950. TITLE CHANGE: *UITBB Information Bulletin* (1950-1972). FREQUENCY: q. PUBLISHER: Trade Unions International of Workers of the Building, Wood and Building Materials Industries, UITBB, Box 281, 00101 Helsinki, Finland. EDITOR: Secretariat. ILLUSTRATIONS. CIRCULATION: 2,000. MANUSCRIPT SELECTION: Secretariat. SPECIAL ISSUES: Occasional. INDEXED/ABSTRACTED: WorAb. TARGET AUDIENCE: GP, HS, SP.

The *UITBB Bulletin* is written by trade union activists, workers, researchers and government employees for members of the trade union. It does advocate the viewpoint of the union. It reports on the activities of the organizations of workers of the building, wood and building materials industries in respect to defending legitimate rights of the workers under different political systems and to promote international cooperation and social justice.

A typical issue has ten to fifteen articles. Editions are published in French, English, Spanish, German, Russian, Swedish and Finnish.

332   *Union Labor News.* DATE FOUNDED: 1937. TITLE CHANGES: *Union Label News* (1937-1942). FREQUENCY: m. PRICE: $5/yr. PUBLISHER: Union Labor News Publishers, Ltd., 1062 S. Park St., Rm. 107, Madison, WI 53715. EDITOR: James A. Cavanaugh. ADVERTISEMENTS. CIRCULATION: 16,000. MANUSCRIPT SELECTION: Editor, Managing Editor. MICROFORMS: State Historical Society of Wisconsin. BOOK REVIEWS. SPECIAL ISSUES: Annually. TARGET AUDIENCE: AC, GP, HS, SP. SAMPLE COPIES: Libraries, individuals.

This tabloid of union news for Central Wisconsin contains news articles such as "University of Wisconsin Graduate Assistants Press For Say Over Working Conditions." Some regular features/columns are "Laborers Report" and "Report to Membership."

It publishes signed book reviews, one-half page in length, and usually one or two per issue. Special supplements on political/economic issues are published each year.

333   *Union Labor Report.* DATE FOUNDED: 1947. FREQUENCY: bw. PRICE: $440/yr. PUBLISHER: Bureau of National Affairs, Inc., 1231 25th Street, N.W., Washington, D.C. 20037. EDITOR: Bill Manville. ILLUSTRATIONS. INDEX. MANUSCRIPT SELECTION: Editor, Editorial Staff. TARGET AUDIENCE: AC, SP. SAMPLE COPIES: Libraries, individuals.

The binder service from Bureau of National Affairs is in the same format as their other products. The main body consists of the texts of laws and their interpretations which are updated biweekly. Most updates also include a highlight of some significant piece of recent legislation affecting unions. A weekly newsletter is part of the subscription. This provides further explanation and amplification of the legislation and other union issues.

334   *United Association Journal.* DATE FOUNDED: 1898. TITLE CHANGES: *Plumbers, Gas and Steam Fitters' Official Journal* (1898-1906); *Plumbers, Gas and Steam Fitters Journal* (1907-1929); *Journeymen Plumbers and Steam Fitters Journal* (1929-1946); *Journeymen and Apprentices of the Plumbing and Pipe Fitting Industry Journal* (1947-1948); *United Association of Journeymen and Apprentices of the Plumbing and Pipe Fitting Industry. Journal* (1948-1967). FREQUENCY: m. PUBLISHER: United Association of Journeymen and Apprentices of the Plumbing and Pipe Fitting Industry of the U.S. and Canada, 901 Massachusetts Ave., N.W., Washington, D.C. 20001. ILLUSTRATIONS. INDEX. MANUSCRIPT SELECTION: Staff. TARGET AUDIENCE: SP.

A monthly magazine designed to communicate with the membership of the Association. A news magazine which is styled like *Time* and *Newsweek*.

It includes with each issue serious, lengthy journalistic features such as "Coal: Why We Can't Make the Best Use of Our Most Abundant Resource." Monthly columns include "Personal Counselor" for financial and retirement issues and "Government Politics and You" which is a series of capsule form news items dealing with labor related government actions.

335   *United Mine Workers Journal.* DATE FOUNDED: 1879. FREQUENCY: m. PRICE: $25/yr. institutions, $100/yr. corporations, $10/yr. personal. PUBLISHER: United Mine Workers of America, 900 15th St., N.W., Washington, D.C. 20005. EDITOR: John Duray. ILLUSTRATIONS. CIRCULATION: 225,000. MANUSCRIPT SELECTION: Editor, Staff. MICROFORMS: State Historical Society of Wisconsin. REPRINTS: Editor. BOOK REVIEWS. SPECIAL ISSUES: Occasional. INDEXED/ABSTRACTED: CoalA, WorAb. TARGET AUDIENCE: SP. SAMPLE COPIES: Libraries, individuals.

Historically important, this major American labor union publication reports on coal miners, coal mining, mine health and safety. It also reports on Appalachia as a region, labor unions in general, and governmental agencies affecting miners such as Bureau of Mines and the Appalachian Regional Commission. The journal is written by specialists who "generally have coal mining experience and/or knowledge of coal mining regions and people."

Each issue runs with two to three major articles such as "The Rank and File Speaks on Acid Rain." It includes a varying number of short, unsigned book reviews per issue.

336   *Voice of African Workers.* DATE FOUNDED: 1975. FREQUENCY: q. PRICE: Free. PUBLISHER: Organization of African Trade Union Unity, Aviation Road, P.O. Box M.386, Accra, Ghana. EDITOR: A.L. Diallo. ILLUSTRATIONS. CIRCULATION: 4,000 (1/2 French; 1/2 English). MANUSCRIPT SELECTION: Editor. MICROFORMS: Publisher. SPECIAL ISSUES. TARGET AUDIENCE: AC, GP, SP.

A "new" Pan African publication devoted to "trade union news, liberation news, and sometimes politics in connection with worker's welfare."

Recent articles, short and "newsy," included: "Geneva: Deliberations and Results of ILO 73rd Session" and "Workers Education."

Written by officers and staff of the OATUU, each issue contains nine to eleven short news articles. All dealt with trade union rights.

337   *Wall Street Journal.* DATE FOUNDED: 1889. FREQUENCY: d. PRICE: $119/yr. PUBLISHER: Dow Jones and Company, Inc., 200 Liberty Street, New York, NY 10281. EDITOR: Robert L. Bartley. ILLUSTRATIONS. INDEX. ADVERTISEMENTS. CIRCULA-TION: 2,026,276. MANUSCRIPT SELECTION: Editor, Staff. MICROFORMS: Yale University Library, Bell and Howell, UMI. BOOK REVIEWS. INDEXED/ABSTRACTED: BankLitI, BoRvI, CADCAMA, ChemAb, CompIndUp, FutSurv, MedCareRev, PAIS, PCR2, PersLit, WorAb. TARGET AUDIENCE: AC, GP, SP.

The *Wall Street Journal* has long been considered the newspaper of record for American, if not the international, business community. It is necessary reading for the business manager and labor leader. It includes general news stories as well as corporate news. It includes very good coverage of labor and industrial relations related subjects.

Each daily issue of this newspaper includes literally hundreds of short news stories. It includes the record of activity of virtually every economic indicator imaginable from all U.S. stock and commodities markets, the price of precious metals to the exchange rate for the dollar.

338   *Weekly Summary of NLRB Cases.* DATE FOUNDED: 1983. FRE-QUENCY: w. PRICE: $75/yr. PUBLISHER: National Labor Relations Board, Division of Information, 1717 Pennsylvania Avenue, Washington, D.C. 20570. EDITOR: Raymond Pikus. CIRCULA-TION: 1,000. MICROFORMS: GPO. TARGET AUDIENCE: AC, GP, SP. SAMPLE COPIES: Libraries, individuals.

Cut and dry, this is the weekly summary of National Labor Relations Board cases. Depending on cases decided, each issue can run from ten to twenty cases.

Each issue also contains a "List of Decisions of Administrative Law Judges," "List of Directions of Elections by Regional Directors," and "General Counsel Memorandum: Submission of Advice Cases." It includes notice of official Board publications.

339   *Western Australian Economic Review (WAER).* DATE FOUNDED: 1981. FREQUENCY: 2/yr. PRICE: $35/yr. PUBLISHER: Confed-

eration of Western Australian Industry, P.O. Box 6209, Hay Street East, Perth, Western Australia 6000. EDITOR: Dr. Paul Moy. ILLUSTRATIONS. INDEX. CIRCULATION: 600. MANUSCRIPT SELECTION: Editor. REPRINTS: Publisher. TARGET AUDIENCE: AC, SP. SAMPLE COPIES: Libraries, individuals.

This journal presents a substantial statistical analysis of the competitiveness of Western Australia and Australian economies in the world economy. There are lists of tables such as employment, retail sales, imports, exports and economic indicators from the United States, Japan, selected European countries, and East Asia. Figures are also provided detailing export/import price, stock market indices for Australia, New Zealand, New York, London and Tokyo, residential and industrial rents, balance of payments, and exchange rates.

Each issue provides an analysis of the comprehensive figures which are accumulated. For some statistics, a five year comparison is made. Each issue contains two feature articles. One recent article was a lengthy piece on the economic impact of the America's Cup Defense series in 1986-1987.

340   *Work and Occupations.*   DATE FOUNDED: 1974. TITLE CHANGES: *Sociology of Work and Occupations* (1974-1981). FREQUENCY: q. PRICE: $72/yr. institutions, $30/yr. personal. PUBLISHER: Sage Publications, Inc., 2111 West Hillcrest Drive, Newbury Park, CA 91320. EDITOR: Curt Tausky. ILLUSTRATIONS. INDEX. ADVERTISEMENTS. CIRCULATION: 1,000. MANUSCRIPT SELECTION: Editor, Editorial Board, Refereed. MICROFORMS: UMI. REPRINTS: UMI. BOOK REVIEWS. SPECIAL ISSUES. INDEXED/ABSTRACTED: ABIn, ASSIA, CIJE, CurrCont, ErgAb, IntLabDoc, LLBA, MgtC, PersLit, PsyAb, SageFamStudAb, SagePAA, SocAb, SOCI. TARGET AUDIENCE: AC, SP.

This journal emphasizes the sociological analysis of issues surrounding work and occupations. Theoretically based articles deal with such topics as: workers participation, authority, job satisfaction, gender difference, technology, and the quality of life. Titles of recent articles include: "Gender as a Moderator of Job Satisfaction," "On the Natural History of Health Care Occupations" and "Technology and Participation in Japanese Factories."

Each issue has five to seven theoretically based research articles of usually under thirty pages in length. Special issues are occasionally published and the most recent was devoted to workers' participation.

Book reviews are signed and appear in most issues. They are usually one to two pages in length.

341   ***Working Life in Sweden***.   DATE FOUNDED: 1941. TITLE CHANGES: *News from Sweden* (1941-1977). FREQUENCY: 3/yr. PRICE: Free. PUBLISHER: Swedish Information Service, 825 3rd Avenue, New York, NY 10022. CIRCULATION: 4,000. MANUSCRIPT SELECTION: Editor. REPRINTS: Publisher. TARGET AUDIENCE: AC, GP, SP. SAMPLE COPIES. Libraries, individuals.

This newsletter is published by the Swedish government presenting topics on Swedish working life which might be of interest to Americans. It is surprisingly well done for its intention and circulation.

Recent signed articles have included "Sweden: Ideological Conflicts in Working Life" and "Why Sweden Has Better Working Conditions Than the U.S." There is usually one article per issue. It includes announcements of material available from the Swedish consulate in New York City.

342   ***Working Woman***.   DATE FOUNDED: 1976. FREQUENCY: m. PRICE: $18/yr. PUBLISHER: Hal Publications, Inc., 342 Madison Avenue, New York, NY 10173. EDITOR: Anne Mollegen Smith. ILLUSTRATIONS. INDEX. ADVERTISEMENTS. CIRCULATION: 850,000. MANUSCRIPT SELECTION: Editor. MICROFORMS: UMI. REPRINTS: UMI. INDEXED/ABSTRACTED: BI, CurLitFamPlan, MagInd, RG, WorAb. TARGET AUDIENCE: GP, SP.

Working Woman is a popular format magazine with a very wide circulation. It is not too unlike *Business Week*, *Fortune*, or even *Forbes*. Only the focus is different. This magazine is directed at what the title implies, the "working woman." Recent issues have included articles such as: "How to Position Yourself as a Leader," "The Corporate Guru of Global Economics," "How Good A Boss Can You Be?" and "Managing the Difficult Employee."

Each issue publishes six major articles of varying length. Regular features include: "Managers Shop Talk," "Career Advice," "Financial Workshop," and among others, "Enterprise."

343   ***Workplace Democracy***.   DATE FOUNDED: 1973. TITLE CHANGES: *Self-management* (1973-1980). FREQUENCY: q. PRICE: $36/yr. institutions, $18/yr. personal. PUBLISHER: Labor Relations and Research Center, University of Massachusetts, 111

Draper Hall, Amherst, MA 01003. EDITOR: Julie Melrose. ILLUS-
TRATIONS. ADVERTISEMENTS. CIRCULATION: 2,000.
MANUSCRIPT SELECTION: Editor. REPRINTS: Publisher.
BOOK REVIEWS. SPECIAL ISSUES: Occasional. INDEXED/
ABSTRACTED: API, SageUrbStudAb, WorAb. TARGET AUDI-
ENCE: AC, GP, HS, SP. SAMPLE COPIES: Libraries.

A publication of the Labor Relations and Research Center of the
University of Massachusetts, this magazine format focuses on the
worker participation movement, employee stock option plans, quality
circles, flextime, project teams and other work alternatives. Recent
articles have included: "A New Dimension in Labor-Management
Relations," "Beyond Taxes: Managing an Employee-Owned Company" and "The Future of Workplace Alternatives."

Each quarterly issue contains seven to eight feature articles of varying
length. There are an average of eight signed book reviews per issue.
Other features include "Bread and Roses: News Briefs" and "Read and
Right: Media Notes."

344   *World Marxist Review.* DATE FOUNDED: 1958. FREQUENCY:
m. PRICE: $40/yr. institutions, $25/yr. personal. PUBLISHER: Prog-
ress Books, 71 Bathurst Street, Toronto, Ontario M5V 2P6. INDEX.
MICROFORMS: UMI. REPRINTS: UMI. INDEXED/AB-
STRACTED: AmerH, HistAb, PAIS, SocSc. TARGET AUDI-
ENCE: AC, GP, SP.

World Marxist Review is the North American edition of the monthly
journal, *Problems of Peace and Socialism* published in Prague. It is billed
as the "theoretical and information journal of Communist and Workers
parties throughout the world." It is published in no less than forty
languages. It is a very good, if somewhat ideological, source of comparative labor/industrial relations. Typical recent titles included: "Reviving
the Co-operative Movement," "Options for Global Economic Development," and "The Only Unemployed We Met." This publication's
focus is less for academic than public appeal.

Each issue of the *Review* publishes five articles from Communist leaders
in a variety of countries. There are ten to fifteen other articles written
under such unifying headings as "For Human Survival," "Viewpoints,"
"The Party" and "The Socialist Way."

345   *Wyoming Labor Force Trends.* DATE FOUNDED: 1963. FRE-
QUENCY: m. PUBLISHER: Wyoming Employment Security Commission, P.O. Box 2760, Casper, WY 82602. EDITOR: Michael Jones

Paris. ILLUSTRATIONS. CIRCULATION: 1,500. MANU-
SCRIPT SELECTION: Editor. REPRINTS: Editor. SPECIAL
ISSUES: Occasional. INDEXED/ABSTRACTED: SRI. TARGET
AUDIENCE: AC, GP, HS, SP. SAMPLE COPIES: Libraries, indi-
viduals.

Trends is considered the best source for comprehensive and timely
information about employment, unemployment and the labor force in
Wyoming and for local areas within the state. It is written by researchers
from the Commission.

There are seven to eight brief, analytical articles in each issue which are
essentially statistical.

346 *Yearbook of Labour Statistics.* DATE FOUNDED: 1936. FRE-
QUENCY: a. PRICE: $98/yr. PUBLISHER: International Labour
Office Publications, CH-1211 Geneva 22, Switzerland. ILLUSTRA-
TIONS. INDEX. TARGET AUDIENCE: AC, SP.

The *Yearbook of Labour Statistics* is a trilingual publication. It is a
comprehensive survey of annual data from all parts of the world relating
to economically active population, employment, unemployment, hours
of work, wages, labor cost, industrial disputes, occupational injuries
(most tables by major division of economic activities) and consumer
prices. In 1988, the 48th annual edition was published.

APPENDIX:
TITLES NOT INCLUDED

The titles listed here were not included because current copies were not accessible in area libraries. Some of the publishers in question did respond to the questionnaire but did not provide sample copies; in most cases no reply was received to any mailings. Information about a few titles was received too late for inclusion in this edition. Readers with information about these and/or other titles suitable for inclusion in a revised edition are invited to write to the authors c/o Greenwood Press.

347   *Around the Bargaining Loop*

348   *Australian Journal of Labor Law*

349   *Bulletin of Labour Statistics*

350   *Canadian Personnel and Industrial Relations Journal*

351   *Changing Work*

352   *Christian Management Review*

353   *Conditions of Work Digest*

354   *Documents of the International Labour Conference*

355   *Eastern Worker*

356   *Employee Responsibilities and Rights Journal*

357   *Hong Kong Journal of Trade Unions*

358   *Indian Journal of Labour Economics*

359   *Indian Labour Journal*

360   *Indian Management*

361   *Industrial Relations Journal of South Africa*

362   *Inside Negotiations*

363   *International Journal of Comparative Labour Law and Industrial Relations*

GEOGRAPHIC INDEX

International, 1, 3, 13, 17, 20, 23, 28, 35-36, 39, 42, 46-47,50-51, 53-54, 57-
    58, 61-63, 67-70, 76-78, 80-83, 86, 93, 98-101, 106, 108-111, 114-116,
    125, 129, 132-133, 137-138, 140-141,143-144, 146, 148-161, 163-165,
    170, 172-174, 176-178, 180, 182, 184-185, 189-191, 193, 195, 198-199,
    201-202, 211-213, 219-221, 224-226, 230, 233, 243, 246-248, 252, 256-
    257, 260, 266, 268-270, 274-275, 277-279,284-286, 293-301, 304, 306,
    309, 319, 321-322, 326-328, 331, 334, 337, 339, 343, 346
Iowa, 315
Ireland, 66, 272, 326

Jamaica, 297
Japan, 165

London, 77, 96, 98, 118, 122, 134-135, 140-142, 245, 258, 271,
    300, 313, 322, 324
Louisiana, 283

Malaysia, 314
Maryland, 121, 146, 156, 169, 204, 218, 292, 318
Massachusetts, 40, 119-120, 216, 234, 270, 279, 296, 343
Michigan, 73, 79, 207, 295, 328
Minnesota, 201, 253, 325
Mississippi, 4-6
Missouri, 10

Netherlands, 70, 99, 148, 158, 174, 177, 180, 195, 275, 286,
    301, 321
New Jersey, 2, 209, 285, 306
New Mexico, 65, 104, 330
New York, 7, 25-27, 42-43, 51, 56, 59-60, 63, 75-76, 81, 84, 88, 94, 108-
    109, 123, 125, 127-128, 130, 133, 166, 175, 192-193, 197, 203, 205, 227,
    229, 239, 241, 250, 254, 260-261, 269, 273, 282, 288-289, 307, 316-317,
    337, 341-342
New Zealand, 90, 131, 278
Newfoundland, 214
North Carolina, 215, 299, 303

Ohio, 8, 12, 267
Oklahoma, 249

PUBLISHER INDEX

International Confederation of Free Trade Unions, 110, 129
International Foundation of Employee Benefit Plans, 86
International Institute for Labour Studies, 211
International Institute of Administrative Sciences, 157
International Labour Office, 154-155, 212, 220-221, 247-248, 298, 347
International Personnel Management Association, 277
International Quality Consultants, Ltd, 278
International Social Security Association, 160
International Transport Workers' Federation, 164
International Union of Bricklayers and Allied Craftsmen, 29
Irish Central Statistics Office, 66

JAI Press, 9, 170, 309
Japan Institute of Labour, 165
Jewish Labor Committee, 166
John Herling, 168
John Wiley and Sons, 127, 193

K. Ophel, 95
Kluwer, 148, 174, 275, 301, 321

Labor Education and Research Project, 207
Labor Herald, 204
Labor Relations and Research Center, 344
Lakewood Publications, 325
Law and Society Association, 216
London School of Economics and Political Science, 80, 386
Long View Publishing Co., Inc., 260
Longman Group, 93

Malaysian Trade Unions Congress, 314
Management Development Centre, 233
Management Publications Ltd., 230
Massachusetts AFL-CIO, 234
Massachusetts Institute of Technology, Sloan School of Management, 296
MCB University Press, 87, 149, 151, 182, 189, 219, 225
McGill University, Centre for Developing Area Studies, 213
McGraw Hill, Inc., 43
Memorial University, Department of History, 214
Methuen, Inc., 83

Van Gorcum, 158

Washington (State) Labor Market and Economic Analysis Branch, 222
Washington, D.C. Department of Employment Services, 235
Western Economic Association International, 61
Williams and Wilkins, 169
Workers' Educational Association, 118, 313, 322
Wyoming Employment Security Commission, 346

Xavier Labour Relations Institute, 224

TITLE INDEX

(Includes current and previous titles for all annotated serials)

SUBJECT INDEX

Brookings Institution, 37-38
Brotherhood of Railway, Airline and Steamship Clerks, Freight Handlers,
    Express and Station Employees, 146, 156, 218
Building Materials Workers, 331
Bureau of Labor Statistics, 237, 244
Bureau of National Affairs, *see* BNA
Business Administration, 44, 53, 119, 172-174, 223, 226, 293, 319
Business Ethics, 174
Business History, 39-40
Business Law, 14, 41
Business, 12, 40, 43, 81, 106, 108-109, 119, 242, 281, 283, 337, 342

Cabinetmakers, 49
California, 44-45
Canada, 47, 103, 126, 172, 214, 217, 255, 329
Canadian Union of Public Employees, 103, 217
Career Development, 48
Carpenters, 49
Caterers, 50
Catholic Worker Movement, 51
Center for Public Choice, 275
Central America, 18
Centre for Employment Initiatives, 93
Civil Liberties, 120
Civil Rights, 120
Clerks, 22
Collective Bargaining, 55, 60, 75, 87-88, 97, 175, 237, 239, 258, 273, 284,
    298, 313
Committee on Canadian Labour History, 214
Communications, 57, 115, 271
Communist, 260, 269, 314
Compensation, 33, 59
Computers, 22
Concerned Educators Against Forced Unionism, 145
Confederation of Western Australian Industry, 339
Conference Board, 60
Conflict Resolution, 176
Contracts, 55
Corporate Law, 64
Corporations, 64, 74
Counseling, 117, 181, 191, 201
Craftsmen, 29
Cullen Egan Dell Australia Party, 31

ABOUT THE COMPILERS

Professor Michael C. Vocino, Jr. is Chair of the Technical Services Department and Political Science Bibliographer at the University of Rhode Island Library.

Professor Lucille W. Cameron is Chair of the Public Services Department and Sociology Bibliographer at the University of Rhode Island Library.